# An Artistic Approach to Virtual Reality

A special quality of the medium of virtual reality is its immersive nature, allowing users to disengage from the physical world around them in order to fully interact with a digital environment. *An Artistic Approach to Virtual Reality* traces the lineage of artist/technologists who have worked with virtual reality in its infancy to the interactive virtual work of contemporary artists such as Laurie Anderson.

Interlaced within a survey of artists whose works fit within the boundary of the interactive virtual medium, this book teases out what qualifies as interactive virtual artworks. The authors discuss the theories behind the basic mechanics required to enter the virtual reality space and investigate theories around visual and embodied conceptual space.

Key Features:

- Explores theoretical and practical aspects of using virtual reality for artistic practice.

- Includes examples and discussion of virtual reality artworks from award-winning artists.

- Discusses topics relevant to virtual reality that are pertinent and persist throughout hardware and software changes.

- Provides historical and contemporary discussion of virtual reality artistic works.

# An Artistic Approach to Virtual Reality

Cyane Tornatzky, M.A., M.F.A. and
Brendan Kelley, M.S.

CRC Press
Taylor & Francis Group
Boca Raton London New York

CRC Press is an imprint of the
Taylor & Francis Group, an **informa** business

First edition published 2024
by CRC Press
2385 Executive Center Drive, Suite 320, Boca Raton FL 33431

and by CRC Press
4 Park Square, Milton Park, Abingdon, Oxon, OX14 4RN

*CRC Press is an imprint of Taylor & Francis Group, LLC*

© 2024 Cyane Tornatzky and Brendan Kelley

ISBN: 9781032426693 (hbk)
ISBN: 9781032420127 (pbk)
ISBN: 9781003363729 (ebk)

DOI: 10.1201/9781003363729

Typeset in Minion
by codeMantra

**Cyane Tornatzky**

*Thanks to artist technologist Steve Wilson and scholar Louis Tornatzky for their inspiration and faith in me.*

---

**Brendan Kelley**

*I dedicate this work to my parents, Sandra Winkler and Thomas Kelley, who have always supported my endeavors, even if they don't always understand what it is I do; my brother, Cameron Kelley, for providing support when I need it; to my cat, Chewy, for the love and care, even if it is conditional on my continued feeding of her, and to all of my other friends and family members for their love, care, and support throughout the years.*

# Contents

# Preface

**Brendan Kelley**

I first met Cyane Tornatzky some 8 years ago when I began my career as a student in electronic art (Colorado State University's name for their new media program) and graphic design. At the time, my main motivation was to gain the skills necessary to develop video games, a dream I had had since my late uncle first gave my brother and me money for a GameCube back in the early 2000s. It was during this time in the electronic art program that I was exposed to virtual and augmented reality technologies. I purchased my first virtual reality headset on a whim, picking up a Rift CV1 from Best Buy on my way home from work one evening. I donned the headset around 5 PM, and the next thing I knew, it was 3 AM – a testament to the way virtual reality sucks its users in. From there, I was hooked.

Through collaborations with Cyane and other opportunities over nearly a decade, I expanded my skillset, learning more and more about virtual reality and its sister technologies along the extended reality spectrum. As I did, her interest grew as well. I and some fellow driven students in the electronic art department began to insist on incorporating more gaming and virtual reality opportunities into our coursework. Eventually, this led to artistic and academic collaborations with Cyane. However, the most pertinent one for this book was our publication *The Artistic Approach to Virtual Reality* (Kelley & Tornatzky, 2019), where the initial ideation for what would become this book began.

After the publication, we began to discuss further academic collaborations, considering conferences, journals, workshops, etc., but we realized that we had far too much we wanted to explore and discuss – far more than even fit into this project. Virtual reality is rich with history, philosophy, technical considerations, psychological and physiological elements, etc. It is a technology built upon hundreds of years of experimentation, exploration, and discovery. But among all of its foundations, there was a lack of discussion on the artistic merits of virtual reality. Many of the books and popular discussions surrounding virtual reality artistic works were 'how-tos' (many of which are now outdated) or explored technologies that were virtual reality adjacent.

It is our hope with this book that we can educate and inspire aspiring virtual reality artists to consider and dream beyond our reality; to provide a foundation for those interested in the technology and all it has to offer. This endeavor was just as much a learning experience for us as we hope it is for those that read its pages.

## REFERENCE

Kelley, B., & Tornatzky, C. VRCAI '19: *Proceedings of the 17th International Conference on Virtual-Reality Continuum and its Applications in Industry November 2019*, No. 36, pp. 1–5 https://doi.org/10.1145/3359997.3365701

# Author Biographies

**Cyane Tornatzky** Digital immigrant Cyane Tornatzky received her Master of Fine Art in new media from San Francisco State University's Conceptual and Information Arts program. In 2015, she started the Electronic Art program within the Department of Art and Art History at Colorado State University in Fort Collins, Colorado. As part of her coursework, Tornatzky teaches an art game class that starts with students creating board games and ends with them crafting digital art games, some in virtual reality (VR). As a CoPI for a VR project with her colleagues in Veterinary Sciences at CSU, Tornatzky is Creative Director for a team developing a VR training application for veterinarians. The application is a digital twin and has been released on Steam as a simulation game. Tornatzky is also on a research project with a colleague from Computer Science at CSU, investing interfaces for a VR sketching tool. Tornatzky is a visiting faculty member for the Richardson Design Center's Design Thinking: Graduate Certificate in Virtual Reality, and teaches a course on Data Visualization in VR as well as co-teaches with Brendan Kelley a graduate-level Serious Games Course. Tornatzky is a member of Colorado State University's Office for the Vice President of Research Virtual Reality Advisory Board. Her own artworks vary from using code to dynamically generate images to creating installation work that uses stereoscopic lenses.

**Brendan Kelley** Digital native Brendan Kelley is currently working toward a Doctorate of Philosophy in Computer Science with a focus on human-computer interaction at Colorado State University (CSU) after completing a Master of Science in Media Communications at CSU. He has worked with VR since the release of the first Oculus headset and has received several awards for his VR, augmented reality, and game design work. His projects span the realms of art, industry, and academia. His projects, such as *Orillas Del Ebro VR* (2019), explore the merging of humanities and science that is possible through VR technologies by visualizing poetic writings and the anthropological hydrology principles they describe. Other works include *The Path We're On* (2018), a collaborative VR project that received the second place award in the 2018 Ram Reality HackAThon at CSU. He also worked as a VR developer for several years with the Colorado State University Office for the Vice President of Research OVPR. During this time, he acted as a consultant for the CSU VR Anatomy and CSU Vet VR projects, as well as assisted and led the development of projects such as the *CSU Environmental and Radiological Health Sciences Interactive Experience* and the *Aug Mag Augmented Reality Magazine Experience for the OVPR*.

In addition, he has conducted research on design theories, social VR use, cognitive perceptions of VR, and the artistic use of VR. This includes publications such as *The Artistic Approach to VR* (2019) co-authored by Cyane Tornatzky and published in the proceedings of the 2019 VRCAI conference. More recently, he has worked on the research paper titled *The Rise of the 'Quarantine Bar Simulator'* (2020), which explores the different ways in which social VR was used during the ongoing COVID-19 pandemic. He has also helped to develop graduate-level courses for the Nancy Richardson Design Center, where he is an adjunct professor, focused around both virtual and augmented reality technologies. More recently, his research has focused on cognitive aspects of virtual and augmented reality technologies, such as his master's thesis work, which compared learning efficacy among augmented reality, paper manual, and online video training modalities, as well as the creation of an augmented reality platform dubbed the Augmented Reality Assistant, or ARA, and an ongoing cognitive cueing research project.

# CHAPTER 1

# Introduction

Contemporary discussions about virtual reality (VR) range from extreme enthusiasm to a belief that VR will never match its hype. The enthusiastic side sees VR infiltrating every aspect of society, from courses taught in headsets to tens of thousands of eager students to the replacement of movie theaters and other entertainment media. The disbelievers state that VR is unable to fulfill its potential and should be relegated to the dustbins of technological history, like its forbearers LaserDisc and Betamax. What's missing from both extremes is an informed conversation about what content sits inside the digital virtual spaces. The VR hardware – headsets, controllers, battery backpacks – isn't an end in itself; what makes a VR experience interesting is the content inside the headset.

Research shows that simulations, training, and digital twins provide solid VR experiences that have stated end goals such as education or preparation (Bolter & Gromala, 2003, p. 126). Other avenues of content generation for VR experiences are manifold and, in some ways, conceptually simplistic; they do not fully capitalize on all that VR has to offer. Some of these more simplistic examples of VR use are multiuser chats, streamed concerts, 360-degree videos that offer a perspective from across the world, architectural renderings, and product showcases. Often left out of discussions around what VR can offer are the works of artists engaging the medium of VR. These works map pathways and offer experiences that investigate what it means to be a physical creature immersed in a digital world. Artists have been using the medium of VR to great effect since the 1980s, and a new generation brings their early video game interactive expertise to its development.

The current resurgence in popularity of virtual and augmented realities is primarily coming from commercial sources and lacks some of the critical theory that necessarily accompanies the integration of such devices into our culture. Unfolding at a breath-taking pace, new developments in VR hardware and software gallop ahead of concept – in part due to the expensive hardware and software needed to develop and view VR. The entrepreneurial enthusiasm for VR as a content delivery method is palpable, yet it is missing purposeful integration. What makes VR different from a mere translation of the 2D digital world into 3D? What possibilities in terms of story and responsiveness are there in the virtual world? Who is missing from the conversation about the development of the virtual world? In the sense that creating content for VR is complicated and requires much skill, how does the end result merit the hard work that its creation requires? Our intention in writing this book is to touch on the history of artists using VR, discuss foundational theory surrounding technical approaches used to create VR projects, and discuss the work of contemporary artists using the medium. Seeking a "meta" approach, the following chapters shy away from fads and trends in order to offer fundamental principles of interaction, examples of content and concepts as appropriate to the medium, and evaluative methodologies that will help avoid the pitfalls of earlier failed technologies. The work of artists such as Lori Anderson and Hsin-Chien Huang has guided us in writing the book – it is through their experimentation and innovation that the intricacies and potential of the VR medium are unfolding. While there are many exciting advances in not just VR but various forms of augmented reality – we have chosen to focus on the immersive environment of a head-mounted device (HMD; a small subsection of the extended reality continuum) as opposed to mediating the physical world with a device that incorporates the digital.

While fads in VR come and go, VR as an artistic medium has been explored continuously since the 1980s. The specifics of code, hardware, and output have varied, but in each era since its unveiling, there have been examples of remarkable artworks that offer a wide variety of conceptual topics. Sometimes these works have explored the nature of humans' relationship to technology; other times, the virtual works are intimate stories of self-portraiture. This book takes a look at the historical influences that brought about the innovations leading up to contemporary VR. These influences are not just technological but also artistic experimentation, which played a central role in uncovering some of VR's potential. The following chapters also break down fundamental concepts in VR as an artistic medium, not just as physical and virtual spaces but also as the ability to interact with virtual digital content. Lastly, the book offers examples of contemporary artists whose approaches to the medium have a wide scope – examples of which range from incorporating artificial intelligence to creating ominous architectural spaces.

## WHAT IS VIRTUAL REALITY?

In his article "Virtual Second Thoughts" Wanger James Au (author of The Making of Second Life) complained that "[m]ost of the new VR technology, like the highly anticipated Oculus Rift that started shipping this week, requires a bulky and expensive headset that literally blinds a user to the outside world." Well, yes, VR headsets are supposed to blind a user to the outside world. That is because the intent of VR is to present an immersive "virtual" experience that convinces the participant through sensory and technical means that they are in fact in another "place."

*Brenda Laurel (2016)*

Extended reality technologies have been challenging the way in which humans interact with computers since their early implementations in the 1990s. An umbrella term that encompasses augmented, virtual, and other mixed reality concepts such as augmented virtuality, extended reality uses combinations of software and hardware to enhance the physical realm through spatial digital content. The output comes through the use of hardware such as headsets, controllers, transparent lens headsets, cave-automated virtual environments, dome theaters, and mobile phones. As technologies advance, an umbrella term is useful in that what constitutes "extended reality" will morph as technology advances. Currently, the various definitions under the extended reality umbrella moniker are augmented reality, VR, augmented virtuality, and mixed reality. Augmented reality is used to describe scenarios where digital virtual elements are overlaid onto the physical environment – usually via a phone or tablet. VR defines situations where the user is fully immersed in the digital environment via a headset and the physical environment is suppressed in favor of the digital stimuli. While the hardware can vary from headsets with controllers to untethered (cordless) headsets, the key element in describing VR is full visual immersion. In a best-case scenario, this immersion comes with an interactive element, meaning that the user can use an input such as gesture, voice, gaze, or controller triggers to interact with digital elements in the 3D virtual space. Lastly, mixed reality allows headset users to interact with their physical surroundings, which means that the user is not fully immersed in the virtual environment.

What is special about the medium of VR is its immersive nature, allowing users to disengage from the physical world around them in order to fully interact with a digital environment. Early VR technical pioneer Frederick Brooks defines the experience "as any in which the user is effectively immersed in a responsive virtual world. This implies user dynamic control of viewpoint" (Brooks, 1999). In his important book *Virtual Art: From Illusion to Immersion*, Oliver Grau describes immersion as being "characterized by diminishing critical distance to what is shown and increasing emotional involvement in what is happening" (2003, p. 13). Grau points out that "intellectually stimulating" and "mentally absorbing" experiences of VR artworks offer artists the opportunity to engage with their audiences in an intimate and profound way (2003, p. 13). Due to the immersion inside the headset and the disconnect from their physical surroundings, users are forced to suspend disbelief and connect immediately with their digital surroundings. Creating an immersive world gives makers the space to create complete experiences for end users, just as an immersive artwork offers artists the possibility to investigate and expand their understanding of space, perception, and immersion.

Creative VR artwork applications "do not seek to escape from our embodied world: on the contrary, VR can be a technology for exploring embodiment" (Bolter & Gromala, 2003, p. 126). For artists, capturing this embodiment within a digital world creates an opportunity for engaging with their audience in ways that mesmerize, envelop, and entrance. The artworks in this book give evidence to this – the artists chosen each bring their personal experience, technical know-how, and cultural background to bear in the development of their VR worlds. The artworks described in the following pages are stellar examples of Jerry Saltz's description of art as "the greatest operating system our species have ever invented, a means of exploring consciousness, seen and unseen worlds" (2022, p. 8).

Harkening back to the 1980s, the term "virtual reality" was used by innovative computer engineer Jason Lanier to describe what he and his friend Thomas Zimmerman developed: a virtual-reality headpiece and interactive data glove that allowed users to manipulate virtual digital objects in cyberspace. In describing applications in the virtual world, there is often the mistaken idea that the best works are the most "virtual" or the works that most accurately reproduce physical reality. This somewhat reductionist approach could be said to value simulation over innovation. Instead, VR development offers "bare potentiality intrinsic to human experience, always subject to technological modulation" (Krebs, 2023). The potential offered by VR can be found in the concept of embodied conceptual space. Embodied space "is the location where human experience and consciousness take on material and spatial form" (Low, 2003). What works well is when users are not asked to forget their bodies but to integrate and experiment within virtual creations. This ability offers a method to alter perception and "does away with the dualism responsible for the modern disenchantment of nature and—decentering the human, placing it as equally part of a rhizomatic and entangled nature" (Krebs, 2023). When an artist like Jacolby Satterwhite invites users to his intimate virtual spaces, interaction occurs not out of a perceived need to explain but out of an offering that opens the door to the unexpected, the surprising, the impermeable to interpretation, and yes, a kinship – the understanding that we as humans are performative, variable, and fragile.

Interactive VR also offers a shift in the roles of content creators and their end users. Compared to passive television viewing or interaction with the flat monitors of the web, VR can offer the end user a sense of personal autonomy. Instead of a solely time-based interaction with visuals, interactive VR offers participants the capacity to explore and shift scenes. Laurie Anderson and Hsin-Chien Huang's work, *The Chalkroom*, is a text-based piece that offers a non-linear approach, which offers a "library of stories, and no one will ever find them all" (Holger, 2017). A digital version of choose-your-own-adventure, *The Chalkroom*, uses text, language, storytelling, and a specific esthetic environment to create an unforgettable experience.

Oliver Grau defines new media art as a "comprehensive term that encompasses art forms that are either produced, modified, and transmitted by means of new media/digital technologies or, in a broader sense, make use of 'new' and emerging technologies that originate from a scientific, military, or industrial context" (2016). By definition, VR sits within the perspective of "new" media art. While the qualifier "new" isn't necessarily appropriate, media artworks do offer something to contemporary notions of art, through explorations of "creativity, medium, system and interaction. It is this tension between apparent exteriority and curious intimacy that lends media art its critical purchase within contemporary art" (Bunt, 2012). Many artists working within the VR environment are at the vanguard of immersive interactive exploration, and their explorations reveal much about identity, notions of real and unreal, interactive decision-making, and juxtapositions between corporeal and non-corporal needs. The artists herein belong because the depth of their work transcends the medium of virtuality.

A major issue with new media works is their maintenance. How to archive when the computers that supported the work are antiques? The intangible nature of digital artworks prompts a host of issues in terms of the work's relevance. Works that rely on the "wow" factor of a new technology can become obsolete once that technology is widely adopted or potentially abandoned. Works whose concept is profound and "asks big questions" require us "to think in languages beyond words…makes us reckon with uncomfortable things, compels us to look for difference, to glean the pressures of necessity and to notice the monumental in details" (Saltz, 2022, p. 8). The artworks in this book are primarily interactive VR experiences, although some early artists' works are 360-degree immersive worlds that are minimally interactive. The 360-degree works chosen for review ultimately helped to guide and inform other artists discussed, who developed immersive, responsive VR works of greater complexity.

## ARTIST TECHNOLOGISTS

In choosing artists for this book, we focused on artist technologists – artists that are well versed in the mediums, tools, and skills that are required to create VR works. This usually includes 3D modeling programs, coding, gaming development platforms, and associated VR hardware. Each of the works curated within Chapters 5, 7, 9, and 11 was created by artists using VR as their medium. In contrast, some artists will "direct" a VR work, allowing a VR company to fabricate the digital experience. Artists who are "makers" within the medium of VR bring their intimate and specialized knowledge to bear when creating their works. In the cases of Rachel Rossin, Jacolby Satterwhite, and Lawrence Lek, their early introduction to interactive technology was through playing video games. This foundation threads through each of their works in very individualistic ways. For Rossin, early video gaming experience means bringing in scenes from popular games and manipulating them for output not just in VR but also in painting form. Lek creates video games as artworks based on his practice of "making worlds for audiences to journey through" (Artnet Gallery Network, 2022). Satterwhite draws on "his technical virtuosity to reclaim the video-game environments of his childhood, re-inhabiting them with his own community all through the sharp lens of art history" (Bullock, 2018).

The artists chosen for this book have all had gallery or museum representation and are a bridge between what galleries and museums more traditionally show and works that require a VR system (such as a headset) in order to be fully enveloped in the virtual experience. While there are many contemporary VR artists working in fantastic ways outside the boundaries of the gallery and museum systems, it's important to acknowledge and highlight those artists that will bring the galleries and museums closer to a fuller understanding of the medium and its practices. It's important to also acknowledge that VR works do not yet garner the big money that more traditional mediums do – the double-edged sword of this is that it means that access to the field is more fluid. Like many of the artists, Ian Cheng and Matteo Zamagni are both represented by galleries, which can provide art-world vetting and a system of support for international exhibitions and art fairs. Lastly, the digital nature of VR also provides access to artworks that are specific to the artist's culture, like the work of Persian artist Mohsen Hazarati and the "post-futurist" themes of Sandrine Deumier, a trained artist-philosopher.

The artists chosen herein have authored multiple works in VR, have done extensive research into immersive VR's development tools as a medium, and/or were important pioneers whose work ultimately contributed to VR as a medium for art. The great Laurie Anderson has worked in experimental technologies since the 1970s. Her collaboration with VR artist Hsin-Chien Huang resulted in "The Chalkroom," an innovative work that draws on a deep foundation of interactive artwork knowledge and is one of the most highly visible VR artworks to date, as well as several other masterful works. Anderson states that VR "does what [she] always wanted to do as an artist from the time [she] started, which is a kind of disembodiment" (Anderson & Huang, 2017). While many talented and technical artists have created one or two VR works, this book is focused on artists who have demonstrated themselves to be committed and invested in furthering VR art as "an instrument, medium, matrix, or miracle that transforms old impressions into new thoughts; that makes a thousand insignificant details light up and draw you out" (Saltz, 2022, p. 8).

## A BIT OF VIRTUAL REALITY HISTORY

Chapter 2 discusses the surprisingly long history of VR's early forms – the types of lenses that are used in HMDs are very similar to the lenses that allowed people in the 1850s to look at images through a stereoscope and see a 3D image. The technological foundations for VR go back to the mid- to late-eighteenth century, with the development of the stereoscope attributed mainly to Sir Charles Wheatstone. Improvements and experiments continued throughout Wheatstone's time, as he often reached out to others for contributions. One such effort was Wheatstone's communication with early photographer Henry Fox Talbot. Wheatstone's early stereoscopic cards were primarily simple drawings; it was Wheatstone's hope that Talbot's imagery would help popularize the stereoscope. While no record remains of Talbot's images, Wheatstone's desire for intriguing artistic content to deepen investment and interest in his technical hardware echoes today's need for artistic approaches for the creation of VR content. The stereoscopic lenses contributed to much later technologies, one example of which is Morton Heilig's *Sensorama* (1956). *Sensorama* allowed people to be "in" a movie rather than just viewing – a participant sat within a machine that included a stereoscopic color display, fans, odor emitters, a stereo sound system, and a motional chair. Around the same time, computer graphics pioneer Ivan Sutherland was conducting research that resulted in *The Head Mounted Display*, "a screen, think of it as a window, a window through which one looks into a virtual world" (Brooks, 1999). Commonly but mistakenly called *The Sword of Damocles*, *The Head Mounted Display* stands out as a very recognizable forbearer for today's headsets.

Stepping outside of commercial or military applications and inviting play, early interactive artworks such as "Videoplace," created by Myron Krueger, ultimately contributed to immersive interactive components in virtual realities. Krueger's books "Artificial Reality" and "Artificial Reality II" were important in understanding how the computer-generated worlds of VR and augmented reality could present "a view of our future interaction with machines, when computer systems will sense our needs and respond to them" (Krueger, 1983). The book discusses Krueger's personal journey in the creation of his human-computer interactive works. Kruger points out that "it is easy to get the impression that the Big Bang occurred at NASA in 1984 and that VR is a triumph of the technical establishment alone. What has been overlooked is the important contributions that artists have made to the development of the field" (Krueger, 1993). Technological advances such as Atari's games and the development of the Apple personal computer also contributed to VR's development. Many of the programmers and engineers, such as Brenda Laurel and Jason Lanier, moved fluidly from company to start-up and brought their teammates with them.

## EARLY VIRTUAL REALITY ARTWORKS

An excellent example of how artists can approach the virtual world with fresh ideas and unusual approaches is found in Chapter 3, a Virtual Reality Modeling Language (VRML) artwork created by artist Char Davies in 1995. Using a HMD and a motion-track vest, Davies' *Osmose* allowed viewers to interact with the artwork through the use of their breath and balance. The low-polygonal worlds the participant experienced were compelling and ethereal – abstract and partially transparent. Davies' approach to developing *Osmose* was not mired in a translation of traditional computer inputs to the virtual space, but instead she incorporated the breath and pulse of the user to navigate the space. Because of this innovative approach and her lack of desire to recreate the physical world into a virtual one, "Osmose" is as compelling today as it was in 1995. This example of creative exploration is based on the medium of immersive VR rather than traditional computer input/outputs such as a keyboard and mouse and a monitor.

Another important virtual artist of this period is Brenda Laurel. After working at Atari, Laurel became interested in working in VR with former colleague Scott Fisher. Laurel went on to co-create *Placeholder* (1992) with MIT architecture graduate Rachel Strickland. *Placeholder* is still innovative in terms of how the user moves through space. Rather than porting more traditional computer interfaces into the virtual digital world, *Placeholder* uses iconography and mythology to guide users through the space. Nicole Stenger billed her work *Angels* (1992) as the first interactive movie. Conceived for three senses: vision, audio, and touch, Stenger's work was miles ahead of the technology at the time, and she had to reconcile herself to using a non-tactile data glove for users to interact with her work.

## WORKING IN VIRTUAL REALITY AS A MEDIUM

Chapter 4 breaks down the basic foundational mechanics and input methods that VR authors use and build on. In the fact that VR software tools and its attendant hardware are constantly in flux, this chapter does not get into specifics about which software to use or how to develop for a particular brand of headset. Instead, this chapter covers the concepts of gesture, interaction, translation, mimicry, concept, and various interaction components. Included in this discussion are the theories and concepts from the field of computer-human interaction that help to guide and inform the interactions enabled and produced by VR systems. Chapter 6 discusses visual conceptual space. Whereas many digital works are displayed on a 2D plane, VR offers an immersive 360-degree space that fills the viewer's field of vision. This "aims at producing a high-grade feeling of immersion, of presence (an impression suggestion of 'being there') which can be enhanced further through interaction with apparently 'living' environments in 'real time'" (Grau, 2003, p. 7). As such, it is important to consider the lineage established by the 2D plane, namely that of metaphorical windows, mirrors, and frames, and how new media technologies, such as VR, challenge and break these prior notions regarding visual artistic works. Chapter 8 investigates how artist technologists use VR as a medium and what it means when authorship of the application is delegated elsewhere. There is also significant consideration on the topic of what constitutes a medium versus a tool when creating artistic works. Chapter 10 discusses embodied artistic space. This chapter investigates what it means to be embodied creatures that interact with others and how the body reacts as "a representational medium for the mind" (Myers & Biocca, 2006). VR is built upon sensory illusions that are interacted with in a corporeal form. This, in turn, creates significant and unique opportunities for artists when properly capitalized upon. Chapter 12 looks at the control of output and access to virtual artistic content. Where do VR artworks get seen, and what are some ways to promote them? What caveats, limitations, and considerations exist when working with necessarily commercialized hardware, tools, and techniques? Lastly, the conclusion discusses the need for a book on VR artworks and some of our aspirations for the future of the medium, as well as a grander discussion of how each of the chapters ties into each other. None of the concepts discussed in the chapters are solitary; each must be attended to create engaging and masterful VR artistic works.

In writing this book, we started with the premise that it is often the artists who offer the necessary critical lens with which to approach the world; whether physical or virtual.

> I think you have your technical form of your art, which is one thing. And it should not ever be confused with the esthetic manipulation of that art, or certainly the content of the art. They are entirely different questions. Cocteau, for example said "What do I care? You know, on what size the paper you write a poem? It doesn't matter to me if the paper is small or big." He said that in response to people such as myself, who were trying to expand the sensory information, going from a small screen of that type to perhaps an IMAX or OMNIMAX screen. One thing has absolutely nothing to do with the other. If you put a very powerful technical medium in the hands of a klutz, you're going to wind up with nothing.
>
> Obviously, no matter what the technical form is, whether it's painting, music, poetry, or whatever, it has to be put in the hands of somebody who has something meaningful to communicate, and who is an artist.
>
> – *Myron Krueger (cited in Barlow et al., 1990)*

## REFERENCES

Anderson, L., & Huang, H.-C. (2017). *Chalkroom*. Laurie Anderson. https://laurieanderson.com/?portfolio=chalkroom

Artnet Gallery Network. (2022, June 15). Spotlight: Artist Lawrence Lek melds video-game technology and eerie films to peer into our A.I.-dominated future. *Artnet News.* https://news.artnet.com/buyers-guide/spotlight-artist-lawrence-lek-vh-award–2130745

Barlow, J., Dyson, E., Leary, T., Bricken, W., Robinett, W., Lanier, J., & Jacobson, B. (1990). Hip, hype and hope—The three faces of virtual worlds (panel session). *Proceedings of the ACM SIGGRAPH 90 Panel,* 1001–1029. https://doi.org/10.1145/328750.328798

Bolter, J. D., & Gromala, D. (2003). *Windows and mirrors: Interaction design, digital art, and the myth of transparency.* MIT Press.

Brooks, F. P. (1999). What's real about virtual reality? *IEEE Computer Graphics and Applications, 19*(6), 16–27. https://doi.org/10.1109/38.799723

Bullock, M. (2018). Interview: Jacolby Satterwhite on how video games, art history, and sleep deprivation inspire his 3d interiors. *Pin-Up, 25.* https://archive.

pinupmagazine.org/articles/interview-3d-queer-artist-jacolby-satterwhite-on-video-game-environments

Bunt, B. (2012). Media art, mediality and art generally. *Leonardo*, *45*(1), 94–95. https://www.jstor.org/stable/41421814

Grau, O. (2003). *Virtual art: From illusion to immersion*. MIT Press. https://direct.mit.edu/books/book/2550/Virtual-ArtFrom-Illusion-to-Immersion

Grau, O. (2016). New media art. *Oxford Bibliographies*. https://doi.org/10.1093/OBO/9780199920105-0082

Holger, D. (2017, October 5). Laurie Anderson's dark VR art makes you "fly through stories." *VRScout*. https://vrscout.com/news/laurie-anderson-vr-chalkroom/

Krebs, V. J. (2023). Digital animism: Towards a new materialism. *Religions*, *14*(2), 264. https://doi.org/10.3390/rel14020264

Krueger, M. (1993). The artistic origins of virtual reality. *SIGGRAPH 1993: Machine Culture*, 148–149. https://digitalartarchive.siggraph.org/writing/the-artistic-origins-of-virtual-reality/

Krueger, M. W. (1983). *Artificial reality*. Addison-Wesley.

Laurel, B. (2016). *What is virtual reality?* https://doi.org/10.13140/RG.2.1.4415.0643

Low, S. M. (2003). Embodied space(s): Anthropological theories of body, space, and culture. *Space and Culture*, *6*(1), 9–18. https://doi.org/10.1177/1206331202238959

Myers, P., & Biocca F. (2006) The elastic body image: The effect of television advertising and programming on body image distortions in young women. *Journal of Communication*, *42*(3), 108–133. https://doi.org/10.1111/j.1460-2466.1992.tb00802.x

Saltz, J. (2022). *Art is life: Icons and iconoclasts, visionaries and vigilantes, and flashes of hope in the night*. Riverhead Books.

# CHAPTER 2

# Early Predecessors

## HISTORICAL INFLUENCES

The elaborate electronic head-mounted displays may seem novel and confuse some, but the foundational concept of viewing a scene through stereoscopic vision is over a hundred years old. Indeed, many of the techniques used in the virtual reality (VR) of the 21st century were first discovered in the mid- to late 1800s. In looking for a definition of VR that bridges today's digital simulacrum to that of its technical predecessors, we can define these experiences as ones that use special equipment and software to create an immersive three-dimensional illusion. They aim to suppress the physical environment and present a virtual one through mediated stimuli. To create this illusion of dimensionality, the brain integrates the spatial information from two visual inputs and interprets this information to create a sense of depth of field. The historical use of overlapping imagery that creates this sense of dimensionality started with hand-drawn images, advanced to photographs, and can now exist in the form of motion-sensing headsets with special lenses to focus digital content. The link between these forms of illusory depth remains consistent in the "stereoscopic" nature of the devices – all of these examples use two eyepieces to impart a three-dimensional effect to two visual inputs of the same scene, each input's snapshot of the scene taken from slightly different angles.

Sir Charles Wheatstone's *Stereoscope* was the first example of the type of device that led to today's VR. Wheatstone's *Stereoscope* differs the most from such mechanisms in that it uses mirrors at 45° angles to trick the

DOI: 10.1201/9781003363729-2

viewer's eyes into combining two separate images to produce a three-dimensional object in the viewer's mind. Built in 1838, the *Stereoscope* originally had hand-drawn, simplistic images that offered an illusion of perspective. In 1840, when the burgeoning field of photography developed, Wheatstone reached out to British photographer Henry Fox Talbot and asked Talbot to consider producing photographic images for Wheatstone to use.

He believed, "one of the most immediately profitable applications of your new art would be to the production of stereoscopic pictures, for which there exists now an immense sale" (Wheatstone, 1858). While there are no records of the images Talbot provided to Wheatstone, we know that Talbot's photographs from this period ranged from still life, trees, and self-portraiture to the facades of buildings (Metherell, 2017). Wheatstone worried about the cost of the images to the end user. In his letter to Talbot, Wheatstone wrote, "My large stereoscope, far superior as it is to the others, has never become popular on account of the expense of the pictures. Were they reproduced by your method, I have no doubt that if some optician <sic> to take it up he would find it to answer his purpose" (Wheatstone, 1858). Even with Talbot's stereoscopic photographs, the *Stereoscope* never reached the popularity of later stereoscopic devices – especially as the devices that followed were lightweight and could be hand held – an improvement over Wheatsone's heavy and bulky mechanism.

In 1849, Sir David Brewster made major improvements to Wheatstone's *Stereoscope* by replacing the mirrors with lenticular lenses – these double-convex lenses consisted "of a single lens cut in half so that the two half-lenses, when appropriately mounted, acted as magnifiers as well as prisms, fusing adjacent stereo drawings or photographs" (Ono et al., 2013). Known for his work in physical optics, Brewer's stereoscope used solid-backed daguerreotypes that didn't need light to filter through them – looking very much like the wooden predecessors of today's VR head-mounted displays. Brewster produced multiple versions of his viewers and was able to offer mid-range and inexpensive renditions (Burford, 2021) (Figures 2.1 and 2.2).

The version of the stereoscope that most people today are familiar with is likely to be the Holmes stereoscope, developed in 1861 by Oliver Wendell Holmes. The success of Holmes' innovation was in part due to its affordability, as Holmes chose not to patent his version to keep the price down. Holmes' hand-held viewer used a single stereo card that contained

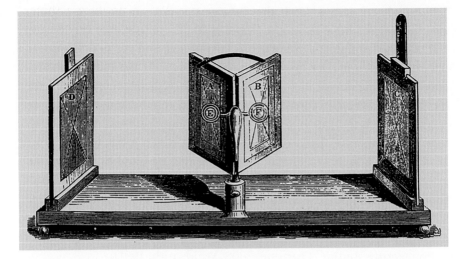

**FIGURE 2.1** Charles Wheatstone. "Stereoscope" (1840s). Woodcut. Public domain, via Wikimedia Commons.

**FIGURE 2.2** Brewster-type stereo slide and stereo photo viewer (second half of the 19th century). Popular Science Monthly Volume 21, Public domain, via Wikimedia Commons.

both images taken from different angles. Stereo card manufacturers also aided in making Holmes' device popular, as they produced thousands of stereo cards compatible with his viewer.

Although created in 1939, the *Viewmaster* did not become popular until the 1950s. This was another hand-held device that gave the illusion of 3D depth through the use of a specialized lens and images. The popularity of the *Viewmaster* followed in the footsteps of the Holmes stereoscope in that the device was inexpensive to produce and there was a wide offering of *Viewmaster* cards. *Viewmaster* card content came from popular sources such as contemporary films of the day and breathtaking views from national parks. The cards also included stereo cards created from elaborate small-scale sculptural 3D sets created by hand by *Viewmaster* artists such as Florence Thomas and her successor Joe Liptak. These sets recreated scenes from animated movies and television series and required skilled set building craftsmanship to develop "special methods of close-up stereo photography and modeling which is now in common use by major motion picture studios" (Torrone, 2008; Waldsmith, 1991).

Stereoscopic viewing as an artistic or entertainment medium did not really appear on the scene until the move away from the hand-held and widely distributed to the very specialized. Morton Heilig's *Sensorama* (1956), which allowed people to be "in" a movie rather than just viewing it. The original flier for the *Sensorama Simulator* states that it is "an entirely new kind of communication device which creates for its user the illusion of being physically present in a different environment" (*Introducing the Sensorama Simulator*, n.d.). *Sensorama* was a machine that included a stereoscopic color display, fans, odor emitters, a stereo sound system, and a motional chair. Sitting inside the booth, a viewer could see, smell, hear, and feel the movie they were watching, making Heilig's work a true multimodal technology.

A 1969 article in the *New York Times* describes the device as "concave and formed of a reflective mosaic. The projector is centrally located, and loud speakers are spaced so as to provide the directional sound…for safety, spectators are to fasten themselves in their chairs with locked bars" (Jones, 1969). The "three-D, peripheral, tactual, aromatic simulator" sold for $6000 in 1964, and "tactual sensations" were felt by the viewer through the seat and the control panel that the hand rested on (*Introducing the Sensorama Simulator*, n.d.). One of the movies offered showed motorcycle rides through New York City – complete with bumps, rushing wind, and a range of vision wider than that of a TV or movie screen. Alternatively, participants could experience water skiing, skydiving, toboggan rides, skin diving, a gondola ride in Venice, bullfighting, a helicopter ride through the Grand Canyon, and an intimate view of Michelangelo's David

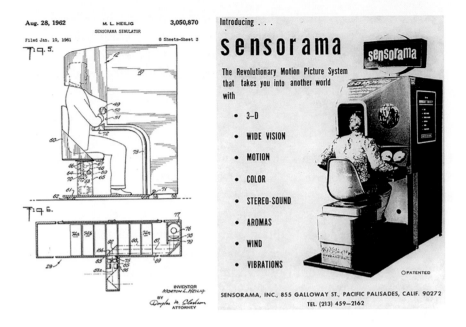

**FIGURE 2.3** Morton Heilig "Sensorama" (1962). The first virtual immersion system, the technical table, and the pictures shown at the presentation of the experimental product. Distributed under a CC BY-SA 4.0 license.

(*Introducing the Sensorama Simulator,* n.d.). Heilig's experiment and invention bring us to one of the first examples of immersive, interactive media. While television invited audiences to passively watch what was on the screen, Heilig's device required user selection and physical response to stimulus on screen. His inclusion of smell makes *Sensorama* avant-garde even today, as few examples of immersive works use the sense of smell to integrate participants (Figure 2.3).

In many ways, it makes sense that Mort Heilig would be the one to adapt the burgeoning technology of immersive reality into an entertainment system. Heilig, 37 at the time of *Sensorama's* invention, graduated from the University of Chicago, the Centro Sperimentate de Cinematographa (Rome), and received a Master's degree in Communications from the University of Pennsylvania. He described himself as an inventor-film-maker, as he produced and directed some 50 documentary films. This background in communications and cinema allowed Heilig to approach *Sensorama* with a narrative foundation and focus. Heilig had grand visions of how *Sensorama* could be used, even describing how astronauts could benefit from *Sensorama*:

"Day after day, with nothing to look at but the black void, the astronauts could sit in the machine and see wheat fields in Kansas, smell the hay, walk down main street of their hometown, see and hear their wives talking to them. I think that would be meaningful"

*(Junker, 1965).*

Heilig's deep belief in his simulation went beyond his dedication to *Sensorama*. In a response to a SIGGRAPH panel held in the 1990s, Heilig stated:

There is a tremendous tradition, going all the way back to the cave-man, of people who, in the arts in one fashion or another, have tried to immerse the spectator in an environment and give him as powerful and complete an illusion of reality as they could. They were limited by the technological means at their disposal at the time. Now, we have this marvelous new medium of video and the computer, obviously enormously extending their power. But, let us not have any illusions that we are operating without a tradition. We have a tremendous tra-dition behind us. The roots are rather obscure, but they are there.

*(Barlow et al., 1990)*

Less well known than *Sensorama*, in 1957, Heilig also developed the *Stereoscopic-Television Apparatus for Individual Use*, a headset eerily pre-scient to today's VR head-mounted displays. More commonly called the *Telesphere Mask*, the headset includes small speakers to fit over the user's ear. Heilig received the patent for the device in 1960, 8 years before the next lens-based headset (Heilig, 1960) (Figure 2.4).

Heilig's patent describes the headset as giving the user "a complete sen-sation of reality, i.e. moving three dimensional images which may be in color, with 100% peripheral vision, binaural sound, scents and air breezes." Unfortunately, the headset was not a commercial success, and Heilig was compelled to stop marketing the device. Arguably, Heilig has not garnered proper appreciation for his endeavors; supposedly, his widow, Marianne Heilig, has the "Telesphere Mask" in a box at home, as the Smithsonian Institution rejected it (Brockwell, 2016).

Somewhat concurrently to Heilig's *Sensorama*, computer graph-ics pioneer Ivan Sutherland developed what was called *The Head*

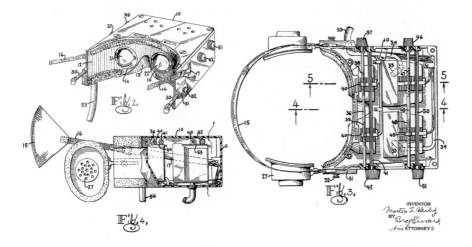

**FIGURE 2.4** Morton Heilig "Telesphere Mask" (1960). Patent – issued in October 1960. Public domain, via Wikimedia Commons.

*Mounted Display* – often mistakenly called "The Sword of Damocles" (I. E. Sutherland, personal communication, March 16, 2023). Created in 1968 while at Harvard, Sutherland had been investigating the virtual realm for many years before. While working as head of the Information Processing Techniques Office at the US Defense Department Advanced Research Project Agency (ARPA), Sutherland wrote an essay in 1965 called "The Ultimate Display," where he envisions "A display connected to a digital computer [that] gives us a chance to gain familiarity with concepts not realizable in the physical world. It is a looking glass into a mathematical wonderland" (Sterling, 2009). In a lecture at the International Federation for Information Processing (IFIP) Congress in 1965 on the same topic, Sutherland asks his listeners to "think of that thing as a screen, think of it as a window, a window through which one looks into a virtual world" (Brooks, 1999; Sutherland, 1965). These ideas regarding the virtual world and how to interact with it helped to establish foundations that would lead to contemporary VR systems.

After his move to Harvard, Sutherland and his engineering students used a computer program to generate stereoscopic displays with simple wireframe graphics of rooms for *The Head Mounted Display* visuals. The head mount tracked the viewer's gaze, to which the computer program generated a responsive perspective. The display itself was tracked mechanically through ceiling-mounted hardware that ran 12 feet in length (Sutherland, 1965). While primitive in terms of visuals and uncomfortable

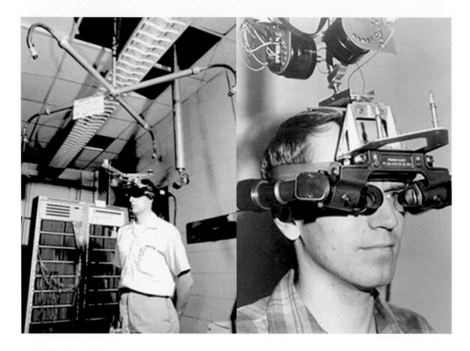

**FIGURE 2.5** Dr. Ivan Sutherland "Head Mounted Display" (1968). Courtesy of Dr. Ivan Sutherland.

in terms of hardware, Sutherland's *Head Mounted Display* marks the first time a user's gaze and head position generate a change in the imagery's perspective – a truly immersive, responsive environment very much like that of today's immersive VR (Figure 2.5).

During the period in which Sutherland and his students were developing efforts to create a stereoscopic "virtual reality," the notion of immersive virtual space existed almost exclusively in academic institutions and government agencies such as the Department of Defense and the National Aeronautics and Space Administration. Heavily invested in the technology's practical applications, the work of these agencies led to developments such as modern flight simulators, remote camera trackers, and night vision piloting systems. Due to the prohibitive size and expense of the equipment and the software needed to run such virtual simulators, the technology was often locked away within these agencies, with only those directly involved working consistently to evaluate its impact and use.

In 1982, Myron Kreuger authored *Artificial Reality*, making him another important pioneer in the virtual world. What sets Krueger apart from other experimenters in the field is his focus on responsiveness in the virtual environment. This responsiveness can be defined as, "a computer perceives the actions of those who enter and responds intelligently through complex visual and auditory displays" (Krueger, 1977). Krueger was also very interested in immersing the participant in an artificial reality that surrounded its users and responded to their movements. Krueger states that while he had considered head-mounted displays, he rejected them as he felt that the immersive environment they offered was offset negatively by the heavy apparatus that users would have to wear. Instead, Krueger wanted the experience to be indistinguishable from "real experience." Kreuger states that "instead of an alien planet accessed through an airlock, it would be like a doorway to a fantasy world that you could enter simply by attending to it" (Turner & Krueger, 2002).

Krueger earned a PhD in Computer Science at the University of Wisconsin-Madison, during which he collaborated on a number of computer controlled environments. These interactive experiments led to Krueger's *Videoplace - An Artificial Reality* which was funded by the National Endowment for the Arts and shown in the Milwaukee Art Museum in 1975. *Videoplace* incorporated projectors, screens, and video cameras, as well as specific hardware, to accomplish Krueger's goal of creating an immersive space. As Krueger sees himself as an artist, *Videoplace* can be seen as an early artwork rather than an experiment in technology for entertainment or military uses (Barlow et al., 1990). The computer-generated graphic environment of *Videoplace* created a live feed of the participant's digitized silhouettes, projecting them into the artificial reality environment. The silhouettes were projected in different colors, allowing for a sense of presence on the screen. As participants' silhouettes intersected with the shadows of others, they would respond in a variety of ways – sometimes reaching out for connection and other times pulling away and avoiding "touch." Additionally, there could be images funneled in from participants in different locations – making Krueger's work an early experiment in telepresence and collaborative computing. Running on a VAX 11/780, the computer cognitive system could also alter the participant's image on the screen, causing it to rotate and be placed throughout (Norman, n.d.-a).

*Critter* was a specific scenario that ran inside of *Videoplace*. In this case, the participant's silhouette is projected onto a screen and is joined by a single graphic creature. The creature's programming is complex and contextually dependent, invoking a sense of anthropomorphism in the participant. If the participant moves toward the creature, the graphic object will move away to avoid contact. If the participant reaches out their hand, only then does "Critter" land – ultimately doing a "triumphant jig" when reaching the participant's head (Krueger et al., 1985).

In a paper presented at CHI '85, Krueger states, "as a greater percentage of the population becomes involved in the use of computers, it is natural to expect the manner of controlling computers to move away from the programming model and closer to the perceptual process we use to accomplish our goals in the physical world" (Krueger et al., 1985). Kreuger (1977) writes that in the *Videoplace* environment, the participant is "stripped of his informed expectations and forced to deal with the moment in its own terms…he does not simply admire the work of the artist; he shares in its creation".

While *Sensorama* and *The Head Mounted Display* had specific audiences and goals, Kreuger's work steps outside of commercial or military applications and invites play. Participants in *Videoplace* had a variety of responses; none were prescribed, but instead the work invited individualistic investigation. Krueger's work in the history of VR is not a departure from immersive reality as a tool for technological advancement but rather a step toward immersive reality as an artistic medium.

Adjacent to Krueger's experiments, VR engineers and developers at Atari's Sunnyvale Research Lab went on to become some of the biggest conceptual and developmental leads in the VR realm. Operating for only 2 years, the Lab's director, Alan Kay, had come from Xerox PARC. Backed by Atari and given a big budget, Kay began to court creative makers to come and work at the Lab. Kay campaigned to bring Scott Fisher, who was at the MIT Media Lab' predecessor, the MIT Architecture Machine Group. Fisher had been working on telepresence, and when he joined Atari's lab, he was tasked with turning "the expensive, handmade equipment that was required for VR in the laboratory, into less expensive plastic equipment that could be mass-produced for the arcade ecosystem" (Johnson, 2016).

Fisher remembers Kay asking, "What was going to be the home of the future? The interfaces?" as well as Kay's encouragement for tech innovation (Johnson, 2016). Atari's VR and interface innovations began to attract a variety of creative innovators. Thomas Zimmerman filed a patent in 1982 on an "optical flex sensor mounted in a glove to measure finger bending" with tactile feedback "used to add realism to interactions between computer-generated (virtual) objects and the virtual hand" (Zimmerman et al., 1987). Calling his device the *Data Glove,* ZImmerman moved to California and joined Atari, thinking that Atari would be excited by the glove and invest in it. When Zimmerman presented the glove, his manager offered him $10,000 for it, but a friend cautioned him that the amount was too low and that he should hold out. Setting the *Data Glove* aside for a moment, Zimmerman joined Atari's Lab in Sunnyvale, where he worked with fellow interactive pioneer Jaron Lanier.

In 1982, Lanier helped create the video game "Alien Garden" for the Atari 800 console, which was published by Epyx Games ("Alien Garden," 2023). When Lanier joined Atari in 1983 and saw Tom Zimmerman's *Data Glove,* he was excited. Lanier had been "using a tablet and a glove sounded like a much better interface". While Atari was generous to the Sunnyvale lab, that generosity in part brought on financial trouble when the gaming market crashed due to market saturation and the rise of the home computer (Schnipper, n.d.). Atari split into two companies, and the Sunnyvale lab was closed. Fisher moved on to NASA Ames Research in Mountain View, and Lanier and Zimmerman found themselves unemployed (Rosen, 2017).

Convinced that they had something in Zimmerman's *Data Glove* Lanier and Zimmerman formed the company Visual Programming Language (VPL) in 1983. At VPL, ZImmerman and Lanier were really technological futurists – providing demos of software and hardware that would come to shape the field of VR. They used 3D glasses to create "prototypes on an Amiga with stereo imagery" and created "an ultrasonic tracking device so we knew where the glove was in five dimensions. That really expanded it. Now you had a hand in 3D. By 1986, 1987, we were on the cover of *Scientific American.*" Reaching out to Scott Fisher at NASA, VPL discovered that NASA was working on head-mount displays (Rosen, 2017). VPL showed progress they'd made with the glove and stated that the meeting demonstrated that the glove and the glasses went together like "peanut butter meeting chocolate" (Norman, n.d.-b; Rosen, 2017) (Figure 2.6).

Even though Atari had split into two companies, innovative research within the divisions continued. In 1982, Cynthia Soloman brought the Logo Programming Language, originally developed at MIT's Artificial Intelligence Laboratory, to the Atari Cambridge Laboratory (Solomon, 2007). Originally designed for the Apple II Plus and developed by Logo Computer Systems, Solomon's intention was to design a programming language more accessible to children. Desiring to continue research, Soloman

**FIGURE 2.6** Thomas Zimmerman "Early Data Glove" (1983). Courtesy of Thomas Zimmerman.

contacted Alan Kay, chief scientist at Atari. Solomon then became director of the Atari Cambridge Research Laboratory, where one primary focus was to look at ways to control computers through gestures. At MIT, Solomon worked with Marvin Minsky, a co-founder of MIT's Institute of Technology's Artificial Intelligence Laboratory. The Minsky family fostered innovation and scientific process in their children, with daughter Margaret parlaying her PhD in haptics to become an artist investigating whole-body interaction. After receiving her PhD from MIT's Media Lab, Margaret was the lead developer for a breakthrough in creating haptic textures. Minksy's research on haptics continued as a member of the research staff at Atari Corporation, then at Interval Research Corporation, after which she taught at University of North Carolina, Chapel Hill. As principal investigator, in 1990, Margaret Minsky's published paper explored haptic inputs and was entitled "Feeling and Seeing: Issues in Force Display." The paper documents "using the sense of touch, the haptic system, as part of our everyday interface with computationally created worlds" (Minsky et al., 1990). The system *Virtual Sandpaper* was designed to experiment with the ability to feel texture through a motor-driven two-degree of freedom joystick. While we still use essentially the same mouse and keyboard system demonstrated in 1968 by Douglas Englebart, Minskey and her research group, led by the University of North Carolina's computer science department founder Fred Brooks, explored ways to translate physical texture and touch to the hand of someone using a controller. In addition to sandpaper, Minsky's force-feedback joystick was used to replicate "stirring virtual ice cubes in virtual molasses" (Holloway & Lastra, 1993). In 1997, Minsky wrote a paper that asked *"will haptics research parallel computer graphics research?"* where she compares the haptics field as "sparse, wide, and wooly as Computer Graphics was 20 years ago" (Minsky, 1997).

In a 2020 paper on the use of VR haptics for blind or low-vision users, the paper's authors point out that "current virtual reality technologies focus on rendering visuospatial effects, and thus are inaccessible for blind or low vision users" (Siu et al., 2020). It would seem that the promise of haptic creation developed out of research like Minsky's in the late 1980s and early 1990s has yet to be fulfilled. Minksy, like Myron Krueger, ultimately defines herself not just as an engineer but as an artist. Both Krueger and Minsky step across the fuzzy line of what's practical into the realm of imaginative experience, and this is reflected in their contributions to interface.

Another debt is owed to the creative visioning offered by science fiction writers, who help societies to envision objects and systems that inform real-world technological developments. Two heavyweights in terms of speculative immersive realities are William Gibson's *Neuromancer* (1984) and Neil Stephenson's *Snow Crash* (1993). Gibson coined the term "cyberspace" for *Neuromancer* as the concept "allowed for a lot of moves, because characters can be sucked into apparent realities-which means you can place them in any sort of setting or against any backdrop you want" (Punday, 2000). In Gibson's cyberspace, a matrix of computers and systems of data are visualized through geometric shapes floating like a "transparent 3D chessboard extending to infinity" (Kelly, 2018). Gibson's vision of cyberspace is important in terms of "elevating the prominence of VR cyber-realms within the public consciousness" (Kelly, 2018). What often gets lost is that the "consensual hallucination" of cyberspace created in *Neuromancer* takes place in a dystopian world, and via some social media outlets, Gibson has expressed some dismay that fans of his technological visions take the work at face value, missing layers of irony. Artistic works can offer this level of criticality – an investigation into something that holds a place for ambivalence. A nuanced critical approach is often missing when a novel technology is touted by commercial or corporate means. How can you unveil a technology's dark side if you need to make money off of its profits?

Released around 10 years later than *Neuromancer,* Neal Stephenson's *Snow Crash* was the first to coin the term "metaverse." The metaverse in "Snow Crash" describes a virtual dimensional world where humans in the physical realm don headsets to interact with others in a virtual space (Stephenson, 1992). Much like Gibson's cyberspace, this metaverse is established as a technology existing in a dystopian reality. Once in virtual space, humans use "avatars" to represent themselves. An old Hindu term describing the incarnation of a deity, Stephenson is credited with popularizing the word "avatar" within the context of a person's virtual representation.

Stephenson avows that rather than looking to previous science fiction for his structure of the metaverse, he was more influenced by the *Apple Human Interface Guidelines* (Kelly, 2018). A draft of the *Guidelines,* written in 1986 and edited by John Huber for Apple Technical Publications, states that "a human interface is the sum of all communication between the computer system and the user. It is the part of the system that presents information to the user and accepts information from the user" (Huber, 1986). While these guidelines can be understood when read at face value, in the hands of an artist, the concept of "sum of all communication" is ripe for exploration. The *Guidelines* also state that while the human interface has features that are "generally applicable to a variety of applications" some of these features must be "hypothetical because they anticipate future needs, and may not be found in any current application" (Huber,

1986). From what appears to be a dry user experience guide, this was an open invitation for fantastical creation for an author of explorative science fiction like Stephenson.

Like so much of new media art's history, many factors contributed to virtual realities' development: fiction, the military complex, technological innovation, and the entertainment industry. In the late 1980s and early 1990s, a corollary technological and conceptual influence was instrumental in the development of VR technology. This was, of course, the rise of video games. At its most basic level, advancements in computer graphical interfaces and imagery for shopping mall video game arcades and home consoles fed into graphical developments for VR. Video games' emphasis on interactivity also contributed to more complex user interactions in the virtual realm. But when the video game world stepped into the realm of the digital interface, VR made its first appearance on an international stage.

With the release of the Atari console in 1977, people could bring video games out of the arcade and take them into their own living spaces to play *Space Invaders* or *Pong*. Just as early cinemagoers adapted to the fantasy of images flickering on a screen and became less frightened and confused by the Lumiere Brothers *Arrival of a Train at La Ciotat Station*, early video game players began to understand and move through digital space. Because of the increased popularity of video games in the 1980s, the broader public learned the digital and visual literacy needed to build complexity in virtual space (Steinkuehler, 2010).

In 1991, the Virtuality Group launched gaming machines equipped with a VR head-mounted display and stereoscopic 3D visuals. These machines also offered interactivity and, in some cases, could be used for multiplayer use (Islami, 2020). *The Virtuality* and its creator, Dr Jonathan Waldern, began in a garage in Leicester, England. Waldern created early VR gaming prototypes in the mid-1980s, using an active shutter system "which literally had a plastic screen that would shutter over each eye in a way that created the illusion of 3D" (Virtual Reality Society, 2018). While those systems didn't take off, Waldern's research earned him recognition. In November 1990 at Computer Graphics '90, *The Virtuality* was demonstrated and made its first sale to British Telecom to use for telepresence experiments. Great interest was generated in a variety of industries, but *The Virtuality*'s timing was perfect for the arcade market (Figure 2.7).

*The Virtuality* sitting and standing machines were more expensive than regular arcade machines and required an attendant to help the player

**FIGURE 2.7** Dr. Jonathan Waldren "Virtuality" (1989–1994). Courtesy of Dr Johnathan Waldern/Virtuality Group. CC BY-SA 4.0.

into and out of the headset. This cost was offset by players paying more to try the machine – up to four pounds for 3 minutes of play time (Virtual Reality Society, 2018). The offerings included a flight simulator, a demo derby racer, and a couple of first-person shooters. The head-tracking on Virtuality's machines was excellent, making up for the roughly 30,000 polygons rendered at 20 frames per second. For comparison, today's VR headsets have a minimum of 60 frames per second for rendering and the ability to display millions of polygons. Hoping to cash in on *Virtuality*'s success, 1980s gaming industry giants Sega and Nintendo jumped into the ring, both developing at-home VR options. Sega developed a headset, the "Sega VR," which never hit stores. Nintendo's *Virtual Boy* was the first portable game console that could show true 3D graphics through the use of parallax (Islami, 2020). To move through 3D space, the *Virtual Boy* needed a controller that could move along the Z-axis. Users could use dual digital pads on the joypad to move along this axis, although if not set up properly, use of the *Virtual Boy* could induce vomiting and even seizures, a problem that sometimes continues with contemporary headsets and is referred to as cybersickness. The fact that usability was intermittent led to much criticism, so even though there were 19 titles, such as "Mario Tennis" and "Teleroboxer." *Virtual Boy* had a very limited release and was a commercial failure.

Back after the gaming market crash of the early 1980s, in 1993, Atari released a home video game console named *Jaguar* with two custom 32-bit processors and a Motorola 68000. While all games and computers used a 32-bit processor until this point, Atari's beta 64-bit processor doubled the number of memory locations to store and fetch data, as well as increasing the number of calculations per second that could be performed. A VR headset was released for the *Jaguar* and worked with a special version of the game "Missile Command" in 3D. Unfortunately, financial difficulties and the exorbitant price tag prevented any sort of widespread adoption (*Atari Jaguar: The Only Functional Virtual Reality Headset Resurfaces in Video*, 2022).

What marks VR history is innovation, experimental thought, and risk. Even with large financial investments, VR history is littered with "almosts." What makes something "successful" or "valuable" to a culture? What contributes to a successful experience in VR? This book offers an examination of artistic approaches to creating experiences in the immersive space that lives within a headset. In many cases, the hardware used to build the VR scenarios has become obsolete, but the experiences themselves arguably stand the test of time. Propelled by a sense of play, exploration, and curiosity, artists bring a specific and compelling vision to the immersive experience. In so many ways, it is up to artists to explore some of the innovative, immersive, moral, idealized, and dystopian possibilities of VR. Mort Heilig spoke up from the audience at a SIGGRAPH panel on VR in 1990. Frustrated with some of the panel participants, Heilig said:

> I mean, if somebody said, 'Here's a club, go out and kill a million people,' he couldn't do it because by the time he killed the third person and heard his screams, smelt his blood, there would be an automatic feedback mechanism operating and he would stop. [In virtual reality] We have no way of controlling our own behavior because it's gone beyond the sensory input. The hope here is that by getting that psychic information to come back to us, we'll have an opportunity to put things more in balance again, so that

our ability to understand our behavior and feel and emotionally respond to our behavior will be proportional to our capacity to act. And that, I think, is the way that we're going to save the human race.

*–(Barlow et al., 1990)*

## REFERENCES

Alien Garden. (2023). *Wikipedia.* https://en.wikipedia.org/w/index.php?title=Alien_Garden&oldid=1136953486

*Atari Jaguar: The only functional virtual reality headset resurfaces in video.* (2022, January 13). Get to Text. https://www.gameblog.fr/jeu-video/ed/news/atari-jaguar-le-seul-casque-de-realite-virtuelle-fonctionnel-refait-surface-en-video-396566

Barlow, J., Dyson, E., Leary, T., Bricken, W., Robinett, W., Lanier, J., & Jacobson, B. (1990). Hip, hype and hope—The three faces of virtual worlds (panel session). *Proceedings of the ACM SIGGRAPH 90 Panel,* 1001–1029. https://doi.org/10.1145/328750.328798

Brockwell, H. (2016, April 3). Forgotten genius: The man who made a working VR machine in 1957. *TechRadar.* https://www.techradar.com/news/wearables/forgotten-genius-the-man-who-made-a-working-vr-machine-in-1957-1318253

Brooks, F. P. (1999). What's real about virtual reality? *IEEE Computer Graphics and Applications, 19*(6), 16–27. https://doi.org/10.1109/38.799723

Burford. (2021, May 23). The Brewster Stereoscope – Its improvements and variations. *The Stereosite.* https://stereosite.com/collecting/the-brewster-stereoscope-its-improvements-and-variations/

Heilig, M. L. (1960). *Stereoscopic-television apparatus for individual use* [United States Patent No. US2955156A]. https://patents.google.com/patent/US2955156A/en

Holloway, R., & Lastra, A. (1993). *Virtual environments: A survey of the technology* [No. TR93-033, University of North Carolina]. http://www.macs.hw.ac.uk/~ruth/year4VEs/Resources/holloway93virtual.pdf

Huber, J. (1986). *Human interface guidelines: Second beta draft.* Apple Technical Publications.

*Introducing the Sensorama Simulator.* (n.d.). https://web.opendrive.com/api/v1/download/file.json/Ml8xNTA4ODQyMzBf

Islami, D. (2020). *Virtual reality – VR* [Bachelor's Thesis, University for Business and Technology]. https://doi.org/10.33107/ubt-etd.2020.2329

Johnson, J. (2016, May 9). Atari's secret VR experiments of the 1980s. *Kill Screen.* https://killscreen.com/versions/ataris-secret-vr-experiments-of-the–1980s/

Jones, S. V. (1969, October 4). A road safety radio. *The New York Times,* 49, 51.

Junker, H. (1965). New perils awaiting the serious drinker. *Film Comment, 3*(3), 34–38. https://www.jstor.org/stable/43753325

Kelly, N. M. (2018). "Works like magic": Metaphor, meaning, and the GUI in Snow Crash. *Science Fiction Studies*, *45*(1), 69–90. https://www.jstor.org/stable/10.5621/sciefictstud.45.1.0069

Krueger, M. W. (1977). Responsive environments. *Proceedings of the National Computer Conference*, 423–433. https://doi.org/10.1145/1499402.1499476

Krueger, M. W., Gionfriddo, T., & Hinrichsen, K. (1985). VIDEOPLACE – An artificial reality. *Proceedings of the SIGCHI Conference on Human Factors in Computing Systems*, 35–40. https://doi.org/10.1145/317456.317463

Metherell, C. (2017). Early 3D. *The Stereoscopic Society*. http://www.stereoscopic-society.org.uk/WordPress/early-3d/

Minsky, M. (1997). Will haptics research parallel computer graphics research? *Proceedings of the ICAT '97 Conference*, 27–32. https://icat.vrsj.org/ICAT2003/papers/97027.pdf

Minsky, M., Ming, O., Steele, O., Brooks, F. P., & Behensky, M. (1990). Feeling and seeing: Issues in force display. *Proceedings of the 1990 Symposium on Interactive 3D Graphics*, 235–241. https://doi.org/10.1145/91385.91451

Norman, J. (n.d.-a). Myron Krueger's Videoplace pioneers "artificial reality." *History of Information*. Retrieved October 9, 2022, from https://www.historyofinformation.com/detail.php?entryid=4699

Norman, J. (n.d.-b). Zimmerman & Lanier develop the DataGlove, a hand gesture interface device. *History of Information*. Retrieved March 29, 2023, from https://www.historyofinformation.com/detail.php?entryid=4081

Ono, H., Lillakas, L., Kapoor, A., & Wong, I. (2013). Replicating and extending Bourdon's (1902) experiment on motion parallax. *Perception*, *42*(1), 45–59. https://doi.org/10.1068/p7269

Punday, D. (2000). The narrative construction of cyberspace: Reading Neuromancer, reading cyberspace debates. *College English*, *63*(2), 194–213. https://doi.org/10.2307/379040

Rosen, J. (2017, February 22). An oral history of Nintendo's Power Glove. *Mental Floss*. https://www.mentalfloss.com/article/91939/losing-their-grip-oral-history-nintendos-power-glove

Schnipper, M. (n.d.). The rise and fall and rise of virtual reality. *The Verge*. Retrieved October 25, 2022, from http://www.theverge.com/a/virtual-reality

Siu, A. F., Sinclair, M., Kovacs, R., Ofek, E., Holz, C., & Cutrell, E. (2020). Virtual reality without vision: A haptic and auditory white cane to navigate complex virtual worlds. *Proceedings of the 2020 CHI Conference on Human Factors in Computing Systems*, 1–13. https://doi.org/10.1145/3313831.3376353

Solomon, C. (2007, March 29). *Atari Cambridge research – part 1*. https://www.youtube.com/watch?v=CR2CwKcuIBU

Steinkuehler, C. (2010). Video games and digital literacies. *Journal of Adolescent & Adult Literacy*, *54*(1), 61–63. https://www.jstor.org/stable/20749077

Stephenson, N. (1992). *Snow crash*. Bantam.

Sterling, B. (2009, September 20). Augmented reality: "The ultimate display" by Ivan Sutherland, 1965. *Wired*. https://www.wired.com/2009/09/augmented-reality-the-ultimate-display-by-ivan-sutherland-1965/

Sutherland, I. (1965). The ultimate display. *Proceedings of IFIP Congress*, 506–508.

Torrone, P. (2008, November 7). ViewMaster artist profile. *Make*. https://make-zine.com/article/craft/viewmaster-artist-profile/

Turner, J., & Krueger, M. (2002). Myron Krueger live. *CTheory*. https://journals.uvic.ca/index.php/ctheory/article/view/14583

Virtual Reality Society. (2018, April 17). *Virtuality – A new reality of promise, two decades too soon*. https://www.vrs.org.uk/dr-jonathan-walden-virtuality-new-reality-promise-two-decades-soon/

Waldsmith, J. S. (1991). *Stereo views: An illustrated history and price guide*. Wallace-Homestead Bk. Company.

Wheatstone, C. (1858). *WHEATSTONE Charles to TALBOT William Henry Fox* [Document number: 7751]. British Library: The Correspondence of William Henry Fox Talbot. https://foxtalbot.dmu.ac.uk/letters/transcriptDocnum.php?docnum=7751

Zimmerman, T. G., Lanier, J., Blanchard, C., Bryson, S., & Harvill, Y. (1987). A hand gesture interface device. *ACM SIGCHI Bulletin*, *18*(4), 189–192. https://doi.org/10.1145/1165387.275628

# CHAPTER 3

# Artists Working in Virtual Reality Pre-2010

## INTRODUCTION

After working at Atari's Sunnyvale Lab from 1981 to 1983, Scott Fisher moved on to NASA Ames Research, where he continued to research and develop virtual reality (VR). While at NASA Ames, a former co-worker from Atari, Brenda Laurel, reached out to Scott for his help "in developing a location-based entertainment environment that would involve Virtual Reality" (Brenda Laurel, 2019; Laurel, n.d.). Laurel was working with a client, Centerpoint Communications, who was "especially interested in developing a location-based entertainment environment that would involve Virtual Reality" (Laurel, n.d.). While this project did not materialize, the youthful tech wizard Joichi Ito encouraged Fisher and Laurel to create their own company, which they did – Telepresence Research. Telepresence Research conducted research and development not only in the field of virtual presence in other locations but also in VR.

The business pursued a variety of potential revenue generators, including artistic ones. Feedback was positive, yet permanent revenue generation was elusive. As Laurel points out, the audience engagement was enthusiastic, but there were problems. Laurel says, "one more memorable moment…a Las Vegas type turned bright green and got…sick. I rushed out and got him some Dramamine, administered with profuse apologies. 'Are you kidding?' he said 'This is GREAT!'" (Laurel, n.d.). In late 1991,

DOI: 10.1201/9781003363729-3

Fisher and Laurel parted ways, with Laurel moving into research on interaction design, the relationship between gender and technology, and the creation of a New Media Program at the Art Center of College and Design. Fisher went on to collaborate with others to develop a virtual environment system "to assess the value of a head-coupled stereo display and direct 3-D manipulation of a surgery simulation application" (Pieper et al., 1991). Fisher then worked at University of Southern California to help create the Interactive Media Division.

The importance of these early researchers and pioneers of new media/interactive art programs cannot be understated. With their openness to taking on risk and their desire to break new ground, Fisher and Laurel are just two examples of how those involved in VR research continue to push the edge of the envelope, resulting in innovative approaches to how we interface with and understand our technology. If it were not for these risk-takers, VR may very well still be relegated to the realm of science fiction and speculation.

## VRML

From early versions of headsets and consoles, VR's next big shift was the move to the internet. In 1994, Mark Pesce and Anthony Parisi presented a prototype 3D web application called "Labyrinth" at the first World Wide Web conference in Geneva. Around the same time, Dave Raggett presented a paper that proposed extending the World Wide Web to support platform-agnostic VR applications, coining the term Virtual Reality Modeling Language, or VRML (Edwards, 2022). Building on the two concepts, Pesce and Parisi went on to create the first 3D web browser, naming it after Raggett's proposed "VRML." Thus, in 1995, VRML became a standard file format for representing 3D interactive vector graphics and virtual worlds on the internet. VRML, like Hyper Text Markup Language or HTML, uses dynamic linking to pull objects into the browser's display interface. At first, the VRML browser only displayed static 3D objects but eventually expanded to include various multimedia functions such as animation and sound. While other formats offered participants access to a dimensional digital space, VRML offered a glimpse of where VR would head, as VRML files could also be viewed with actual VR hardware. Unfortunately, the VR headsets that could display 3D VRML worlds were very expensive, and the resolution was low (Edwards, 2018). While popular with those in the know, such as companies like Microsoft, Wired, and

Silicon Graphics, the average personal computers and home computing systems did not have the capacity to process VRML at its full capacity (CNET, 1996).

Around the same time as VR's move to the internet, there was an alternative system for viewing VR – the cave automatic virtual environment or CAVE, a project spearheaded by Carolina Cruz-Neira et al. (1992). Along with Daniel Sandin and Thomas DeFanti, Cruz-Neira CAVE consisted of a room "whose walls, ceiling and floor surround a viewer with projected images" (Cruz-Neira et al., 1992). Cruz-Neira felt that, like the head-mounted displays, the CAVE allowed users to suspend disbelief "give in to a situation – to ignore its medium." CAVE also gave the user a "viewer-centered perspective," allowing for a 360-degree field of vision within the virtual world from the observer's location (Cruz-Neira et al., 1992). Arguably less accessible than VRML headsets, Cruz-Neira insisted, "what I want to shout from the top of mountains is that VR is not one singular technology. It's not a single implementation: VR has so many possibilities" ("VR Pioneer Carolina Cruz Neira," 2018).

The advent of VRML offered exciting possibilities for the burgeoning fields of new media art and art games. The idea of using interactivity to create compelling narratives appealed to creative coders and interactive experience providers. One venue that successfully navigated the demands of a three-dimensional web was online multiplayer gaming. OnLive! produced a 3D authoring kit to develop a VRML game called *Traveler* (1995) that allowed participants to travel to other worlds and chat with online visitors. The main objective of these spaces was to operate within the virtual community "represented by 3D head avatars within community locations represented as bounded 3D spaces" (*Traveler*, n.d.). Using 3D modeling software of the person's choice, participants would "conceptualize and design spaces according to social and technical guidelines outlined by OnLive!'s manual." Participants could use audio, background textures, and ambient lighting and to the attributes of the avatar's entry into the space (Figure 3.1).

In 1998, Finnish artists Andy Best and Marja Puustinen used VRML to create the interactive work *Conversations with Angels*, a multiuser project where users were able to navigate 3D worlds using their home PCs. These worlds were interactive – "the user is able to trigger sound effects, animations and video clips by clicking the mouse and chatting with the chat programmes that represent the avatars inhabiting the world" (MEET Factory,

**FIGURE 3.1**  OnLive *Traveler* (1995). Onlive Technologies, CC BY 3.0 US, via Archive.org.

When Artists Use VRML, n.d.). Tooling around in a low-polygonal red plane, users navigated to find the characters and spaces within the world. Spaces included the inside of a serial killer's house, the garden of a lesbian princess, and a fishbowl inhabited by Bob the Redneck (MEET Factory, When Artists Use VRML, n.d.). Participants were represented by avatars, with visual embodiments for various characters and environments built using VRML and using Netscape browser plug-ins. Co-produced by BANFF Centre for Arts and Creativity in Canada and exhibited at KIASMA, The Museum of Contemporary Art in Helsinki, this work demonstrated an openness and curiosity about interactive 3D space as an art form.

Both *Traveler* and *Conversation with Angels* were VRML experiences that created interest in the virtual space, although the strongest part of these works was the ability for community members to join and collaborate in that space. When VRML moved onto single servers, it allowed individuals to don headsets that offered more graphical and interactive capabilities. One of the most remarkable of these early immersive VR experiences is found in the work of artist Char Davies. Davies is the founding director of 3D graphics company Softimage, later acquired by Autodesk. Regarding her transition into VR, Davies states that "as a painter, I was looking for ways to cross over the 2D picture plane, to find a way to work on the other side of the picture plane. That led me to the virtual space of 3D computer graphics. I got involved in building a software company, Softimage, because I wanted good access to the tool" (Schnipper, n.d.).

## OSMOSE

Davies' *Osmose* (1995) was an artistic installation created using VRML that used a head-mounted display and a wearable vest as an input device. The head-mounted display takes the user through environmental graphics with interactive sound, while the participant's breathing motion is tracked by a custom-built vest that they wear. Davies states that "'Osmose' is a space for exploring the perceptual interplay between self and world, i.e., a place for facilitating awareness of one's own self as consciousness embodied in enveloping space." *Osmose* viewers interact and move through the low-polygonal world by taking a deep breath to move "up" in the 3D space. Participants would then exhale to "lower" themselves in the environment. Tilting to the right or left allows participants to fly through the space in the direction they lean, tying movement in the physical realm to the participant's movement in the virtual. The graphics that the participant sees when entering the digital environment are compelling and ethereal – abstract and partially transparent, with polygonal trees and landscapes etched against a three-dimensional Cartesian grid. Eerie synth music gives way to interdimensional forest sounds – there is a sense of entering a world shimmering with irreality – similar but in essential ways unlike our own. Davies' graphics are extremely effective in that they "avoid representational realism in the creation…of worlds, although the environments are partly representational, they also have an element of translucency and use textures that suggest a constant flow of particles" (Paul, 2003, p. 127) (Figures 3.2 and 3.3).

Leaning forward to move through the space, participants can cycle through eight different biomes – ones such as "leaf," "cloud," and "abyss." Each has its own unique music and particular visual elements. Taking a deep breath, the participant soars into the "cloud" biome – expelling air brings one back down to/and below the ground. Where most contemporaneous VR experiences are tethered to the concept of a controller or hand gestures, Davies explored innovative approaches to user interactions. What's remarkable about Davies' approach is that, in so many instances, users enter the virtual space and lose their bodies. Users usually find disembodied hands floating in the air, but when they look down, there is nothing to see. Early VR pioneers touted the virtual space's freedom from

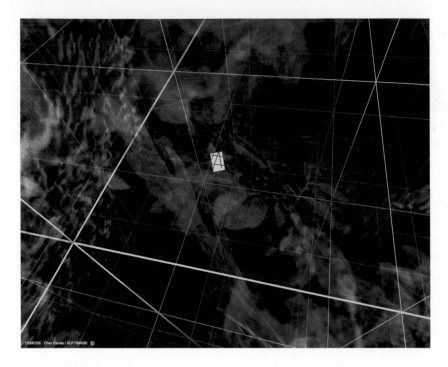

**FIGURE 3.2** Char Davies. Forest Grid, *Osmose* (1995). Digital stills captured in real time through HMD (head-mounted display) during live performance of immersive virtual environment *Osmose*. Image and permission courtesy of the artist.

the physical body, arguing that it will become "a great liberator of the mind and a place to 'ultimately open up possibilities for creating new and autonomous identities'" (Tanasyuk, 2008). While Simon Penny accuses this mindset about VR of "blithely reconstituting a mind/body split that is essentially patriarchal and industrialist," Davies works to create an experience that "depends on the body's most essential living act, that of breath—not only to navigate, but more importantly—to attain a particular state-of-being within the virtual world" (Davies, n.d.).

Because Davies chose artistry over realism in terms of the 3D objects, *Osmose* is as compelling visually now as it was when Davies and his team first made it. What makes *Osmose* so successful is that "our minds provide such tremendous flexibility in interpreting what is outside of us, realism in virtual reality is simply not necessary. Our cognitive plasticity permits even simple cartoon worlds of 500 polygons to be experientially satisfying. We must design worlds that respect our physiological

**FIGURE 3.3**  Char Davies. Tree Pond, *Osmose* (1995). Digital stills captured in real time through HMD (head-mounted display) during live performance of immersive virtual environment Osmose. Image and permission courtesy of the artist.

needs" (Bricken, 1990). This is a testament to the notion that high graphic fidelity is not necessary to create compelling artistic works. *Osmose* participants described the experience of interacting with the work as profound, as if they had found a part of themselves that they had lost and felt more alive in the world after taking the headset off. These participant experiences confirmed "the artist's belief that traditional interface boundaries between machine and human can be transcended even while re-affirming our corporeality, and that Cartesian notions of space as well as illustrative realism can effectively be replaced by more evocative alternatives" (Davies, n.d.). Davies says that when she started developing *Osmose* in 1993, most games "…were shoot-'em-up games. They all involved either a gun, or a pointer, or a mouse. They all involved a hand. I believed that if you made the interface centered on the hand, it reinforced a way of approaching the world in terms of doing things to things as an instrument — either shooting it or manipulating it in some way. So we introduced a hands-free interface that relied on breathing and balance. This shifted the experience from one of "doing" to one of "being". People cried, usually men" (Schnipper, n.d.).

In the case of *Osmose*, it is the artist, not the technologist, that plays the pivotal role in inventing ingenious concepts for the VR experience. Artistic investigations often focus heavily on the viewer's intellectual and physical responses to their work. These responses invite the viewer to participate in an artwork and navigate the virtual environment, emphasizing interaction, immersion, and participation – all of which break down the barrier between the creator, the viewer/performer, and the audience (deLahunta, 2002). Author of the human-computer interaction text Computers as Theatre, interactive media expert, and co-founder of VR company Telepresence Research Brenda Laurel describes Davies work as "poetic … a new art form and I take my hat off to her. I was looking at it as a structuralist, 'Okay, what can we turn inside out here about this?' But her sensibility is much more of a fine artist, and so the stuff that she did was just outrageously beautiful. One of the guys who installed it at the museum in Toronto, I think, got his head in it and came out 10 minutes later weeping and saying that his life had been changed forever" (Schnipper, n.d.).

## *PLACEHOLDER*

Laurel's own VR project, *Placeholder* (1992), was co-created with MIT architecture graduate Rachel Strickland and invites participants to investigate the notion of spaces. Co-produced by Interval Research Corporation and The BANFF Centre for the Performing Arts, *Placeholder* explores the relationship between locations and inhabitants through multiperson narrative action. Accommodating two people at a time, *Placeholder* has digital representations of three real-world locations based in the Canadian Rockies, all while drawing upon spiritual practice, stories, and myth to enhance the interactive experience. Participants are placed in the landscape together as distorted voices speak to them, while symbols inspired by mythological stories dance around in the virtual atmosphere. Portals allow the viewer to move from space to space as the narrative progresses. Several places are recreated, albeit to a limited degree given the processing power available in the 1990s, ranging from mountains to caves. Users were also capable of leaving "voicemarks" – fragments of spoken narrative for future participants, thus dynamically changing the landscape for future

**FIGURE 3.4** Brenda Laurel and Rachel Strickland *Placeholder* (1992). Image courtesy of the artists.

viewers and creating opportunities for co-creation of the work with not only the artist but other users as well (Figure 3.4).

The work explores multiple connections: human to human, human to nature, and human to technology. It analyzes how humans interact with each other and the natural world by using narrative and visual motifs that incorporate indigenous symbols and iconography. The virtual space is established in three "locations," each connected by a portal. In addition to being able to move through the space, participants could "take on the bodies and some of the sensory-motor characteristics of animals. The worlds had affordances for voice communication between participants with some vocal distortion to distinguish the various animals" (Laurel et al., 1994).

*Placeholder* analyzes how humans connect with various concepts of technology – investigating not just novel digital technologies but also historic or even ancient technologies. Pulling from mythology, Laurel and Strickland look at how early humans used tools in order to make a connection between how handheld tools of the past compare to the digital tools of now. Like the use of one's hands to crash one rock into another, *Placeholder* users use their hands to gesture in space to interact with the digital medium. The meta narrative about human-computer interaction deepens when using VR as the participatory medium. Essential to the immersive nature of entering a headset, participants lose the view of the physical world around them in order to enter the digitally created world of the headset (Laurel et al., 1994).

Artistic choice is an integral part of *Placeholder*'s conceptual framework – Laurel and Strickland chose not to use any kind of visual user interface elements to guide participants through the virtual space. This choice invites curiosity and exploration on the part of the participant – instead of an obvious way to move through the virtual, Laurel and Strickland opt to invite as artists do: graciously open-ended. The freedom that *Placeholder* gives the participant creates a sense of being, a sense of inhabitance. The lack of user interface in the virtual space means that there is no breaking the illusion within the VR environment. As Brenda Laurel stated, "VR is harmed by authorial control, it works best when people can move about and do things in an unconstrained way" (Laurel et al., 1994). Instead of a structured path the participant must follow, *Placeholder* creates a technologically mediated environment that allows people to *play*. Unlike works restricted by their physical and rectilinear bounds, in VR, the audience dictates their experience and consumption of the art, working in collaboration with the creator to experience the artwork.

Char Davies had seen *Placeholder* while working on *Osmose*. Davies states that "I think Brenda was one of the few people who was trying to do something with VR outside of the commercial mainstream. Everyone else was basically doing games; entertainment and military, basically" (Schnipper, n.d.). In many ways, *Placeholder* was a proof-of-concept to demonstrate that "virtual reality could be used for things besides training [it was] also an experiment, digging into issues of presence and representation" (Laurel et al., 1994).

## BUSH SOULS

Rebecca Allen is an artist and has worked with VR as a medium since the 1990s. In addition to her studio practice, Allen is a research professor at UCLA and the founding chair of UCLA's Department of Design Media Art. She received a BFA from the Rhode Island School of Design in 1975 and went on to study at Massachusetts Institute of Technology Cambridge's predecessor to the MIT Media Lab – the Architecture Machine Group. Spanning four decades of artmaking, Allen's pedigree as an artist technologist is outstanding. Beginning with research in the early 1980s at the New York Institute of Technology Research's Computer Graphics Laboratory, Allen investigated 3D computer animation, human motion simulation, facial animation, nonverbal communication, and new forms of dynamic digital art. Allen's *Bush Souls #1, #2, and #3* is a series of interactive works that were made for differing versions of VR and/or immersive installations. The works "explore the role of human presence in a virtual world inhabited by artificial life" (Allen, n.d.). The concept of Bush Soul is based on the belief that "a person's second soul" is, in some cultures, able "to inhabit a wild animal of the bush" – for this VR work, the user enters a desert-like space with lush, sunset colors painting the background mountains (Merriam-Webster, n.d.). In Allen's VR work, the *bush souls* are in some cases represented as star creatures, or more like a stack of starry, flowing shapes that seem to joyously laugh and dance around. There are also thorny figures, more like thistles, as well as bird-like arrays. All of the "creatures" are brought to life through AI – the AI "defines their behaviors and desires" (Allen, n.d.). Participants move through the work using a force-feedback joystick – in fact, Allen was familiar with Margaret Minsky's research on joystick haptics when developing the feedback device for *Bush Souls* (personal communication, April 14, 2023). This joystick "provides both navigation and tactile sensations and serves as a connection between the physical body and the virtual soul" (Allen, n.d.). Allen was particularly interested in connecting the body to the mind within the context of VR. The idea that the body is outside or ancillary to the mind was antithetical to Allen's thinking – as an artist working within a technological field, she felt that the mind/body connection was an important part of being human. She also knew all too well how representation of the female body plays out in terms of the male gaze and wanted to subvert this notion of being subject or object, instead being interested in integrating the viewer's experience with what they saw and felt (personal communication, April 14, 2023).

While the latest version of Bush Soul was completed in 1999, Allen has continued to create artwork and research VR. Allen's contemporary approach has its foundation in the works of early artistic movements – while in art school, she was interested in the work of the Futurists. She sees parallels between the Futurists' obsession with the machine age and her own curiosity about how technology has affected humanity (Figure 3.5).

**FIGURE 3.5** Rebecca Allen *Bush Souls #3* (1999). Image and permission courtesy of the artist.

## *ANGELS*

Nicole Stenger was a research fellow at MIT's CAVS & Visual Arts Program from 1989 to 1991 before she became a visiting scholar at the Human Interface Technology Laboratory in Seattle. Her 1992 artwork, Angels, was the first interactive movie created using VPL's Virtualization Interface during Stenger's tenure as a visiting scholar in Seattle. Participants would don a VPL "Data Glove" and HRX goggles to enter the virtual narrative. As Stenger writes, the work follows "Tom Furness' theory … conceived for the 3 senses: vision, audio, and touch, though only vision, audio, and a nontactile data glove could be implemented at the time" (Stenger, n.d.). Known for his work building helmet-mounted displays for the US Air Force in the 1960s, Furness developed the Super Cockpit. The "Cockpit" was a prototype that was built and allowed "a total spherical world to be generated so that information is conveyed in spatially relevant positions" and made use "of the 3-D information processing abilities of the projecting information directly operator by into the eyes using miniature components" (Järvinen, 2021). Leaving the military, he helped found the Human Interface Technology Lab and worked to form a nonprofit, the Virtual World Society (VanFossen, 2019).

In *Angels*, the computer-generated visuals morph the recognizable into colorful abstract 3D forms. Some forms are textured with tortoiseshell or moire patterns, creating a sense of complexity. Participants start at a carousel that allows for passage into other VR worlds - interactivity comes through touching the hearts that dangle in the center of the carousel. The hearts morph into artistic interpretations of angels – somewhat like candles, the angels dance in the virtual space, enticing participants to reach out. Stegner's experiments with early VR hardware became "impracticable, if not utterly dangerous," impeding her from making the move to VRML (Stenger, n.d.).

## DYNASTY

Stenger's *Dynasty* came out in 2007–2009 using the VRML platform. A song from Tchaikovsky's *Nutcracker Suite* plays in midi note as the main scene opens. A house in the distance invites users to reveal a pink waiting room. A dragon with Buddah's head assists the participant, directing them to an elevator that brings the user to an upper floor, revealing the ancestors, who voice in unison, "we loved you before you were born." Composed of silver and gray low-poly forms, the ancestors sport antlers and hazy halos. Looking down from a dias with an accented voice-over, they speak to the user before gently floating into space. Originally developed for VR in the late 1980s, Stenger was only able to port the experience into the proper immersive format in 2017. Stenger's ability to create an emotional connection with her audience means that even though her original renderings relied on the 3D modeling technology of the time, her work still holds impact today (Figure 3.6).

In 1998, Steve Ditlea wrote an article for the New York Times Technology section entitled *False Starts Aside, Virtual Reality Finds New Roles* (Ditlea, 1998). The article is about Sun Microsystems announcement that they had acquired the patent portfolio of VPL Research Inc. VPL had accepted funding from Thomson-CSF and used its patent portfolio as collateral. When Thomson foreclosed on its loans in 1993, VPL went into bankruptcy. The VPL patent portfolio never made it into the public domain again – a sorry end to a bright star in the VR universe. When asked about this particular faltering of VR, Jaron Lanier responded: "I bear some of the blame for it. I always talked about VR in its ultimate implementation and when that didn't happen, interest declined. Because everyone wanted the holodeck from Star Trek, virtual reality couldn't fulfill its promise so quickly" (Ditlea, 1998). With the implosion of VPL, Atari, and the crash of the headset market, the late 1990s saw a dip in VR research and exploration.

**FIGURE 3.6** Nicole Stenger *Dynasty* (2007–2009). Image and permission courtesy of the artist.

The introduction of Netscape's Mosaic browser meant that a much broader swath of participants on the internet could author not just text-based works but visuals as well. In 1994, "Garage Virtual Reality" author Linda Jacobson stated that "the web really changed things. The fact that there was a proliferation of online access to 3D design tools meant a lot of people started focusing there and not on the hardware." Jacobson's book offered "virtual world technologies for the rest of us," offering resources for creating and distributing software that "redefine virtual reality, yet support sensory immersion." Ten years later, when the Oculus Rift appeared, Char Davies wrote:

> "I was very pleased when the Oculus Rift appeared, because I have always believed that a sense of immersion is most fully enabled via a headset with a wide field of view. I had been waiting a long time for such technology to reappear. I say "re-appear" because the last wide-field-of-view helmets I used were from the mid-90's, and nothing suitable has come along since, until the Oculus Rift. But when I heard that Facebook had bought the company,

I was disappointed. Twenty years after Osmose, I still believe that immersive virtual space has rich potential for enabling people to step outside their habitual assumptions about reality to see freshly: that the technology will be used instead to maximize advertising revenue is a profound technology will be used instead to maximize advertising revenue is a profound shame (Schnipper, n.d.).

The interactive and immersive nature of virtual reality technology allowed artists of the 1990's to translate media from the second dimension and pseudo three dimensions to a fully immersive embodied three dimensional experience. They explored virtual reality through the use of VRML headsets and pushed the boundaries of interaction by subverting audience expectations. In *Placeholder* this was done through an unexpected and interpretive menu system – in *Osmose* boundaries were pushed by the use of a vest and the body, not a mouse or controller, to allow directional control in the immersive space. The sense of playfulness brought to virtual reality by these artists took place in what feels like almost a parallel universe to the fast paced and capitalistically driven developments in commercial and gaming virtual reality applications. Early virtual reality software and hardware hype often felt as Nathaniel Bletter wrote in 1993, "a solution looking for a problem" (Bletter, 1993). This is in part due to the technical limitations of the hardware at the time, but also due to the lack of publicly salient artistic experiments. And yet Bletter's idea that virtual reality "has a long way to go before every sight, sound, touch, taste, and smell of virtual reality replicates true reality" has it wrong (Bletter, 1993). Virtual reality does not solely exist to replicate reality. Instead it offers opportunities for magic; ways to experience realities beyond our physical reality. Traditional development of a digital application usually involves creating specific information architecture and user interface elements. In commercial application, these elements carefully guide participants through a clear, goal oriented, and specific path. Interactive artworks supersede this narrative by offering the participant a chance to find their own paths; to explore and investigate. Virtual reality builds on this by putting the viewer in the role of an active creator, requiring them to become active participants in crafting their artistic experiences. In turn, the digital developer of the virtual reality project loses total control of the experience, which may be the shift that proves to be virtual reality's greatest strength.

Virtual reality artworks that innovate in terms of input (*Osmose*) or interface (*Placeholder*) or redefined social and technical roles (OnLive's *Traveler*) don't require virtual reality to be a simulation of reality, in fact they would suffer had they opted to attain simulated realism. These artworks offer exceptional vantage points for experiencing the both physical and digital worlds as they *aren't*. It is time that we reevaluate the roles of creator and the viewer, and this technology affords us that opportunity. As Myron Krueger writes in *Artificial Reality II* "Indeed, one of the strong motivations guiding this work is the desire to compose works that surprise their creator".

*(Krueger, 1991)*

## REFERENCES

Allen, R. (n.d.). *Bush Soul #3*. https://www.rebeccaallen.com/projects/bush-soul-number-3

Bletter, N. (1993). The virtues and vices of virtual reality. *Design Quarterly, 159*, 38–44. https://doi.org/10.2307/4091331

*Brenda Laurel*. (2019, May 14). *Atariwomen*. https://www.atariwomen.org/stories/brenda-laurel/

Bricken, W. (1990, September 10). *Virtual reality: Directions of growth*. https://web.stanford.edu/dept/HPS/TimLenoir/MilitaryEntertainment/Atari/WilliamBricken/VirtualRealityDirections.html

CNET. (1996, June 28). *VRML not quite ready for real world*. https://www.cnet.com/tech/services-and-software/vrml-not-quite-ready-for-real-world/

Cruz-Neira, C., Sandin, D. J., DeFanti, T. A., Kenyon, R. V., & Hart, J. C. (1992). The CAVE: Audio visual experience automatic virtual environment. *Communications of the ACM, 35*(6), 64–72. https://doi.org/10.1145/129888.129892

Davies, C. (n.d.). *Osmose*. http://www.immersence.com/osmose/

deLahunta, S. (2002). Virtual reality and performance. *PAJ: A Journal of Performance and Art, 24*(1), 105–114. https://www.jstor.org/stable/3246463

Ditlea, S. (1998, March 23). False starts aside, virtual reality finds new roles. *The New York Times*, D3. https://www.nytimes.com/1998/03/23/business/false-starts-aside-virtual-reality-finds-new-roles.html

Edwards, B. (2018, April 27). The wacky world of VR in the 80s and 90s. *PC Magazine*. https://www.pcmag.com/news/the-wacky-world-of-vr-in-the-80s-and-90s

Edwards, B. (2022, January 12). Remembering VRML: The metaverse of 1995. *How-To Geek*. https://www.howtogeek.com/778554/remembering-vrml-the-metaverse-of-1995/

Järvinen, A. (2021, October 27). The Reality Files #10: The Super Cockpit (1986) by Thomas A. Furness. *The Reality Files*. https://medium.com/the-reality-files/the-reality-files-10-58325e3d891d

Krueger, M. W. (1991). *Artificial reality II*. Addison-Wesley.

Krueger, M. W. (1993). The artistic origins of virtual reality. *SIGGRAPH 1993: Machine Culture*, 148–149. https://digitalartarchive.siggraph.org/writing/the-artistic-origins-of-virtual-reality/

Laurel, B. (n.d.). Telepresence research. *Tao Zero*. http://tauzero.com/Brenda_Laurel/Resume/TelepresenceResearch.html

Laurel, B., Strickland, R., & Tow, R. (1994). Placeholder: Landscape and narrative in virtual environments. *ACM SIGGRAPH Computer Graphics*, 28(2), 118–126. https://doi.org/10.1145/178951.178967

*MEET Factory, When artists use VRML*. (n.d.). Sandy Ressler. https://www.sandyressler.com/about/library/weekly/aa021698.htm

Merriam-Webster. (n.d.). Bush soul. In Merriam-Webster.com dictionary. Retrieved April 19, 2023, from https://www.merriam-webster.com/dictionary/bush%20soul

Paul, C. (2003). *Digital art*. Thames & Hudson.

Pieper, S. D., Delp, S., Rosen, J., & Fisher, S. S. (1991). Virtual environment system for simulation of leg surgery. *Stereoscopic Displays and Applications II*, 1457, 188–197. https://doi.org/10.1117/12.46307

Schnipper, M. (n.d.). The rise and fall and rise of virtual reality. *The Verge*. Retrieved October 25, 2022, from http://www.theverge.com/a/virtual-reality

Stenger, N. (n.d.). *The virtual reality trilogy*. Retrieved October 21, 2022, from http://www.nicolestenger.com/trilogy.htm

Tanasyuk, P. (2008). Social implications of virtual worlds: Duality of mind and body. *ISChannel*, 3(1), 4–6.

*Traveler*. (n.d.). *Digital space*. https://www.digitalspace.com/traveler/

VanFossen, L. (2019, May 31). Virtual reality pioneer: Tom Furness. *Educators in VR*. https://educatorsinvr.com/2019/05/31/virtual-reality-pioneer-tom-furness/

VR pioneer Carolina Cruz Neira. (2018, July 17). *ACM SIGGRAPH Blog*. https://blog.siggraph.org/2018/07/vr-pioneer-carolina-cruz-neira.html/

# CHAPTER 4

# Mechanics, Input, and Output

## INTRODUCTION

Before delving fully into a discussion of virtual reality (VR) artworks, it is important to understand the technological underpinnings that drive the technology. This includes not only the technical definition of VR (and related technologies) but also the different development, interaction, and output techniques. Many of these techniques are rooted not only in the traditions of computer science, specifically the subdomain of human-computer interaction, but also in psychology. Of course, these techniques also find their foundation in human communication.

## UNDERSTANDING HUMAN-COMPUTER INTERACTION

The three fundamental functions of a computer are to accept input, manipulate data, and produce output. Built around these fundamentals is human-computer interaction or HCI, a subfield of computer science. HCI is concerned with the way in which individuals and groups use, interact with, and respond to computer systems. As with most computing subfields, HCI was developed over time in response to technological and scientific advances. Computer interactions such as hypertext, direct manipulation of interactive digital graphics, graphic user interfaces (GUIs), and the desktop metaphor all played a role in HCI's development (Baecker, 2008). These advances also led to more accessible computing,

DOI: 10.1201/9781003363729-4

prompting the adoption of computing for broad and general purposes in nearly every conceivable field. This continuing demand led to the integration of design and usability testing as part of the HCI field (Baecker, 2008). Further HCI developments have centered around embedded computing, where the desktop form factor falls away for seamless integration with our lives – examples of this can be found in smart devices and the use of augmented reality, where a device reacts to an object in the physical world (Fitzpatrick, 2005). In embedded computing, minicomputers combine with hardware to perform one task. Digital watches are a prime example of embedded computing – they are meant to tell time and little else.

In the case of augmented reality, users can do something similar to a VR headset with the exception of having a clear vision of the physical world – the user can see the physical space surrounding them through the lens or a live video feed, yet their hand gestures trigger events and affect digital objects that appear within the displayed output. Both of these examples are a far cry from the traditional keyboard and mouse input that the Xerox Star personal computer offered. Instead, these newer inputs provide specific and diverse solutions for interaction methodologies. The idea that interface advancements offer ways to solve problems in terms of interacting with computers doesn't negate the fact that with each advancement, it is important to remember the *human* element. The prioritization of computing systems over what systems are most easily adaptable, interesting, or intuitive to humans means that the creator runs the risk of alienating their audience. Instead, consider what hardware is comfortable or what response users might expect when a certain event is triggered. Applying these sorts of solutions is a step in the right direction toward developing solid foundations upon which VR systems are built and integrated (Fitzpatrick, 2018).

## BASICS OF VIRTUAL REALITY

There are a variety of definitions for VR, but for the purposes of this book, it is defined as "computer mediated system that suppresses the physical environment and presents a simulated digital environment that can be interacted with *as if* it were physical" (Jerald, 2016; Bamodu and Ye, 2013). While this describes a variety of technologies that fall under the umbrella of VR, much of the discussion in these pages will refer to head-mounted display systems (HMDs), sometimes called headsets. However, much of the discussion provided can be applied to any VR technology and some of its sister technologies. One major aspect of VR technology is that it affords "new explorations of experimental user interfaces in the pursuit to 'identify natural forms of interaction and extend them in ways not possible in the real world'" (Pfeuffer, 2017).

VR is part of a larger collection of technologies that create interaction between physical and digital components. This combination was first proposed by Milgram and Kishino (1994) and is referred to as the "virtuality continuum" or "mixed reality continuum." The general concept of this continuum is that on one end of the spectrum exists our physical environment with no augmentations or computer-driven influences, and on the other side of the spectrum is a completely virtual environment. In between these two extremes lie not just augmented reality and VR but a host of other conceptual "realities" centered around a computer-mediated world. These conversations are being used to include concepts such as immersion, the role of the user, and the extent to which the computer device can affect or understand the physical environment (Skarbez et al., 2021).

In the case of VR experiences that use a head-mounted display, there are a few conventions that are assumed for each interaction. First is the ability to move with "six degrees of freedom." This concept applies to both the headset and any motion controllers present and means that the user is able to move along and around in three-dimensional space: "forward/backward (surge), up/down (heave), left/right (sway) … combined with changes in orientation through rotation about three perpendicular axes, often termed yaw (normal axis), pitch (transverse axis), and roll (longitudinal axis)" (Lang, 2013).

The head-mounted display also offers a level of immersion that provides a space for the user to lose themselves in the experience. Another convention assumes that the user can interact with and affect the environment in some way. There may be limitations to their ability to affect, but the user should typically go beyond being a passive observer. This ability to interact is typically facilitated by motion controllers; however, this is not required as many systems are moving to supporting hand gestures, speech, or even physiological markers as input. Examples of the user's ability to affect can range from simple, limited interactions, such as the ability to zoom in and out on an object in a scene to serious interactions with the work – sometimes resulting in completely different outcomes for each experience.

## GESTURE IN COMMUNICATION

Even when using motion controllers for input in a VR system, there are many practices and conventions around gesture interaction that should be considered. Central to this idea is that the controllers don't replace our hands but instead augment them. Some expected gestures are **deictic**, **gesticular, manipulative, semaphoric, pantomimic**, or **iconic** in nature (Karam et al., 2005; Aigner et al., 2012). **Deictic** or pointing gestures are typically used to call attention to an object or indicate a direction. **Gesticulation** is a natural process of communication where gesturing is used in combination with language – an example could include a waving of the arm while yelling "come quickly" (Karam et al., 2005). **Manipulative** gestures describe some form of change and are often used in computer interaction, such as "swiping" left to indicate moving an object to the left (Karam et al., 2005; Aigner et al., 2012). **Semaphoric** gestures signify a specific meaning, such as the peace hand sign with the index and middle fingers up and slightly parted or the OK hand sign (Ainger et al., 2012). These signs may be static or dynamic in nature and depend on a shared learned culture (for example, the peace sign in the United States takes on a much more vulgar tone in the United Kingdom). **Pantomimic** gestures demonstrate a specific action to be performed (Ainger et al., 2012). These often reference a specific object, such as "throwing a ball" or "on the phone" gestures. **Iconic** gestures are typically used to communicate an aspect of an object, such as size or shape, and can be used to give an estimation or evaluation of an object (Ainger et al., 2012).

Participants' gestures within the VR experience can be recorded through several methods, with the most basic being tracking where a user's hand is in space. This sort of tracking can occur through user input into a controller, but some headsets can record the details of a user's hand movement through the use of cameras in the headset. Others may use specialized sensors, such as data gloves or infrared sensors, to track gestures. How the gesture is interpreted – whether or not the virtual application can recognize the movement as semaphoric or iconic all depends on how that application is implemented, and whether or not the interactivity is built to respond to any or all of the above ranges of movement.

## BUILDING INTERACTIONS

In terms of implementing interactivity for any VR application or artwork, there are a wide variety of different approaches to developing interactions.

Some of the most essential interactive forms are **translation, mimicry,** and **conceptual.** Each of these approaches is composed of other interaction components, some of which can be based on gestures and affordances from both the user and the motion controller devices. In fact, most interaction systems are typically not just composed of translation, mimicry, or conceptual approach but instead are a combination of all three.

## TRANSLATION

One method for VR interaction design is **translation,** often a first method of approach for designers coming from other user experience and user interface fields, such as game design or web design. The translation method takes ideas and concepts regarding user interaction from other established fields and translates their approaches into the VR space. For designers coming from other fields, using the translation method can provide some security while designing for the new space of VR. A danger of using this method that often arises is that other user experience frameworks will not function in a VR space. This requires the designer to pivot from what they are familiar with and may result in incompatibilities in the virtual space.

One potential example of poor translation is found in the use of locomotion-based movement. Locomotion in the VR space is taken from video game design and refers to using a joystick or other input, such as the WASD keys on a keyboard, to move a player around a scene. If a player wants to move forward in a 2D game, they can thrust the joystick away from them, and in turn, their character will move forward in the game space. When used in the original design context of video games, locomotion is a staple of first-person experience design. When locomotion is applied to VR, it is often cited as the principal cause of simulation sickness. Better methods for moving around in the VR space exist (such as teleportation), but they require familiarity with the virtual medium.

Very often, menu systems are derived using the translation approach, as menu systems are found throughout videogame applications and in web design. In these mediums, the menu system is designed for and built around interaction with a flat screen. It is common in the translation of these menu systems to VR for a menu screen with dropdowns, checkboxes, and input fields to float in front of the viewer, who then uses a controller to act as a laser pointer to select an action. This movement is based on a mouse acting as a pointer on a computer monitor. In some cases, a narrative metaphor calls for the use of embedded virtual screens depicted within the diegetic (or the world that is depicted in a work of art) user interface. Examples of this can be found in Lawrence Lek's *Notel*, where the 3D architectural space has flat monitors and screens sprinkled throughout the various rooms. Because the building surrounding the immersed participant is meant to replicate the feeling of a high-end, austere hotel, the metaphor of the screen makes sense in the virtual environment. Conversely, if flat screens are incorporated anachronistically into the VR scene, while it may still result in menu systems that are usable, these menus can feel clunky and awkward to navigate, especially if the experience depends on frequent use of the menu.

## MIMICRY

The **mimicry** approach is more abstract than the translation approach, as the designer is no longer referencing user experience and interface examples from the 2D world but is instead looking to physical world interactions in order to build an interaction system. Examples of this could be picking up a cup or throwing a ball – both actions found in the physical world, meaning that users in the virtual space would have expectations around these behaviors. Mimicry only refers to movements or interactions that can be found in the physical world. Typically, the mimicry approach creates interactions that feel similar to movement and interaction with physical objects and can be used to create systems that are second nature to the user and require little to no guesswork, familiarity, or prior knowledge of the user interface or VR systems. Often, this approach can be integrated for users unfamiliar with VR hardware, as the user will experience and approach the technology similarly to how a child might approach a new toy or tool. Mimicry can also allow experienced users to approach a virtual scene with a sense of familiarity that can reduce learning curves with specific application mechanics. Based on the idea that most humans will expect that their movements in the virtual environment will trigger certain realistic physics and reactions, use of the mimicry method can benefit training and commercial applications due to its accurate interactive representations. Several virtual games are digital twins that offer step-by-step simulacra that use the same tools, motions, and actions required for procedures in the physical realm. These mimicry situations provide not just a sense of familiarity but also experiential learning opportunities for task-based training or skill mastery.

## CONCEPTUAL

The **conceptual** approach is a non-conventional approach to interactions. Both the translation and mimicry approaches offer specific digital or physical world references that creators can reference when developing their applications. A conceptual approach affords experimentation and exploration with alternative interaction systems developed directly for a VR system. These interactions are not necessarily functional or useful outside the bounds of VR interaction, but instead the creator tests the bounds of user experience to determine what is and is not possible. A conceptual approach is not typically found in commercial products but can provide valuable information about the medium, especially in the hands of artist technologists. Artist Char Davies and game developers Owen Harris and Niki Smit use what could be considered a conceptual approach, as these artists use diaphragm expansion as a method for VR input. Davies' *Osmose* uses a vest to track the user's breath in order to control how the user moves within the virtual artwork. In Harris and Smit's VR game *HERE*, a user's breath is measured using an experimental device, which is then translated into visual feedback in the virtual space.

Both of these examples highlight ways to fully include a user's physical body within the immersive space, further embedding them within the immersive world. It is hard to predict and define examples of the conceptual approach, as these interaction systems are often created for either experimental purposes or to address interaction or accessibility problems in the emerging and changing technologies of VR. Some of the issues around trying to define conceptual approaches to VR arise because the ideas are novel and unconventional. For an example of this, we need not look further than the arrival of the first iPhone, which would usher in the smartphone revolution. Before 2007, most of our interactions with mobile phones included buttons, knobs or joysticks for input. When the iPhone was introduced, it moved the keyboard behind a glass screen and made all inputs digital, responding to the user's finger gestures with haptic responses. Instead of the familiar methods of input such as pressing a button, inputs included tapping on a screen, pinching, and swiping with fingers. The result was that the proliferation of this new technology required new interaction design solutions without many precedents, often taken from academic and commercial research conducted decades prior. These issues require conceptual approaches to be solved.

## INTERACTION COMPONENTS

Breaking down some of the ways that users can interact with VR systems provides insight into the basic structure of inputs. The inputs that are available to an artist for implementation start with the use of a few basic components: **grip**, **pinch**, **move**, **point**, and **button.** By combining one or more of these, complex interactions can be described. The combined use of these components (or multimodal inputs) can allow for complexity in terms of immersive interaction and is often a way to add a multiplicity of event triggers that signal different responses from the work. A list of some of these essentials is as follows.

## GRIP

Grip uses multiple fingers, typically the middle through pinky, and allows a user to firmly grasp virtual items in the immersive world. In an interaction, this would be used to hold onto an object, such as a scalpel for an operating room training simulation. This translates to "holding" something in the physical realm.

## PINCH

A pinch uses a few fingers – typically the thumb and index – to loosely hold onto an object. Using a hand-held motion controller, this would be achieved with a trigger squeeze and is often helpful for objects that don't require excessive transportation or interaction.

## MOVE

Move interactions originate from the wrist and move up to the shoulder and throughout the user's body. This interaction includes both the position and rotation of the person and each of their appendages within space. Here, the real-world position is translated to the virtual space, typically, but not necessarily, on a one-to-one scale. Movement in these spaces is defined by changes in position.

## POINT

Point interactions are created by an extension of a person's appendage or gaze within the virtual system. Often used in conjunction with raycasts, originally conceptualized by the gaming world, this interaction uses a participant's primary action as the focus to project into the virtual space.

Thus, following a user's gaze through headset input devices, 3D objects in the virtual environment can react or respond. Finger pointing or specific ray selections are useful for menu interactions and ultimately help determine player intentions.

## BUTTON

Buttons are interaction components unique to human interface devices, such as a keyboard or game console controller. These include not only two stage toggle buttons (such as on and off) but also multiaxis inputs such as a joystick. Buttons are the least natural and intuitive of the VR interaction components, but they are helpful for some interactions that would be far too difficult or complex to track properly using the other basic components. Some examples would be: activating a lightsaber or turning a surgical saw on and off. Both of these require several gesticular and interactive inputs to happen all at once – having a button as an option reduces the number of variables needed.

## COMPLEX INTERACTIONS

The lightsaber and surgical saw are good examples of complex interactions. By combining two or more of the basic interaction components, a designer can build more complex interactions, allowing for more complicated and defined input. For instance, using Grip or Pinch and Move, a user is able to carry an object. Using Point, Grip, or Pinch, and Move, a user can throw an object. Teleportation typically uses a combination of Point and Button.

## FEEDBACK

As with any interaction system, responsive and immediate feedback from inputs is critical. Feedback can happen via haptics, visual or auditory responses, or a multitude of other methods. Instances where a user would want feedback can range from: objects being carried that need their positions updated; a visual response to a thrown hand gesture; an auditory click played in response to a menu choice. Even when crossing the street, a button press should be accompanied by feedback to assure the user that their input was received. Poor feedback can lead to user frustration and discomfort, and for an emerging technology like VR, this can be detrimental to the user's experience and turn them off completely.

## POSITION, SCALE, AND ROTATION

Given that VR exists as a three-dimensional system, it is important to consider the three properties of objects in a virtual three-dimensional environment: **position**, **scale**, and **rotation**. **Position** refers to the digital coordinates of an object in space. This property often uses a three-dimensional cartesian coordinate system consisting of an offset value along the X, Y, and Z axes in reference to the world origin (typically denoted as position 0, 0, 0). **Scale** refers to the overall size of the object along the X, Y, and Z axes and is typically altered locally, which is self-referential rather than globally, which references the world's origin. **Rotation** is the degree of tilt around any given axis. For example, a cube rotated 45 degrees around the Z axis would have two of the corners of its face aligned with the axis.

## OBJECTS

In addition to considering the position, scale, and rotation, it is also useful to consider objects in virtual space. This is similar to how computer scientists consider how "objects" work from a coding perspective. Consider, for example, a cup. A cup has several properties, or things that describe the cup, and functions, or things the cup can do. It may be made of glass or ceramic; it may have a specific height and circumference; it may have a print; or it may have other properties that describe it. It can hold liquid (which can be considered another object that the cup interacts with), it can be held, and it can be emptied, assuming it has liquid or some other object filling it; each of these are functions that the cup can perform. It may also have a handle, in which case it may be a mug, which is itself a special kind of cup. By considering objects, their properties, and their functions, as well as how these objects interact with other objects, revelations regarding how the virtual world works in tandem with the user can be discovered.

## CONCLUSION

Throughout the years, human-computer interface research has developed and tested a multitude of interaction techniques that are now commonly used in everyday technologies. These established interaction techniques may or may not be appropriate for the world of VR. While the exact design and implementation of VR interaction will depend on the nature of the artwork being created, it is important to understand some of the foundations of computing interaction, VR systems, and interaction techniques.

Not everything will be applicable, but as with every design endeavor, it is important to understand the generally accepted rules to know which and when to bend and break them.

## REFERENCES

Aigner, R., Wigdor, D., Benko, H., Haller, M., Lindlbauer, D., Ion, A., & Zhao, S. (2012). *Understanding mid-air hand gestures: A study of human preferences in usage of gesture types for HCI* [MSR-TR-2012-111].

Baecker, R. M. (2008). TIMELINESThemes in the early history of HCI – Some unanswered questions. *Interactions*, *15*(2), 22–27. https://doi.org/10.1145/1340961.1340968

Bamodu, O., & Ye, X. M. (2013). Virtual reality and virtual reality system components. *Advanced Materials Research*, *765–767*, 1169–1172. https://doi.org/10.4028/www.scientific.net/AMR.765-767.1169

Fitzpatrick, G. (2018). A short history of human computer interaction: A people-centred perspective. *Proceedings of the 2018 ACM SIGUCCS Annual Conference*, 3. https://doi.org/10.1145/3235715.3242569

Fitzpatrick, G. (2005). Evolving HCI… From Where to Where? *Proceedings of the 17th Australia Conference on Computer-Human Interaction: Citizens Online: Considerations for Today and the Future*.

Jerald, J. (2016). *The VR Book: Human-centered Design for Virtual Reality*. United States: Association for Computing Machinery.

Karam, M., & Schraefel, m.c. (2005). A taxonomy of gestures in human computer interactions. *Electronics and Computer Science*.

Lang, B. (2013, February 12). An introduction to positional tracking and degrees of freedom (DOF). *Road to VR*. Retrieved March 30, 2023, from https://www.roadtovr.com/introduction-positional-tracking-degrees-freedom-dof/

Milgram, P., & Kishino, F. (1994). A taxonomy of mixed reality visual displays. *IEICE Transactions on Information Systems, E77-D*(12), 15.

Pfeuffer, K. (2017, October 16). Gaze+pinch interaction in virtual reality. *ResearchGate*. Retrieved March 30, 2023, from https://www.researchgate.net/publication/320312970_Gaze_pinch_interaction_in_virtual_reality

Skarbez, R., Smith, M., & Whitton, M. C. (2021). Revisiting Milgram and Kishino's reality-virtuality continuum. *Frontiers in Virtual Reality*, *2*, 647997. https://doi.org/10.3389/frvir.2021.647997

# CHAPTER 5

# Artist Gallery – Lawrence Lek, Mohsen Hazarati, Sandrine Deumier

## LAWRENCE LEK

Lawrence Lek was born in Frankfurt, Germany, and received a BA in Architecture at Trinity College, University of Cambridge, England, a Master of Architecture II from The Cooper Union in New York, and a PhD in Machine Learning from the Royal College of Art, London, England. Lek describes himself as an "artist, filmmaker, and musician working in the fields of virtual reality and simulation" (Lek, n.d.). Lek's works draw on his architectural background, allowing him to "explore worldbuilding as a form of multi-dimensional collage that can incorporate elements from both material and virtual worlds while developing narratives that reflect on alternate histories and possible futures" (Lek, n.d.). Lek's works demonstrate a wide range of material knowledge, from the physical to the virtual. Architectural installations complement videos, simulations, games, and virtual reality (VR). From his early work, *Bonus Levels* Lek demonstrates an expansive range of multimedia – video, performance, software exploration, and installation – in order to construct a utopian

DOI: 10.1201/9781003363729-5

world that investigates presence and memory in digital space. Working in multiple forms of immersive space, including several VR artworks, Lek's youth was spent playing video games. During this time, in addition to the rise of video games, Lek was immersed in "different forms of digital media or space that didn't have to do with physical bricks and mortar." This influenced what he calls "the eternal idea of society, society having its own spatial expression," which has been a conceptual inspiration for his experimental works (Ong, 2021).

Lek's recent work focuses on building a "sinofuturist cinematic universe" envisioned through a series of films, games, soundscapes, and VR works that "explore the strange and turbulent beauty of the world to come" (Lek, n.d.). The word sinofuturism is "an obscure term formulated by authors working at the fringes of philosophy and speculative fiction in the early 2000s" (de Seta, 2020) and references exploration of Chinese "cultural, economic, and industrial development" within a technological context that is part science fiction and part futuristic guesswork (Gaskins, 2019). Lek's invocation of the word sinofuturism is multilayered in that it is often described in terms of a singularity – meaning that China's cultural embrace of technology will bring Chinese culture, politics, and economy to the fore in terms of being a trans-national power player. Lek discusses inspiration for this series coming from his readings, where he found "a mirror image between how Chinese industrialisation is portrayed as well as AI. They're both often seen as a threat to civilization, or like it's going to save civilization … there's this weird paradox between these two" (Ong, 2021). Lek goes on to say that "the future has been represented as dehumanized, so it's slightly problematic to use the same human standards on a completely different future, whether that future is Chinese, or AI or intelligent or whatever" (Ong, 2021).

## NØTEL

Work in this series contains a CGI film (*AIDOL*) that "revolves around the complex struggle between humanity and artificial intelligence"; a video game (*2065*) where "all work taken care of by algorithms, people spend all day playing video games against AIs"; another GCI film (*Geomancer*) where "an adolescent satellite AI escapes its imminent demise by coming down to Earth, hoping to fulfill its dream of becoming the first AI artist" and a video essay (*Sinofuturism (1839–2046 AD)*) that explores "the parallels between portrayals of artificial intelligence and Chinese technological development" (Lek, n.d.). In the series, there is a luxury hotel VR simulation entitled *Nøtel*. A trailer for *Nøtel* starts by following a drone down onto a sleek cityscape, with a massive neon-edged, glowing torus-shaped building set in the middle. The camera swoops down to take us to the building's lobby – a shiny, hard-edged, gleaming environment replete with surfaces of polished marble and glass. A digitally generated narrator guides us through the lobby, welcoming the "global nomad" and assuring the listener that they can feel safe and secure in the knowledge that *Nøtel* values and protects their anonymity and security.

Other drones move throughout the lobby and are, in fact, found hovering surreptitiously throughout all of the building's spaces. From the lobby, the drone takes us to the "thermonuclear" Third-Ear Spa, complete with a bed resting on a mirrored floor amidst a moat. Named the "Third Ear" the spa is meant to soothe its patrons – referencing the third ear can mean listening to what's not said, "observing the tonality of the speaker, his or her intellectual as well as emotional emphasis, and his or her body language, plus other nonverbal signals" (What Is "Listening with Your Third Ear"?, n.d.). In fact, this concept of the third ear is referenced in moving from the spa to the piano bar, as the narrator informs us that an "intelligent sound system" uses face recognition and body translation systems to record the user's mood and plays back a responsive soundtrack that is only heard by that specific Nøtel inhabitant. Echoing the spa's reference to the third ear, we see that a stay in Nøtel means taking "the friction out of living, no more second-guessing your wishes." The AI decides what you need and delivers it to you.

Moving along, the architectural showroom assures users that Nøtel can keep them safe from all sorts of terrors, from civil unrest to natural disasters. The greenly lit marketing suite displays screens that show rotating schematics that say "built by algorithms" and "built by robots," all "made for humans." A CEO suite sits next to the network room, with computer banks lit and stacked as tall as a human. Lastly, a disclaimer points out that Nøtel "transcends standard classification, and that the absence of any human workers allows for another dimension of privacy, Nøtel holds a ø star rating as there are no human workers to rate" (Lek, 2016) (Figures 5.1 and 5.2).

Central to the VR work is Lek's collaboration with electronic musician Kode9 (AKA Steve Goodman). Founder of the Hyperdub record label, Goodman's textured soundscapes belie the glistening allure of Nøtel's

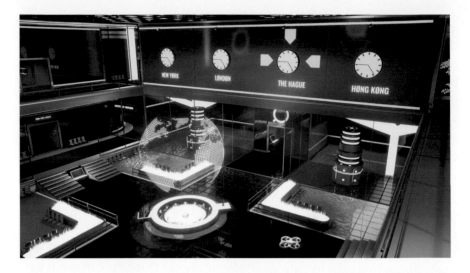

**FIGURE 5.1** Lawrence Lek. *Nøtel* [still] 2016–2019 multimedia installation, HD video, open world video game, and VR experience dimensions variable © Lawrence Lek. Courtesy of the artist and Sadie Coles HQ, London.

**FIGURE 5.2** Lawrence Lek. *Nøtel* [still] 2016–2019 multimedia installation, HD video, open world video game, and VR experience dimensions variable © Lawrence Lek. Courtesy of the artist and Sadie Coles HQ, London.

interiors. Decaying synthesizer notes weave into and among the digital pulse of the electronic beats – the "shiny yet repellent surfaces" of the visuals "complement the sense of discomfort, disconnection and overwhelming emptiness that pervades" Goodman's music (Kafka, 2016). Written as a solo album entitled *Nothing*, Goodman's music creates a dynamic and critical counterpoint to Lek's beautifully rendered architectural spaces. In that book, Goodman discusses how sound can be "deployed to produce discomfort, express a threat, or create an ambience of fear or dread – to produce a bad vibe." The disquieting soundscape of *Nøtel* can be interpreted as a guide for user response and interaction. While Nøtel's spaces are luxuriously appointed, Goodman's atmospheric soundscapes hint at a darkness embedded within this cold new reality (Goodman, 2012). Anthropologist Mark Augé writes that "if a place can be defined as relational, historical and concerned with identity, then a space which cannot be defined as relational, or historical, or concerned with identity will be a non-place" (Augé, 1995). In interviews, Lek invokes Augé in discussing *Nøtel*, as *Nøtel* is itself a non-place "where the individual becomes anonymous and so is divested of responsibility: do what you are told, follow the signs and all will be well" (Hill, 2010). Described as a "fully automated, evacuated luxury hotel simulation" the exhibition of *Nøtel* transforms the space in which it is exhibited into a "pseudo-marketing suite" for the faceless corporation represented in the VR experience (Schwarz, 2018).

## *PLAYSTATION™*

The sinofuturistic continuum of Lek's dystopian approach takes on a different form in *PlayStation™* (2017). *PlayStation™* envisions a "future postwork society with a new virtual reality video game" (Lek, 2017). The game takes place in a physical world, and through these installations, Lek invites collaborators to design and fabricate. The installations vary in execution from one museum space to another, but each contains couches for those waiting, LED strips in the floor to direct the audience to the flat screen display of the VR head-mounted devices. Immersed in the headsets, the participant is placed inside a brightly colored environment that at first reminds one of a restaurant's playspace. More time spent in the virtual architecture shifts the user's perspective; in fact, the space seems to be the massive interior of a computer; what looks like tubular slides is in actuality more closely related to the wiring inside a server. Enclosing the area is a scrim with circular holes; reminiscent of a computer's back vent.

A trailer advertises "funployment forever" within the fictional parent company "Farsight" in the *PlayStation*™ experience. *PlayStation*™ advertises automated workplaces as "earth's most customer-centric company." Once joined, "Farsight" offers "movement up the corporate ladder, bionic enhancement, computer-brain interfaces, life-extension credits, deferred salary in order to put in for a raffle for an eHoliday at Farsight's Casino and Theme Park" (Lek, 2017). *PlayStation*™ is a video game "job simulator" where human labor is billed as fun.

The word robot was introduced by playwright Karl Čapek in his 1920 play *R.U.R.* or *Rossum's Universal Robots*. The word's origin comes from an old slavonic word: robota, which means servitude or forced labor (Intagliata, 2011). The play is about the mass production of fully functional humanoid workers made from synthetic materials. These workers, or robots, perform all the work that humans don't want to do, leading to the company's success. At the end of the play, the robots rebel and kill all humans, whereupon the robots then realize that the humans held the secret to producing more robots and that there was no way to reproduce (Intagliata, 2011; "R.U.R.," 2023). In *PlayStation*™, participants in headsets were taken through tutorials in order to carry out tasks that would gain them credit within the "Farsight" world. Work is then gamified and the workplace automated – it becomes a 9-to-5 work life of leisure.

While the traditional notion of a robot is an automated worker completing acts of drudgery, *PlayStation*™ invites participants to willingly submit to Farsight's training, where "employees outsource their jobs as much as possible, rewarding top performers with access to exclusive entertainment and e-holidays." In his darkly envisioned future, "a group of AI bots, set to always let their human opponents win every e-game they play, collectively decide to break free of their programmed bonds, choosing to become artists" (Bailey, 2018). In an article entitled *What Happens When Capitalism Decides Humans are Useless?*, Lek is asked if artists could ever be replaced by artificial intelligence. "Absolutely," says Lek, "There's this romanticized notion that we associate with creativity, but from my point of view, what is creativity apart from following the rules and then trying to break them? Breaking rules is a rule in itself" (Leonard-Bedwell, 2017).

## MOHSEN HAZRATI

Venturing further into the collaboration of AI and VR is the work of Mohsen Hazrati. Rather than dystopian, Hazariti's work focuses on the integration of Persian culture, specifically Persian culture from the town of Shiraz in Iran. Hazarati graduated with a BA in Graphic Design and Visual Communications from the Institute of Higher Education in Shiraz, Iran, minoring in New Media and Digital Art. In addition to exhibiting his own art, since 2013, he has been the co-founder and curator of Dar-AlHokoomeh Project, a new media art non-profit "with a vision to create a space dedicated to emerging artistic practices, workshops, talks, presentations and exhibitions…[seeking] to expose the creative community and general public to the potentials of Contemporary Arts based in Shiraz" (Hazrati & Forouzandeh, n.d.).

Working in the new media tradition, Hazrati's works explore digital culture and "new aesthetics," integrating these themes into an examination of Shiraz culture and literature. Originally coined by James Bridle in a 2011 blog post, Bridle defines "new aesthetics" as visual references that seem to translate the digital into the physical – examples of which could be an intentionally pixelated pattern printed onto a pillow, digital glitches rendered into physical architecture, or street sculpture that represents fluids in low poly forms. As the concept of new aesthetics was investigated on subsequent SXSW panels and essays, it went on to become more collaboratively defined as "an attempt to draw a circle around several species of aesthetic activity – including but not limited to drone photography, ubiquitous surveillance, glitch imagery, streetview photography, 8-bit net nostalgia" (*New Aesthetic*, 2023) (Figure 5.3).

## FAL PROJECT

Hazrati's VR work *FAL Project* (2017 to ongoing) takes this new aesthetics concept of media translation into deeper territories. The VR work is a glorious symphony of traditional Shirazi music, integrated into a dynamically generated landscape of textured arrays and forms. *FAL Project* is founded on the concept of bibliomancy, or divination through the use of randomly selected text from a book. To do this, Hazrati combines machine learning with living Iranian traditions. Hazrati uses AI to pull from various databases for the visuals, all inspired by the randomly selected texts from *The Divan*, a collection of poems from Persian poet Khwāja Shams-ud-Dīn Muḥammad Ḥāfeẓ-e Shīrāzī, more commonly known by his pen name Hafez ("the memorizer; the (safe) keeper" 1315–1390) (The Divan-i-Hafiz, 2007). Once words and phrases from the poem are selected, they are converted into algorithms that scan the internet in search of visuals that the

**FIGURE 5.3** An example of *New Aesthetics* (2015). Image and permission courtesy of James Brindle.

AI interprets as relating to the original text. The images are pulled into the VR space, where gravity, scale, and position are randomly controlled in order to create movement. The rendering of the visual data and text fragments from *The Divan* allows users to make individual interpretations and predictions about the future (Hazrati, n.d.-b).

*The Divan* is a collection of poems primarily in Persian, but there are also poems in Persian and Arabic. The poet Hafez also hails from Shiraz, and his works are regarded as a pinnacle of Persian literature "often found in the homes of people in the Persian speaking world, who learn his poems by heart, and still use them as proverbs and sayings. His life and poems have been the subject of much analysis, commentary and interpretation, influencing post-14th century Persian writing more than any other author" (Bekhrad, 2018; Hafez Archives, n.d.). Many Iranians use the text for fortune telling, especially during important holidays, where family members will open the collection of poems to a random page and read the poem found therein with the belief that the poem they find will foretell the future ("Hafez," 2023).

Hazarati's choice of Hafez's work as a textual source to generate a digital mystical prediction is important in that Hafez's work can be understood not just as ecstatic mysticism, but as serious works that use satire

**FIGURE 5.4** Mohsen Hazrati's *FAL Project* (2017–ongoing). Image and permission courtesy of the artist.

to critique governmental essays. In *FAL Project*, a pitch-shifted narrator tells the story of Hafez's funeral – where no religious figures would come to pray over him. Instead, his devotees took pages of his unbound book and put them randomly into a box. They then asked a young child to pull a page from the box, and when that page was read, it said, "do not worry about Hafez, he is on his way to heaven" (Hazrati, n.d.-b). The random text selection Hazrati creates with AI is an echo of a Shiraz legend – a beautiful re-telling and re-interpretation of their combined culture, each in a specific place on the timeline of history (Figure 5.4).

## QQQ

While Hazarati has many VR works, he continues his exploration and research of Iranian literature and poetry in the work Hazrati, n.d-b. In non-linear surrealist fashion, *QQQ* sets the scene with a vehicle as a metaphor for humanity initiating a journey "equipped by some terrestrial elements, decorated by different kinds of senses, fed by a pure fuel, to start its mortal journey on the ground" (Mohsen Hazrati: QQQ, 2021). More loosely based on Iranian literature and poetry, Hazrati's conceptual scope still aims to draw from his immediate environment and culture to create a work that "explores the possibilities of digital creation" (Hazrati, n.d.-b). In the work, the visuals flicker between a walking scene

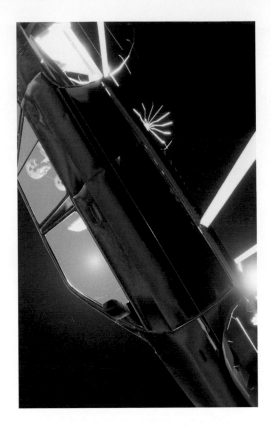

**FIGURE 5.5** Image of Hazrati's *QQQ* (2021). Image and permission courtesy of the artist.

with what looks like a futuristic vending machine and moments where radial waves come toward the viewer – each with brightly colored gradient backgrounds found in what could be described as a "sea punk" aesthetic. Suddenly, a car appears – in one case with wings apparently about to be cut off by giant rotating saw blades; in another from the car's rocking interior. The car at one point contains passengers; the next moment, the passengers are outside holding the car up with drone-like propellers on their heads (Figures 5.5 and 5.6).

## SHIRAZ NATIONAL DAY

In the shorter work *Shiraz National Day* (2021), a scene opens up with a figure in the distance, enveloped by a gray fog. Upon closer look, the scene reveals a photogrammetry figure of Hazarati wearing a VR headset marching around searching, encircled by flat panels. The figure holds

**FIGURE 5.6** Image of Hazrati's *QQQ* (2021). Image and permission courtesy of the artist.

a flashlight, and as it walks in front of each panel, a beautiful building is revealed. The buildings belong to the city of Shiraz, which celebrates *Ordibehesht 15* in the Iranian calendar. Famous sites such as the Afif-Abad Garden, Tomb of Hafez, and Persepolis are visited by tourists and locals alike. Hazarati's small piece must have been displayed in an exhibition celebrating Shiraz's history. This is an example of how Hazarati's work in VR isn't relegated to a one-off, but is the primary medium that he uses to explore his identity and culture.

From longer works like a self-portrait he started in 2017 and continues on, to shorter pieces like *QQQ*, Hazarati demonstrates a confidence in the materials that can only help to push the medium not just in terms of visuals and integration with AI, but in terms of an artistic practice that can imbue contemporary technologies with mystery and cultural identity.

## SANDRINE DEUMIER

Sandrine Deumier was born in Carcassonne, France, in 1978 and received an MA in Philosophy from Toulouse II University in Toulouse, France, as well as a DNAP from the National Institute of Fine Arts in Tarbes, France. Deumier describes her work as belonging to the fields of performance, poetry, and video art, with a focus on post-futurist themes explored "through the development of aesthetic forms related to digital imaginaries" (Deumier, n.d.). Deumier was first interested in video art installations and experimental poetry, but after transferring from philosophy to a study of the arts, she refocused her artistic practice on 3D computer animation. Her work has a standout visual language, wherein the pieces speak directly using Deumier's particular artistic voice.

Instead of letting the latest technology drive the visual rendering of her work, Deumier's personal aesthetic is dominant across any medium she works in. Her objects are usually found within a crisp, clean white environment; her subjects are muted in terms of color but are well rendered and intricate. They also tend to run to the bizarre – Deumier's use of a restricted neutral palette lulls viewers into a calm complacency, and her use of the uncanny valley sets them on edge. Her work investigates technological change, with many of her VR pieces working toward the development of the "imaginary, centered on a form of post-futuristic animism" (Deumier, 2021). Deumier creates an emotional connection with her audience – in her statements, she describes her desire to lead "the audience to immerse themselves in the artistic conception of poetry," allowing for space to "find the connection between contemporary social behavior and new technology," as well as "to put forward a dystopian discourse" (Sandrine Deumier, 2022).

## DELTA: IF EVERYTHING IS CONNECTED, EVERYTHING IS VULNERABLE

Deumier's work *Delta: If Everything is Connected, Everything is Vulnerable* (2020) "attempts to explore/anticipate processes of technological witchcraft." The work opens to a white fog that reveals a clean space – a white sky backdrop with gray softly reflective flooring. Realistically rendered pink feminine figures inhabit distorted bodies that are reminiscent of anamorphic displays. Most of the figures are encased in embryonic, white, slightly frosted plastic sacs, while an astronaut of sorts slowly steps through the space. Some of the fully grown bodies floating in the environment are attached to the walking figure. A closer examination reveals that the figures in the scene share the same face. A later scene shows a mother figure surrounded by the distorted bodies of her face-sharing offspring, and a thought bubble of what appears to be plexiglass contains a flesh-colored jellyfish. Producing a futuristic device with a light-emitting radius, the mother-figure places it on the heads of her children each time her thought bubble transfers to their heads. Finally, she reaches out with the device to the viewer in an effort to transmit her thoughts. *Delta's* subtitle, *If Everything is Connected, Everything is Vulnerable*, emphasizes the delicate nature of the subjects but, perhaps more importantly, invites viewers to examine how technology makes society susceptible to the consequences of viral ideas and words. As a poet, Deumier is particularly aware of words' ability to influence meaning and perception – and in "Delta" Deumier invites viewers to use their interconnectedness to generate empathy and understanding (Figures 5.7 and 5.8).

Deumier states that "by imagining future technological tools centered on phenomena of empathy and interconnections between species," her work "proposes to invent forms of multi-consciousness and strategies for reappropriating animist imaginaries" (Deumier, 2020). Technological witchcraft can be understood as being open to the magic that human computer interaction brings, in that "magic is the science of the imagination,

**FIGURE 5.7** Sandrine Deumier *Delta* (2020). Image and permission courtesy of the artist.

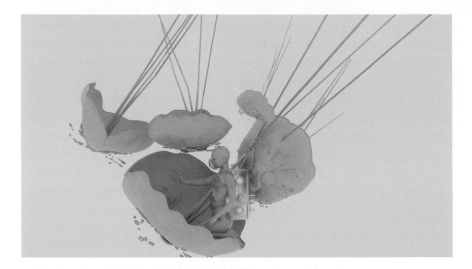

**FIGURE 5.8** Sandrine Deumier *Delta* (2020). Image and permission courtesy of the artist.

the art of engineering consciousness and discovering the virtual forces that connect the body-mind with the physical world" (Davies, 1995). Deumier invokes this apparent dichotomy of witchcraft and technology as a corollary to how we understand art. Art invites us to have a fundamental, personal relationship with a piece. When art is good, it provokes in us an understanding that goes beyond what we thought we understood before (Hirst & Burn, 2001). Artworks based on technology are often judged for their externals – the hardware, the efficacy of the software, their position in the ever-consuming maw of the new. Deumier's work invites its audience to let go of their expectations and to open themselves up to the magic that the weird, the non-linear, and the inexplicable can provide.

## LOTUS EATERS

Deumier also invokes the idea of animism in her descriptions of her VR work. Not a religion but a theory of religion, animism originated in the attribution of life, soul, or spirit to inanimate objects. The original meaning of animism was colonialist and made assumptions about animists; since then, that definition has evolved. In 1985, physicist Nick Herbert put forward a theory of "quantum animism." Herbert's theory moves away from the dualistic approach to animism – rather than a spirit that inhabits the material, Herbert's idea focuses on the "idea that every natural system has an inner life, a conscious center, from which it directs and observes its action" (Krieglstein, 2002, 118). Deumier's virtual artworks indeed seem to have an inner life or a consciousness that directs and observes. In the interactive immersive work *Lotus Eaters* (2021), Deumier describes an environment where "a minimalist aesthetic, intended to position the user in a form of altered perception in order to refocus on minor and infinitesimal things" (Deumier, 2021). The work's title implies "the notion of forgetfulness as a process of appropriating transient identities" (Deumier, 2021).

Monochromatic, as if in a darkening twilight, the user enters a world that offers no traction, nothing obvious to hold on to. Gray manta rays appear in various shades until they become solid black. Scanning the 360-degree space, giant Buddha-like figures appear, towering above the viewer's range of vision. Off in the distance but slowly moving closer are figures of feminine form, slightly akimbo, their movement fluid but intermittently jerky. From a distance, the figures are easy to appreciate, but over time they drift closer and closer until they are atop the viewer. The result is suffocating, with the figures overlapping with the manta rays to create abstract shapes that appear vector and flat in form. Finally, these forms move past to reveal abstract, mountainous, castle-like walls. These walls come closer and closer until the viewer is enclosed with only a narrow passage overhead. In the sky, the manta rays appear again, floating overhead.

Dreamlike in that there is a sense of the familiar but somehow forgotten, and the vision fades. *Lotus Eaters* is an interesting example of a goalless interaction – an experience to be felt and seen rather than a specific pathway to understanding the art. VR applications outside of the artistic realm are often tied to how closely they imitate empirical experience in the physical realm. Immersion in art offers a new level of audience interaction, and the best works invite and provoke in ways that aren't always available to other forms of technological artwork. Deumier's work demands that its audience look beyond simulation and think in terms of potentiality. She states that

> virtual space can be used as an imaginative and creative space… the interaction between these two mental spaces constructs new perceptions of the world and transforms our human identities. More than just the reflection of our own reality, virtual space can be used to examine the mutations of our behaviors influenced by new technologies.
>
> *(Sandrine Deumier, 2017)*

Deumier's vision of her artwork as "post-futuristic animism" requires some conceptual unpacking. Artistically, "post-futurism" is a term used "by a small collective of artists and academics to describe a project of computer based art, poetry and writing" ("Post-Futurism," n.d.). In relation to science fiction, author Jeff Noon uses "post-futurism" in relation to novels that incorporate "mixed media and overlapping storylines" ("Post-Futurism," n.d.). In discussing technopaganism, VR pioneer Mark Pesce says that "magic is the science of the imagination, the art of engineering consciousness and discovering the virtual forces that connect the body-mind with the physical world" (Davis, 1995). In divining what both the digital and magical realms have in common, Pesce goes on to point out that both "cyberspace and magical space are purely manifest in the imagination…both are constructed by [one's] thoughts and beliefs" (Davis, 1995).

## REFERENCES

Augé, M. (1995). *Non-places: Introduction to an anthropology of supermodernity* (J. Howe, Trans.). Verso.

Bailey, S. (2018). Stephanie bailey on Lawrence Lek. *Artforum*. https://www. artforum.com/print/reviews/201806/lawrence-lek-75611

Bekhrad, J. (2018, October 24). Iran's fascinating way to tell fortunes. *BBC*. https:// www.bbc.com/travel/article/20181023-irans-fascinating-way-to-tell-fortunes

Davis, E. (1995, July 1). Technopagans. *Wired*. https://www.wired.com/1995/07/technopagans/

de Seta, G. (2020). Sinofuturism as inverse orientalism: China's future and the denial of coevalness. *SFRA Review*, *50*(2–3), 87. https://sfrareview.org/2020/09/04/50-2-a5deseta/

Deumier, S. (n.d.). *Sandrine Deumier*. https://sandrinedeumier.com/Sandrine_Deumier_CV_EN.pdf

Deumier, S. (2020). *Delta*. https://sandrinedeumier.com/DELTA_Sandrine_Deumier_EN.pdf

Deumieri, S. (2021). *Lotus eaters*. https://sandrinedeumier.com/XRlotuseaters.html

Gaskins, N. R. (2019). Techno-vernacular creativity and innovation across the African diaspora and global south. In R. Benjamin (Ed.), *Captivating technology: Race, carceral technoscience, and liberatory imagination in everyday life* (pp. 252–274). Duke University Press. https://doi.org/10.2307/j.ctv11sn78h.16

Goodman, S. (2012). *Sonic warfare: Sound, affect, and the ecology of fear*. MIT Press.

Hafez. (2023). *Wikipedia*. https://en.wikipedia.org/w/index.php?title=Hafez&oldid=1137469980

*Hafez Archives*. (n.d.). Sufi: Journal of Mystical Philosophy & Practice. https://www.sufijournal.org/tag/hafez/

Hazrati, M. (n.d.-a). Fāl. *New Viewings.* https://sketchfab.com/models/5a911559f3 634b3981bb43a7c2e243d1/embed?autostart=1&ui_theme=dark

Hazrati, M. (n.d.-b). *Mohsen Hazrati.* https://mohsenhazrati.com/#

Hazrati, M., & Forouzandeh, M. (n.d.). *Dar al Hokoomeh project.* http://www.dah-project.com/

Hill, D. W. (2010). Book review: Non-places: An introduction to supermodernity: Marc Augé, 2008 London: Verso. *Urban Studies, 47*(11), 2482–2484. https://doi.org/10.1177/00420980100470111105

Hirst, D., & Burn, G. (2001). *On the way to work: 12 Interviews* (1. publ). Faber & Faber.

Intagliata, C. (2011, April 22). *The origin of the word "robot."* https://www.science-friday.com/segments/the-origin-of-the-word-robot/

Kafka, G. (2016, June 20). ScareBnb: Step into Kode9 and Lawrence Lek's post-human hotel. *Fact Magazine.* https://www.factmag.com/2016/06/20/kode9-lawrence-lek-notel-nothing/

Krieglstein, W. J. (2002). *Compassion: A new philosophy of the other.* Rodopi.

Lek, L. (n.d.). *About.* https://lawrencelek.com/About

Lek, L. (2016). *Nøtel.* https://lawrencelek.com/Notel

Lek, L. (2017). *Play Station.* https://lawrencelek.com/Play-Station

Leonard-Bedwell, N. (2017, July 17). What happens when capitalism decides humans are useless? *Dazed.* https://www.dazeddigital.com/artsandculture/article/36673/1/lawrence-lek-playstation-dystopian-world-human-employ-ment-future

Mohsen Hazrati: *QQQ.* (2021). *Radiance.* https://www.radiancevr.co/artists/mohsen-hazrati/hazrati-qqq/

New Aesthetic. (2023). *Wikipedia.* https://en.wikipedia.org/w/index.php?title=New_Aesthetic&oldid=1146014387

Ong, J. (2021, January 12). *Lawrence Lek talks simulation art and his interest in the ambiguity between two paradoxes.* It's Nice That. https://www.itsnicethat.com/features/lawrence-lek-in-conversation-digital-art-120121

Post-Futurism. (n.d.). *In the art and popular culture encyclopedia.* https://www.artandpopularculture.com/Post-Futurism

R.U.R. (2023). *Wikipedia.* https://en.wikipedia.org/w/index.php?title=R.U.R.&oldid=1144521512

Sandrine Deumier. (2017, July 26). De:Formal. https://www.deformal.com/artists/sandrine-deumier

Sandrine Deumier. (2022). Taipei artist village. https://www.artistvillage.org/artist-detail.php?p=4537

Schwarz, G. (2018, July 26). 'Nøtel' by Lawrence Lek and Kode9. *Apollo Magazine.* https://www.apollo-magazine.com/dystopia-lands-in-londons-docklands/

*The Divan-i-Hafiz* (H. Wilberforce Clarke, Translated and Edited) (2007). Washington, DC: Ibex, p. 1096.

*What is "listening with your third ear"?* (n.d.). Quora. https://www.quora.com/What-is-"listening-with-your-third-ear"

# CHAPTER 6

# The Visual Conceptual Space

## INTRODUCTION

Humans use a variety of internal measures to interpret the space around them. Visual, aural, and psychological clues combine to offer a sense of their surroundings. Of course, there are ways to confuse one's perception – imagine the visual of the vase, which can also be read as the profile of two faces, and other classic illusions. Images like this optical illusion play with what can be interpreted as background and what is foreground. The brain's perception of the figure-ground relationship requires more than a simplistic, quick assessment of the image – instead, the brain looks at more than the sum of what the sense of vision inputs and tries to make sense of the whole. Optical illusions have been with humans for a long time; many early paintings used a high degree of realism to give the illusion of 3D space.

One such example is called "trompe l'oeil," a form of painting that intentionally creates a realistic optical illusion of 3D space on a 2D surface. Trompe l'oeil paintings exploit how human vision works in order to produce the sensation that the painting is real. Closer inspection allows one to see that the paintings were really 2D, just playing with perspective. The digital world inside a headset also uses illusion to convey a sense of depth to the person immersed in that space. At first blush, it would seem

DOI: 10.1201/9781003363729-6

that the illusion is created by the trompe l'oeil painting or the digital perspective, but "perceiving the space around us is not just about passive perception but is important for actively moving through the world" (Jerald, 2016, p. 112). The human brain uses a variety of senses, calculations, and perceptions to build a response in order to interact with the world around it – bringing meaning and depth to what the senses input.

This interpretation of sensory input allows humans to perceive a wide assortment of details that are then given context and narrative. Creators in the flat, 2D world of screens create meaning through the use of specific cinematographic approaches to presenting subject matter. The distance of the camera to the subject and the amount of visual information the audience receives about the subject can impart a wide variety of information: it can convey an emotional connection between audience and character, it can indicate the environment the subjects encounter themselves in, and it can reveal aspects of the character's physical reaction. This information is generally conveyed through the composition of shots that appear on the screen: the establishing shot (this is usually a first shot that sets the stage/ gives context for where the subjects are), the extreme close-up (a shot that tightly focuses on the subject's face), the close-up (a shot that starts at the subject's neck and includes the top of their head), the medium close-up (a shot that starts at the chest and includes the top of the subjects head), the medium shot (usually from the waist up to the top of the head), the long shot (a shot that includes an entire figure, or two figures), and the extreme long shot (this shot covers the entire situation or space around the subjects). In virtual reality (VR) space, the content is not packaged and presented to the viewer; rather, the user has the option to move through the space and encounter the 3D subjects from whatever perspective they desire. Of course, not all objects within the 3D space are approachable – some are in the distance and may not be 3D but give the illusion of dimensionality.

In his book *The VR Book: Human Centered Design for Virtual Reality*, author Jason Jerald discusses "object-relative judgements," which are some of the tools that the brain uses to understand the space around it. Object-relative judgments describe the internal psychological evaluations that occur in order to process where objects are in space in relation to other objects and how the objects move in relation to one another. Jerald has a very helpful description for how to think about space in VR – and in considering the space in the way Jerald describes, artists gain a tool for development – tools that enable them to convey some of what shots do for film.

Jerald describes three layers of the space perceived by the brain: **personal space**, **action space**, and **vista space**. **Personal space** is the intimate surroundings around each of us – at most just beyond arm's length. Personal space tends to be intimate in that very few other people would enter it – only family, close friends and loved ones. Extreme close ups and close ups are used in film to create a close, informal relationship with the subject because it is rare for others to enter this personal space. Jerald's "personal space" can be thought of as a corollary to a close-up. **Action space** can be understood as the space in which we can connect with others more broadly: a conversation across a table, a ball thrown, a short sprint. Action space correlates to medium and long shots in film – it can be thought of as the room around the subject. Lastly, **vista space** is grander – this could be a scene in the distance or the sky around us. A skybox that gives a sense of daylight, nighttime, or outer space is an example of vista space. In film, establishing and extreme long shots are the best parallels to this third space. Jerald's three levels of personal space are very manageable ways to approach development for VR. There are objects that a user can pick up and throw (personal space), there are characters or objects that the user can interact with (action space), and there are greater scenes that the user is placed in (vista space).

1. **Art as a Window, Art as a Mirror**
2. **Renaissance Roots**

Two key concepts that continue to shape and influence western art to this day emerged from the renaissance period: *Brunelleschi's Mirror* and *Alberti's Window*. Both were methods created by artists of the time in order to capture accurate linear perspective in their artistic works. *Brunelleschi's Mirror* was both an artistic and a scientific experiment in which Filippo Brunelleschi used linear perspective techniques to paint an image of the Baptistery of the Florentine cathedral.

In this technique, lines appear to merge at a single point in the distance, rendering what looks like spatial depth on the flat surface of a painting. To achieve this, Brunelleschi created a grid, and much like muralists do today, he copied the scene he looked into a corresponding square in the grid. This produced a perfect perspective version of the original scene, although in reverse, as if the scene were reflected in a mirror. Then, Brunelleschi put a small hole in this reverse image, allowing him to peer through this first painted image at a mirror held by an assistant. Reversing the reversed image, Brunelleschi looked at his original painting through the mirror and was able to repaint the scene correctly with a high degree of accuracy in perspective (Edgerton, 2006; Warwick, 2016). Brunelleschi viewed a combination of the reflected painting and the physical environment that served as the reference for this second painting. His claim was that the "painting could perfectly reproduce the visible world like a mirror reflection" (Warwick, 2016). While there is historical evidence to suggest that *Brunelleschi's Mirror* may not be the first instance of artists using linear perspective, it is a key instance of mirrors being linked to artistic works and helped to set the bar for perspective in western art for decades to come. Using a pinhole to gaze at a mirror evokes the metaphor of painting as a window – in Brunelleschi's case, a literal window to a window on his work.

Following Brunelleschi's lead, Leon Battista Alberti documented a rendering technique dubbed *Alberti's Window*. In addition to writing up Brunelleschi's approach to creating perspective, Alberti was important to the painting community of his time for his treatise called *De Pictura* (1435). In his treatise, Alberti proposed that painting try to achieve a "convincing three-dimensional space" through the use of "light and shadow to create bodies that look three-dimensional" and that figures be "in varied poses to create a compelling narrative" (Kilroy & Graham, n.d.). Like Brunelleschi, Alberti used a technique with a gridded frame whose coordinates were then translated onto the canvas using accurate scaling (Edgerton, 2006). The use of this method allowed artists to translate their perceived environment into a rendered image using whatever medium they practiced (during the renaissance this was typically paint).

Alberti then took this method one step further by directly establishing the metaphor of painting as a window (Friedberg, 2006). Using realism in rendering the figures and the use of a single vanishing point, Alberti taught users to look at paintings as if they were looking through a window frame (Kilroy & Graham, n.d.). Not being exposed to photography or photo-realism, the early painters of perfect linear perspective sought to create images that were so believable they could have been photographs (Bolter & Gromala, 2003). This use of illusion in painting to create a simulacrum of reality continued from the time of Brunelleschi and Alberti until the Impressionists first began to deconstruct how paint is laid on a canvas.

They moved away from a painting as a direct, realistic copy of the scene before them and investigated how paint could capture color and light.

## THE MIRROR METAPHOR

There is existential debate surrounding mirrors, specifically surrounding what is seen in them. One camp proposes that the reflection is a different object from its point of origin; in a sense, it is a copy (Casati, 2012). Another camp argues that what is seen in the mirror is an image; a snapshot of what is being reflected. In many ways, it is akin to a window (Casati, 2012). While the discussion of whether mirrors duplicate or capture an environment and objects is beyond the scope of this book, engaging in the digital world can be both a window into a different world and a mirror of the physical world.

In VR, the context for this book, it is important to consider the cultural, philosophical, and metaphorical meanings given to mirrors and windows. A common assumption among artistic practices in the renaissance is that artistic images are of the same nature as images that appear in mirrors (Calabi et al., 2022). But what is the nature of these reflected images? In general, it can be assumed that mirrors, whether filtered through the lens of technological advancement allowed by optics studies or in a metaphorical artistic sense, reflect the visual properties of an environment (Warwick, 2016). Mirrors show a snapshot of the world at a specific moment and in a specific place. However, artistic works can capture more than simply what is seen.

Artistic works can be considered "mirrors of society" (Böhme, 2015). That is to say that artistic works not only present reflections of a physical space (whether fictitious or not), but they also present a reflection of the societal values, beliefs, and realities during their creation (Gromala, 2003). Examples of mirrors as a reflection of society are, of course, found in artistic movements from different periods in time. For instance, Dadaism arose shortly after The Great War (World War One) and was a direct response to the introduction of a technological war, the treatment of veterans, the corruption of politicians, and other social, cultural, and political aspects of the time (Loggia, 2016). Dadaism as a movement hosted artistic works that were mirrors of the postwar social environment, just as contemporary artistic works are reflections of our own contemporary social environments. In response to the senselessness and devastation of war, Dadaist performances broke narrative conventions – poems were read on stage while musicians played discordantly, fights were started between audience members, and there was no clear beginning or end to the entire scenario. The postwar rage and despair of the artists and their community brought them to a place where they had lost faith in all that went before, and their output matches their sense of hopelessness.

Later on, artists of the 1960s built on the Dadaist performances to create Happenings. Happenings were also non-linear performances and, like Dadaist performances, required the involvement of all who attended. Instead of "viewer" and "object," participants were encouraged to join in and engage with any one of the many events occurring: singing, chainsawing ice, climbing over tires – each event was different in terms of what happened and how long it took. The ephemeral nature of Happenings meant that instead of a physical object that was destined for the gallery, the experience was emphasized, positing itself as "real life" ("Happenings" Performances Overview | TheArtStory, 2012). These examples of audience participation in terms of generating and/or affecting the artwork are important predecessors to later new media artworks; in fact, participation in a wide range of forms is essential to interactive VR artworks.

## THE WINDOW AS METAPHOR

In addition to a mirror, the metaphor of artistic works as windows suggests a specific interplay between the work, the audience, and the artist. Specifically, the window metaphor regards the work as a window with which to view the subject matter (Calabi et al., 2022). It is a metaphor that assumes that the audience is external to the work and views the intangible depictions from afar. These depictions, while subject to some perceptive renegotiation by the viewer, are primarily driven and constructed by the artist. In both the mirror and the window metaphors, there are underlying assumptions that drive the interaction between the artist, the work, and the audience. These assumptions are then reinforced by the physical qualities of the works and their presentation. An excellent example of how the physical quality of a work reinforces how the work is meant to be viewed is framing.

In the past hundred years, the most common way for a broad section of the general public to see artwork was to attend a museum or a gallery. Coming to these spaces to view the art objects, viewers would most commonly see works that take the form of a medium laid on a planar, rectangular surface. Often the medium's visual content was representative of something found in the physical realm – a pastoral scene, a portrait, or a still life. These framed realistic illusions sat on walls, with viewers coming in to look, ignoring or looking past the museum walls, the room itself, and sometimes even the people within. The issue with the artwork-as-window way of seeing art is that it continues to influence the ways in which novel technologies are developed and designed. Luckily, advances in philosophical ideas regarding human-centered perspectives as well as advancements in technology (especially digital technology) have challenged these views. These advances have allowed artists to break away from the window metaphor and the pervasiveness of *the rectangle*. While VR is not the first advancement to do so, it is part of these transitions and challenges to classical views on artistic practice.

It is not clear exactly when framing artistic works became commonplace. It is suggested that frames began to accompany artistic works once the works became independent of a particular surface – rather than a permanently installed fresco on a chapel wall, artists would paint on wood panels (Friedberg, 2006). Regardless of their temporal introduction, frames serve to reinforce the flat, planar qualities of the artistic works they are coupled with. They serve as an enclosure that literally bounds the work, much like the frame that bounds a window in a home. A framed work is meant to be separate from the surrounding wall, to separate an object from its background, so a viewer can approach the work and stand before it. These bounds reinforce the idea that what the viewer is looking at is a portal, an entry to something that is not a wall, something that requires *looking past and into* rather than an integration of the surrounding space. The choice of frame also influences how the work is interpreted – heavy gold frames can indicate value and worth; they can tie a work to a specific time period; and they can be as complex and interesting as the work itself. Frames are often added to works long after they leave an artist's studio – they can be changed according to the desires of the museum or collector. Indeed, considering how much frames can change a work, it is interesting to note how little choice and input artists usually have over which or what frames are used.

## SHIFTING PERSPECTIVE

While many aspects of western artistic practice have emphasized window and mirror metaphors in pursuit of renderings involving singular linear perspective, some historic work did play with the notion of 2D space. For instance, the 1533 work *Jean de Dinteville and Georges de Selve* by Hans Holbein the Younger appears at first to be a prototypical portrait of two ambassadors. Upon further examination, there is a large white and gray shape running across the depicted floor. If the art viewer repositioned themselves to view the painting from the lower left corner of the work, the shape revealed itself to be a skull. The skull, an optical illusion that references mortality, is a particular kind of illusion called anamorphic. Anamorphic images are distorted or extended when viewed from the front, but when viewed from the proper angle, they snap into a visible, recognizable shape.

Holbein's use of anamorphic shapes in his paintings breaks the illusion of looking at work as if through a window. While the hyper-realistic rendition of the two figures adheres to Alberti's dictums for paintings, the anamorphic skull indicates that a straightforward evaluation of the work with the viewer standing in front of the work is a limited perspective. Instead, Holbein's work "challenges the illusion of transparency, so that the painting is no longer a window into the world…[viewers instead] take an active role in constructing the meaning of the painting" (Bolter, Gromola). Holbien's work merges two different perspectives into a single plane, a theory of painting further explored by the Cubist movement.

The original goal of the cubists was to present the world in a new way (Gray, 1953). This was accomplished by rejecting realistic rendering techniques, utilizing geometric abstraction, and collapsing multiple perspectives into one flat image (Gleizes & Metzinger, 1913; Apollinaire & Read, 2004). Collapsing multiple perspectives meant that cubists translated various perspectives of their 3D subject matter onto the flat plane of the canvas. One painting might render a boat from a head-on perspective, but included within the same painting would be other views of the same boat rendered from different positions: a side view from a farther distance away, the subject, and its surrounding settings. Instead of choosing a singular moment in time to capture, Cubist works capture multiple moments and superimpose them. Capturing the multiple moments adds a temporal aspect to the work, allowing documentation of the subject matter over time.

## TEMPORAL PERSPECTIVE

The addition of temporal elements to an artistic work is perhaps the most important aspect of cubism for the context of this book, and indeed, Cubist works have been demonstrated to affect audiences' perceptions of time (Nather et al., 2012). It isn't until the adoption of experimental film and video as artistic mediums that the fourth dimension, time, finds its place as an artistic medium (Ross, 2014). The use of time-based technologies for artistic works, whether film or digital, affords an impermanent element to the work. In any work where one frame follows another, time is integral. This holds true for the history of time-based mediums – even in some of the earliest works, such as *Demolition of a Wall* (1896) by Louis Lumiere. Lumiere's work echoed the passing of time through the filming of the process of knocking down a wall. The film is projected in real time – that is, it takes as long to watch the wall being torn down as it did to actually tear the wall down. Lumiere subverts what appears to be the documentation of a moment by reversing the film – the wall is shown being "built" backward. At the end of the short loop, the wall is erect and fresh – playing with time and with audience expectations for events. This playing with time is in contrast with the typical renaissance-restricted artistic work using mirrors and windows as a guiding principle of the artistic process (whether actual or metaphorical). In these classical works, a singular perspective locked in a singular moment in time is captured. Conversely, both time-based mediums and the earlier example of cubism use multiple temporal perspectives presented within the context of a single artistic work.

## USER-GENERATED PERSPECTIVE

While there has been significant debate on the artistic merits of "video games" (Murphy, 2010; Bourgonjon et al., 2017), one aspect of the technology driving the gaming experience merits further discussion – the notion of *interactivity*. Interactivity, first seen among performative artworks like Dadaism and Happenings, begins its integration in earnest. As audience participation and engagement become more broadly explored through games, users become more accustomed to having their input change the work's perspective. The creator who designs a game imbues the experience with content and, therefore, some semblance of their perspective. However, this perspective can be morphed by the user, as any given frame rendered is at the mercy of the user's input. There is no guarantee that the viewer will be exposed to all elements of the game. Additionally, there is no guarantee that two viewers will experience the same content in the same temporal sequence – creating two separate perspectives driven by each user. In this sense, artists who choose games as a medium must make a choice to share the artistic process with the viewer (Pearce, 2006). On the continuum of 2D artworks, most video games – like most other digital media – are still primarily displayed on flat rectangular screens. While the temporal aspects of time-based mediums (Barnes, 2009) and interactive elements of games can help to break away from the classical notions of perspective, they are most often still bound by a similar layout: the viewer looks *into* the work *through* a flat planar rectangle.

## PERVASIVENESS OF METAPHORS

It should come as no surprise that these metaphors, with roots established by artists like Brunelleschi and Alberti, have influenced not only artistic endeavors but also technological advancements. This is especially true of computer technologies. Perhaps one of the most profound and long-lasting examples of this influence on technology is that of the computer "window."

> When interface designers chose windows to describe the framed rectangles on the screen that present text or graphical data, they made a choice that had vast cultural significance. As a result we have spent the past [fourty] years opening, staring at, resizing, minimizing, and closing 'windows'.
>
> *(Bolter and Gromala, 2003)*

It is worth noting that these computer interface windows are part of a larger metaphor, one that allowed for the vast adoption of computer technology and continues to shape how digital interactions take form: *the desktop*. The desktop metaphor was originally established for the Xerox 8010 Star Information System (Smith et al., 1982). Its interface was designed to resemble the top of an office desk with accompanying "furniture" and equipment (Smith et al.,1982). When something is selected using this desktop metaphor (using the now common mouse and keyboard input convention), desktop icon shortcuts expand into *windows*, with each window containing contextually sensitive information such as a word document or a file explorer. The icons on the desktop resemble common office objects such as folders, files, and trash bins. Still attached to this office notion of interaction, current computer culture harbors semiotic ghosts – such as the floppy disk icon for saving. Out of use since the early 1990s, a floppy disk was a rectangular portable object used to record and save data from one computer to another, a predecessor to flash drives and SD cards. Contemporaneous computer users know the outline of the floppy disk's form from the outlined icon that is still used to indicate "saving," even if they've never seen a physical floppy disk their entire lives.

To most, these conventions and interactions may seem obvious and trivial, but at the time of the Xerox Star's release, most computer interfaces utilized something akin to a command line. It would not be until the Macintosh Apple Lisa™ adopted this same desktop metaphor that its use became more widely popularized (Smith et al., 1985). The pervasiveness of the desktop metaphor, with its portals into various applications, led directly to the name "Windows" for Microsoft™'s operating system. In *Windows and Mirrors: Interaction Design, Digital Art and the Myth of Transparency*, David Bolter and Diane Gromoala urge interface designers to "think of the computer screen as a window, opening up onto a visual world that seems to be behind or beyond it" (2003, pp. 26).

## BENEFITS OF METAPHOR

This is not to say that metaphors like the metaphor of the office desktop do a disservice; quite the contrary. Metaphors serve the beneficial purpose of providing conceptual frameworks to guide users and ease difficulties with technological adoption (Colburn & Shute, 2008). For instance, the use of a *shopping cart* when ordering items online reminds users of their prior experiences in a brick-and-mortar store pushing a shopping cart around and placing selected objects for checkout within the metal body. Calling the list of items selected for purchase on a digital website a "shopping cart" allows users access to their personal experiences, and from this they can infer what to do. The exact nature of a metaphor consists of both a target (the digital list) and a source (the brick-and-mortar shopping cart). The target and the source can be used for comparison, with one being used as a translation of the other (Colburn & Shute, 2008).

At its core, the use of metaphor for understanding is linguistic, cultural, and semiotic in nature. An unfamiliar object is related to familiar objects, words, or symbols (Mehrpooya & Nowroozzadeh, 2013). However, familiarity with objects, words, or symbols depends on cultural familiarity with the referred object. One example is that of the floppy disk – while older individuals understand the metaphor of the floppy disk icon as being linked to the object to which data is saved, younger individuals who are unfamiliar with floppy disks often don't know that the "save" icon is representative of something integral to the origins of computing. The desktop metaphor proved to be successful in its early inception, as the primary audience was those engaging in workplaces and offices; those to whom the desktop metaphors made literal sense. The fact that the metaphors made sense led to their widespread adoption.

## BREAKING THE RECTANGLE

For artists, technological advancement may allow for a breaking of the conventions established by windows, mirrors, and rectangles. An initial step can be seen in the use of film, which allows for multiple successive perspectives to be presented; however, as discussed, there is still an orientation toward a screen – the rectangular plane – that dictates much of the artistic engagement. This issue, where access to the artwork is gained through the rectangle, exists in gaming as well as other interactive artistic forms. While users dictate some of the perspective from which they interact with the work, the rectangle is still ever-present and inescapable.

VR presents an opportunity to truly break away. Rather than viewing the artwork through the rectangular frame, VR creates a situation where the viewer is situated squarely inside of the work. Breaking the conventions of the frame as container, VR has the opportunity to meld the viewer with the work. Instead of looking through a window into an artistic world, users in VR become part of the world. Furthermore, the embodied nature of VR connects the participant's physical experience with visual, aural, and other sensory inputs. This creates new possibilities and potential for artistic expression.

Authors Saker and Frith point out that "the experience of being placed in a virtual space that ocularly appears disconnected from the physical environment…is precisely the phenomenological effect of this technology, and what makes it feel distinctive from other media" (Saker & Frith, p. 1431). Immersion in a work allows for a direct connection between the immersed and the digital environment in a way that work viewed through a screen does not. To have one's entire range of vision filled with a fabricated environment is relatively novel in terms of human evolution – the effect is highly charged and offers an intense experience. To reiterate, the VR experience offers "a computer-mediated simulation that is three-dimensional, multisensory, and interactive," and leaves those who participate in the experience feeling "*as if* [they are] inhabiting and acting within an external environment" (Burbules, 2006, p. 37).

The virtual space shuts out most external stimuli in a way that can focus attention on the virtual. Time passes differently for those engaged with the content in the headset – often there's a sense of putting things on pause while one figures out what is going on and sorts out how to bring their bodily movements to bear on the scenario in front of them.

In many ways, this sensation is due to some aspects of self-consciousness – how does what "I am" doing in the headset affect the immersive world around "me"? In discussing how she approaches her work, artist Rachel Rossin states that "in terms of Virtual Reality as a medium (I feel this is important as a framework for discussions around my work in Virtual Reality and the medium itself), I do regard it's best-use as a phenomenological tool and that is what I am aiming for in the way I program my works. Of course, that is not the exclusive purpose in and of itself but it is important to note that every VR work I've made employs the user's perspective as the game mechanic or 'arbiter'" (R. Rossin, personal communication, March 17, 2023). This makes sense in that phenomenology studies the "structures of consciousness as experienced from the first-person point of view. The central structure of an experience is its intentionality; its being directed toward something, as it is an experience of or about some object. An experience is directed toward an object by virtue of its content or meaning" (Siewert et al., 2003). Rossin's desire is to give those who experience her artwork some level of authorial control and/or interactive consequences. The ability for participants to experience this within a situation that promotes immediacy and intimacy is extremely powerful and is arguably currently best experienced in an immersive VR system.

## CONCLUSION

Much of western art has been dictated by the metaphors of windows, mirrors, and frames. While these metaphors are useful, they do impose limitations on our thinking toward innovative, immersive, artistic works. What is important for artists using VR to understand is that these metaphors of window, mirror, and frame have established a clear positionality for both the viewer of the artistic work and the work itself. These metaphors place the viewer as an external party that is looking into the work, often with a singular perspective. Various technological developments, such as time-based experiences or video games, have challenged some of these established paradigms; however, like their planar artistic predecessors, they are still meant to be surrounded by portals meant for viewing through. Primarily due to the immersive, embodied nature of the technology and the possibilities offered by the visual conceptual space, VR artworks start to truly break away from the division between the artwork and the audience.

## REFERENCES

Apollinaire, G., & Read, P. (2004). *The cubist painters.* University of California Press. https://books.google.com/books?id=qYATQ3Rw6qgC

Barnes, D. (2009). Time in the Gutter: Temporal structures in watchmen. *KronoScope*, *9*(1–2), 51–60. https://doi.org/10.1163/1567715 09X12638154745427

Böhme, C. (2015). Film production as a 'mirror of society': The history of a video film art group in Dar es Salaam, Tanzania. *Journal of African Cinemas, 7*(2), 117–135. https://doi.org/10.1386/jac.7.2.117_1

Bolter, J. D., & Gromala, D. (2003). *Windows and mirrors: Interaction design, digital art, and the myth of transparency.* Cambridge, MA: MIT Press. ISBN 978-0262025454.

Bourgonjon, J., Vandermeersche, G., Rutten, K., & Quinten, N. (2017). Perspectives on video games as art. *CLCWeb: Comparative Literature and Culture, 19*(4). https://doi.org/10.7771/1481-4374.3024

Burbules, N.C. (2006). Rethinking the virtual. In: Weiss, J., Nolan, J., Hunsinger, J., Trifonas, P. (eds) *The international handbook of virtual learning environments.* Springer, Dordrecht. https://doi.org/10.1007/978-1-4020-3803-7_1

Calabi, C., Huemer, W., & Santambrogio, M. (2022). Mirrors, windows, and paintings. *Estetika: The European Journal of Aesthetics, LIX/XV*(1), 22–32. https://doi.org/10.33134/eeja.200

Casati, R. (2012). Mirrors, illusions, and epistemic innocence. In C. Calabi (Ed.), *Perceptual illusions* (pp. 192–201). Palgrave Macmillan UK. https://doi.org/10.1057/9780230365292_11

Colburn, T. R., & Shute, G. M. (2008). Metaphor in computer science. *Journal of Applied Logic, 6*(4), 526–533. https://doi.org/10.1016/j.jal.2008.09.005

Edgerton, S. Y. (2006). Brunelleschi's mirror, Alberti's window, and Galileo's "perspective tube." *História, Ciências, Saúde-Manguinhos, 13*(suppl), 151–179. https://doi.org/10.1590/S0104-59702006000500010

Friedberg, A. (2006). *The virtual window: From Alberti to Microsoft.* MIT Press.

Gleizes, A., & Metzinger, J. (1913). *Du Cubisme.* Paris.

Gray, C. (1953). The cubist conception of reality. *College Art Journal, 13*(1), 19. https://doi.org/10.2307/772389

*"Happenings" Performances Overview | TheArtStory.* (2012, January 21). The Art Story. Retrieved March 30, 2023, from https://www.theartstory.org/movement/happenings/

Jerald, J. (2016). *The VR book: Human-centered design for virtual reality.* Association for Computing Machinery.

Kilroy, L., & Graham, H. (n.d.). *Alberti's revolution in painting (article)*. Khan Academy. Retrieved March 30, 2023, from https://www.khanacademy.org/humanities/renaissance-reformation/early-renaissance1/beginners-renaissance-florence/a/albertis-revolution-in-painting

Loggia, R.D. (2016). THE LEGACY OF DADAISM.

Mehrpooya, A., & Nowroozzadeh, N. (2013). Metaphor-laced language of computer science and receptor community users. *Journal of Technical Writing and Communication, 43*(4), 403–423. https://doi.org/10.2190/TW.43.4.d

Murphy, S. (2010). Can video games be art? *New Scientist, 207*(2778), 46–47. https://doi.org/10.1016/S0262-4079(10)62287-7

Nather, F. C., Fernandes, P. A. M., & Bueno, J. L. O. (2012). Timing perception is affected by cubist paintings representing human figures. *Proceedings of Fechner Day, 28*(1), 292–297.

Pearce, C. (2006). *Games AS Art: The Aesthetics of Play*, 24.

Ross, C. (2014). The temporalities of video: Extendedness revisited. *Art Journal, 65*(3), 82–99. https://doi.org/10.1080/00043249.2006.10791217

Smith, D. C., Ludolph, F. E., Irby, C. H., & Johnson, J. A. (1985). The desktop metaphor as an approach to user interface design (Panel Discussion). *Proceedings of the 1985 ACM Annual Conference on The Range of Computing : Mid-80's Perspective: Mid-80's Perspective*, 548–549. https://doi.org/10.1145/320435.320594

Smith, D. C., Irby, C., Kimball, R., & Harslem, E. The Star user interface: An overview. *National Computer Conference*, (1982, 515–528).

Siewert, C., Kelly, S., Hofstadter, A., & Woodruff, D. (2003, November 16). *Phenomenology (Stanford Encyclopedia of Philosophy)*. Stanford Encyclopedia of Philosophy. Retrieved March 30, 2023, from https://plato.stanford.edu/entries/phenomenology/

Warwick, G. (2016). Looking in the mirror of renaissance art. *Art History, 39*(2), 254–281. https://doi.org/10.1111/1467-8365.12237

# CHAPTER 7

# Artist Gallery – Ian Cheng, Matteo Zamagni, and Rebecca Allen

## IAN CHENG

Ian Cheng graduated from University of California, Berkeley, in 2006 with a dual degree in cognitive science and art practice. Cheng went on to attend Columbia University, where he earned his MFA in 2009. When deciding which artists to discuss for this book, it was important to include some of the first virtual reality (VR) works to pioneer exhibiting in galleries and museums, as these pioneers paved the way for contemporary VR works to be shown.

## ENTROPY WRANGLER

Cheng's work *Entropy Wrangler* was one of those first works, premiering at Frieze London in 2013 with a follow-up exhibition at Off Vendome in Düsseldorf, Germany. Cheng's work was created for the first Oculus Rift headsets, specifically one of the development kits offered before the first consumer model (the CV1) was released. The requirement that Cheng's work mandate viewers don a head-mounted display is notable – in most cases, it was the first time audiences had ever experienced VR, let alone a VR artwork. By putting on the headset, viewers are immediately confronted with a cacophony of objects in

DOI: 10.1201/9781003363729-7

free fall. These objects include, but are not limited to: a globe, a female figure in a bikini, cement blocks, a potted cactus intermittently on fire, what look like planks of lumber, garden tools, a giant (in relation to the rest of the objects) articulated hand, a dolphin, a dildo, a leopard skin rug, swords, a tree limb, a pink cube, and a model of Venus of Willendorf. In the distant background are fireworks; their blasts resonate throughout the viewing of the work. There are also sounds of tinkling or breaking glass, cymbals crashing, and clanking metal. The scale of all the objects is smaller, indicating that the objects are either in the distance or are around the scale of large toys.

The viewer is amidst this chaos, and as the viewer moves their gaze in the headset, the objects are ruffled into action. Reminiscent of a kaleidoscope or snow globe, upon closer examination, the physics that guide the objects seem closer to the movement of small shells on the bottom of the ocean, swirling in an unseen current. This sense of fluidity implies that the objects are housed in water or a more viscous fluid, such as mineral oil. Crashing into each other, each creature has physics and movements of their own. Sometimes one character gets wrapped around another in the virtual space – other times they cling to one another as if magnetized. Each model has its own inherent movement when appropriate – while the pink cube does nothing, one figure struggles to free itself from any entanglements – trying to move away from the pile of objects as if to escape (Figure 7.1).

Programmed with motion capture techniques, Cheng's figures actually owe their original references to actual humans. Motion capture works by rigging a real person up to multiple sensors that track how their body and limbs move in space. This movement is then applied to a 3D model of a human. In many ways, it is this ghost of the human source that is most disconcerting – viewing the figures' struggle inspires empathy for the awkward "person" in the headset. Mirroring the "wild west" state that early contemporary VR systems often espoused. Barging into each other and into the objects around them, the figures react "to one another in unpredictable ways; encounters produce frightening jerks and sudden glitches. Leopard skin convulses as if caught in an invisible web, as a blue sphere stretches out across the screen" (Bailey, 2015).

What was remarkable about Cheng's work when it first appeared was that it was truly an *artwork*. Cheng didn't decide to make a work that was easily accessible to everyone, that had an obvious interface, or that had an

**FIGURE 7.1** Ian Cheng *Entropy Wrangler* (2013). Image and permission courtesy of the artist.

obvious physical world corollary. Instead, Cheng describes his thinking around the time he created the work as a feeling that

> the straight story can no longer normalize the complex, unpredictable forces of reality that intrude with greater and greater frequency, let alone the incessant stream of big data reporting on these complexities. What is the intuitive story of climate change? Shifts in the market? Mutations in your brain? Your browsing history?
>
> *(Rhizome, 2013)*

Indeed, the chaos of the objects in the headset boggles the mind when viewed – they are recognizable and yet irreconcilable. How do they relate to each other? Why were these particular objects chosen? When asked about his choices, Cheng states:

> there's no strategy inherent in the work, in the sense that these objects of culture - the vibrating dildo, the robotic animatronic

medical hand, the flatscreen, the smartphone - were left to their own devices, left to swim in [the primordial] soup.

*(Kerr & Ashford, 2013)*

Instead of choosing prescribed objects to point to a certain concept, Cheng instead talks about how data scientists use some versions of narrative to interpret various forms of analysis, simulation, and statistics. The scientists then use this narrative to make predictions and models for what will happen in the eminent future. But he also talks about how the foundations of this kind of narrative – numerical, binary, inorganic – mean that the stories told are "counterintuitive" to how humans intuit and experience the world. Cheng points out that while we receive the story, "we don't feel it, so we can't embody it. Anxiety takes hold when embodied narration fails" (Rhizome, 2013). While still using the software and some of the hardware that are the foundation for creating VR, Cheng has moved on to focus on work that more broadly investigates his background in cognitive science. His *Emissaries* (2015–17), a trilogy of live-simulation works, is based on computer-generated simulations in a world populated with artificially intelligent characters. Setting the stage as the artist, Cheng doesn't see what he does as the same as an artist like Sol LeWitt, who would create a set of rules for others to follow, but rather that he composes "the right initial conditions and rules, and seeing what breaks but also what unexpected behaviors emerge...fixed deterministic models no longer suffice to make sense of the complexity inside and around us" (Kerr & Ashford, 2013) (Figure 7.2).

**FIGURE 7.2** Image of Cheng's *Entropy Emissaries* (2015–17). Image and permission courtesy of the artist.

## MATTEO ZAMAGNI

Born in Italy in 1992 and currently based in London, Matteo Zamagni's VR work, *Nature Abstraction* (2016), is an immersive experience – a gallery installation that houses three VR works. When viewers enter the gallery, they see a small "room" with slightly opaque screens. Abstractions from nature are projected onto the screens and are seen from outside and within the small space. Upon entering the "room," a participant sees a headset. The VR experience is composed of fractals that were created by Zamagni and then processed in Google Deep Dream, a computer vision program that uses artificial intelligence to find and then enhance aspects of images and videos. The visual experience is mesmerizing, and the end result toes the line between dreamscape and nightmare. Users entering the space encounter three different worlds: **Birth**, **Communion**, and **Aether**. Each of these "planets," as Zamagni describes them, offers a deep dive into a mathematically generated space. Whereas one section of the experience starts with what appears to be massive dystopian buildings that house thousands, another offers fractals that seem to be organically grown – echoing living organisms that might be found in the ocean or on the surface of a pond.

The patterns generated in the first segment, **Birth** appear to be a flat grid of rectangles laid inside rectangles – reminiscent of a repeating vector pattern. The view changes, plunging into the structure and revealing that what appears to be a flat surface is actually the top of fractal architecture surrounded by deep wells of in-between space. Bars jut out and form sharp angles, finally turning back to meld into a circuitous form. The gray palette of the landscape creates an atmosphere where the shapes become evocative of server farms or conduits. Conversely, **Communion's** palette is warm and pink. The base of the fractals is circular rather than angular in origin. As the view moves along, new forms bloom like some sort of algae or brain coral. Larger structures in the background look like an Eiffel Tower conceived in madness, processed in Google Deep Dream the images take on a pixelated oceanic vibe. Lastly, **Aether** immerses one in a blue-green landscape with looping long edges that, seen from the correct angle, are reminiscent of the wind-swept caves of the American West. Processed in Google Deep Dream, the landscape gains the characteristic rainbow-colored "eyeball" often found in other AI-generated visuals.

To appreciate the complexity that fractals offer in terms of 3D structure generation, it is worth unpacking what a fractal is. For starters, fractals are not typical geometry. In non-fractal shapes, such as a pyramid, the edges are smooth. We might think of a geometric shape's "edge" as the part of the pyramid an artist might draw: the black lines that outline the shape. These artist lines, or "edges" converge into points, or "vertices," "faces" are then bound by these edges and vertices to create flat planes. The further we zoom along the edge of this pyramid, the more it becomes clear that the edge is smooth, or what we might call "locally linear." Of course, in the physical world, not all shapes have locally linear edges. Some shapes have wild and chaotic edges that don't seem to register any sort of recognizable pattern. What stands out in the world of geometric edges are cases where instead of being chaotic or smooth, the "geometry shape's roughness may conceivably *fail* to vanish as the examination becomes more searching" (Mandelbrot & Blumen, 1989, p. 3).

What does "fail to vanish" mean? Whereas some shapes have edges that are completely chaotic and some are smooth, there is an unusual middle ground between the two. In 1989, Benoit B. Mandelbrot authored an article entitled *Fractal Geometry: What Is It, and What Does It Do?* where he conceived of this geometric middle ground of "orderly geometric chaos" – giving it the name "fractal geometry." Fractals, as Mandelbrot defines them, are shapes whose "roughness and fragmentation neither tend to vanish nor fluctuate up and down" but are unchanged when zoomed in (and out) (Mandelbrot & Blumen, 1989, p. 5). This means that when you zoom in on the edge of a fractal shape, you will find what appears to be a replica of that shape. When you zoom in further on the edge of the "replica" you will find…yet another "replica." Mandelbrot explains that "the structure of every piece holds the key to the whole structure…an alternative term is 'self-similar'" (Mandelbrot & Blumen, 1989, p. 4). In fact, fractals "display inherent and repeating similarities," so they aren't necessarily exactly the same – but similar enough that the brain tries to recognize and interpret each shape as it comes into form (Figures 7.3 and 7.4).

In Zamagni's *Nature Abstraction,* immersion into the world created by fractals is akin to having a hallucination – it feels as if one's visual senses are mistaken. Traveling among the textured surfaces, the visuals read like plant life or buildings, but moving closer doesn't bring a viewer closer to understanding; instead, the patterns are repeated in miniature – maybe they are recombined in one way or another, but they don't bring anyone

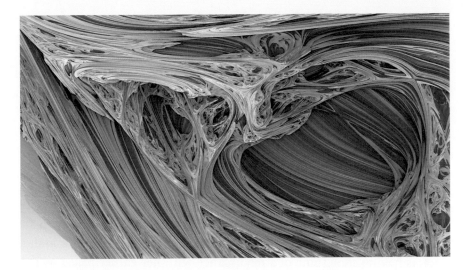

**FIGURE 7.3** Matteo Zamagni's *Nature Abstraction: Aether* (2016). Image permission courtesy of the artist, via Gazelli Art House.

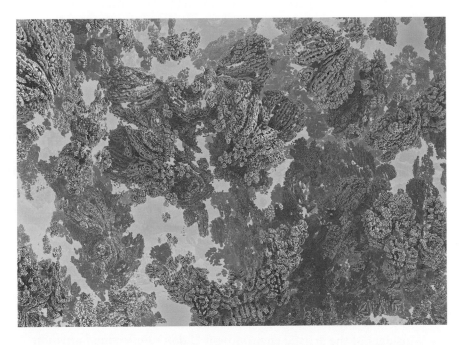

**FIGURE 7.4** Matteo Zamagni's *Nature Abstraction: Communion* (2016). Image permission courtesy of the artist, via Gazelli Art House.

to solid ground. Instead, Zamagni's work builds on this notion of generative form within a "non space" – inside the headset the patterns of fractals create an endless sense of nothingness in between the somethingness. Overstimulated in part by the psychedelic imagery, the viewer must let the patterns wash over them, ultimately relaxing into a meditative state. In talking about *Nature Abstraction*, Zamagni states that "there is no absolute truth in the way we see, and more generally, in the way we perceive. Our experiences are always biased from our sensory perceptions, our tools to relate to the world" (Szilak, 2016).

## REBECCA ALLEN

Rebecca Allen's VR work *Bush Souls #3* is detailed in Chapter 3 as an artwork made prior to 2010. Allen has continued to make VR work and, in fact, is having something of a renaissance with her earlier pieces as they are being shown internationally. She continues to make artwork focused on the immersive and interactive. Her more recent VR work involving the UCLA Brain Mapping Center, UCLA's Neuroscience Research, and UCSF's Neuroscape Labs continues to marry scientific research with artistic output. Her research, artmaking, and community building have had a profound effect on the VR art community; in fact, her portfolio is a testament to a life dedicated to the craft of using computers as an artistic medium. Currently, Allen has turned back more fully to her studio practice in order to create VR art installations. She continues to use VR in her work with prestigious labs like the ones listed above to gain more information on neuroanatomy, a testament to her dual role as an artist and a scholar.

In interviews where she discussed the early days of her studio art/computer research, Allen is very clear about the difficulties she encountered, in that artists at that time didn't consider anything created by a computer as artwork, and technologists in the field didn't see the value in art.

> Yes, it was very frustrating. The computer in the art world was not considered as a means of expression. And yet, I repeat, I believe that artists must indicate the future, give it shape. Instead, it was impossible for me to show my work, and I was often told by the insiders of the artistic environment "*I don't understand anything about it*". But there was nothing to understand, it was still an aesthetic experience. You don't need to understand how marble is

carved to appreciate a marble sculpture. It's the same thing. This resistance lasted throughout my career.

*(Piga & Monti, 2022)*

One place where this mindset was not present was at MIT's Architecture Machine Group, where she studied under architect and computer scientist Nicholas Negroponte. Housed in the School of Architecture rather than in the School of Electrical Engineering, where computer science lived, the Architecture Machine Group was unusual in that, in addition to publishing research, both students and faculty needed to *innovate*. This inspired technology leaders such as Alan Kay and Marvin Minsky to come and conduct research at the lab, creating an environment of cutting-edge research and learning (Featherly, n.d.). Eventually, the program became the MIT Media Lab, whose mission is "to create transformative technologies, experiences, and systems that enable people to reimagine and redesign their lives" (*About the Lab Who We Are + What We Do + Why We Do It*, n.d.). As an artist in the Architecture Machine Group's lab, Allen made headway not just because they needed someone to create visual imagery, but because she had "technical preparation and knew computer languages" (Piga & Monti, 2022).

## LIFE WITHOUT MATTER

The subject of Allen's more recent work, *Life without Matter* (2018), is particularly relevant to Chapter 10's discussion of the dis/embodied nature of one's corporeal representation in virtual space. Describing *Life without Matter*, Allen writes that the work "considers a future life in VR where material things – physical matter – have mostly disappeared and our identity must be redefined" (Allen, n.d.). The artwork starts at what appears to be a religious site or temple. Layers of carved rock tower overhead as the structure appears to be buried underground, somewhat like a cenote or naturally occurring sinkhole. Allen states that the idea for the environment in the virtual space came from Silbury Hill – a paleolithic chalk mound found in the English countryside. These mounds were found to contain stepped stone structures and are thought to be places of spirituality. Allen states that she is interested in how humanity shares common beliefs across cultures – one example is that the mound of Silbury Hill has corollaries found in the Mexican jungle. Origin stories also have similarities across cultures – and technology allows us to share our commonalities in new ways (R. Allen, personal communication, April 14, 2023). Spheres carved out of shiny rock appear littered throughout the space, and at the center, a light blue beam of light, as wide as a human torso, shines up to the sky. Floating in front of the viewer is a sphere, but this one is slightly transparent and seems to breathe. Reaching out to touch the orb causes it to change to the aqua color of the beam, and slowly, with an air of magic, a section of the ray glows and a disc appears within. This disc escapes its boundaries and spins slowly, flipping over from top to bottom. The disc floats until it is in front of the viewer's gaze. The disc is then revealed to be a mirror. As it settles in front of the immersed participant, the user is surprised to find a reflection. Sometimes female, sometimes male, a disembodied head and hands mirror the movements of the user in the physical world.

In Allen's work, hands held up in physical space trigger the same response in the mirror. Hands reaching out to the mirror see their reflection come nearer. The physical proximity of one's virtual hands to the mirror causes an increase in the sound of a vibrating or buzzing object. Removing one's hands quiets the tone. In the mirror, behind the user, is a portal or door to a hallway that leads into darkness. Turning away from the mirror, the VR participant sees that there is indeed a hallway behind them. Out of the corner of one's eye, another figure appears and disappears quickly. At other times, peering into the hallway away from the position of the mirror disc allows for glimpses of a big cat. Suddenly, the mirror starts to spin horizontally and, with its dark side facing the viewer, grows closer.

The screen then goes black, and then the scene is a forest outside, far away from the ray – which still shines up out of the ground and into the sky. In the foliage, a big cat approaches. To be so close to the animal is fear-inducing – one's instinct is to stay perfectly still as the cat's unflinching gaze comes nearer. Staring intently, the cat comes close enough that one's primal instinct is to run, but there is no body to fear for. No hands, feet, or virtual representation appears…instead it is just the forest, the cat, and the sounds of the breeze and the birds. In a moment, the viewer finds themselves again back in the temple, but this time when the mirror comes close, instead of a face, a stylized mask appears. The mask is the face of a giant cat. Allen states that what she is interested in is "the relationship between the virtual and the physical body, the physical immersion in the virtual," and nowhere is this clearer than in *Life without Matter* (Piga & Monti, 2022). It is easy to become engaged with the detailed virtual environment,

**FIGURE 7.5**   Rebecca Allen *Life without Matter* (2018). Image and permission courtesy of the artist. Additional thanks to Gazelli Art House.

but there is no way to forget one's physical body when their actual hands are replicated *and* mirrored in the VR work (Figure 7.5).

This detailed world of Allen's is beautifully and sophistically rendered. This high-resolution imagery doesn't interfere with or supersede the content of the work but rather creates a feeling of familiarity that allows the participant to relax into the spiritual nature of the VR experience. Allen herself describes the scenario as "mythic," not a representation of an external world but a mirror of our interior worlds. Allen states, "since a virtual world is immaterial, a virtual mirror need not reflect one's physical appearance...animal in all of us" (Allen, n.d.). *Life without Matter* is an out-of-body experience layered within what could be considered a different kind of "out-of-body experience." The mystery comes from the reality that "rather than interacting with something alien, you come face to face with yourself in the virtual landscape" (Abrams, 2019). VR artworks offer many kinds of experiences to those who immerse themselves in it – one can experience something of another person's intimate familial narratives; it can remind us of the masks we sometimes wear; and it can provide digital hallucinations. What is hard to do is to marry a feeling of spirituality with a digital experience that requires immersion in a cumbersome headset and avoidance of anything that could invoke a feeling of uncanny valley in the viewer. That Allen's work is able to achieve a sense of quietude, a feeling of awe, a shiver of fear, and a sweet melancholy is a real testament to her technical and artistic mastery, both of which most likely come from her long history within the field of new media art.

## INSIDE

Allen's VR artwork *Inside* (2016) is in many ways the flip side of the ghostly *Life without Matter*. Composed of three parts: **The Night Desert**, **The Brain Cave**, and **Nature**, the VR artwork opens with the nude, smooth, and hairless female form walking on a dry, deserted landscape at night in fog. The landscape is rendered at a high resolution, and even though the work was made in 2016, it still reads as very realistic. Moonlit, the form looks over her shoulder in what appears to be a calm, curious manner. Allen states that the woman's figure is meant to return a gaze in response to the "male gaze" – a term that is used to discuss the historic nature of artworks subjects being female and being objectified (R. Allen, personal communication, April 14, 2023). Suddenly, out of the fog, a miniature electric storm sends static into the atmosphere. The figure disappears, and a brain is left – floating in space. The viewport approaches the brain, moving methodically toward it until it is inside.

This scene cuts to **The Brain Cave**, which is a space that is both the interior of a brain and a cave. Veins jut up from the brain's floor like stalagmites – as the viewer's gaze roves over the brain's wrinkles as a flashlight's circular beam lights up the nooks and crannies. Looking around, bright concentric circles appear, emanating red runes that soon fill up the space. Pinhole beams of light then arc across the space, their bright glare contrasting with the soft and warm light of the brain's interior. Following the beams to their source, the field of vision is overwhelmed with a bright light. Just as it fills up the headset and threatens to become too intense, the scene deposits the viewer into a beautiful valley, where the early morning sun reveals a natural valley like the ones found in the forests of the northern hemisphere (Figure 7.6).

In creating *Inside,* Allen hoped to "explore provocative questions around VR and its uncanny ability to confound our sensory perception. What is the role of the body in VR? What happens inside of us when inside virtual worlds?" (Allen, n.d.). Allen investigates this relationship between humanity and technology through not just the visual concepts found in her work but an "examination of the body in motion, perception, interaction and consciousness" (Watson, 2020).

**FIGURE 7.6** Rebecca Allen *Inside* (2016). Image and permission courtesy of the artist. Additional thanks to Gazelli Art House.

## THE TANGLE OF MIND AND MATTER

*The Tangle of Mind and Matter* (2017) is an earlier work of Allen's that, like *Inside*, also focuses on the brain. In *The Tangle of Mind and Matter*, VR is used to investigate "the mysterious relationship between the mind and the brain" in order to study the mind (Allen et al., n.d.). In human form, the mind awakens the conscious brain and encourages interaction with the viewer. This manifests itself at first by entering the space and encountering a brain – each different part a slightly different shade of fleshy pink. Floating in a bright blue space and encased in a ghostly, transparent golden shell, a participant quickly discovers that selecting each part of the brain allows them to remove and inspect it. After carefully picking up several parts, the rest become animated and fly up and away – while at the center of the brain-shaped shell lies a ghostly sphere with a female figure folded up like an embryo. Slowly, the form of the brain disappears, and the figure takes off, flying through the parts of the brain. Notes play when the user selects any part – and at one point the sphere that housed the golden figure falls to create a body of water. The gentle flying of the figure, the blue sky, and the tree limbs that grow as night falls – all create a meditative experience that allows a user to bring their own perceptions to bear in interpreting the work.

Allen created the model for the brain using real MRI scans, and for other visual assets, he used creative commons objects found on the web. Interested in "developing an aesthetic unique to the medium of virtual reality," Allen wanted to create a world where "some components of the work are generative" and the objects "subtly change each time" as users access the experience (Allen et al., n.d.). This integration of computer aesthetics into her artwork has been something Allen has been interested in since her youth – she writes that while in undergraduate school she became specifically interested in early artistic movements like the Dadaists and Futurists as these groups were specifically thinking about how machines were affecting society. During this time, Allen found that the art worlds she was surrounded by were ignoring computers as a technology that could influence or author artworks. While at the Rhode Island School of Design, she conducted an independent study at Brown University to do some early work in computer animation. Her professors tried to dissuade her from working with computers (Watson, 2020). In fact, until the 1990s, Allen found she had to place herself "in research environments to get access to equipment and software for her artistic practice" (Watson, 2020). As Allen points out – artists are inventors just as much as scientists. In both cases, problem solving and innovation are essential to finding whatever path is needed to achieve a goal. Artists and scientists are both likely to "approach problems with a similar open-mindedness and inquisitiveness — they both do not fear the unknown, preferring leaps to incremental steps" (Maeda, 2013) (Figure 7.7).

The idea of integrating diverse voices into societal dialogs is essential to growing and knowing ourselves as humans. What a diverse voice can offer is a different perspective on issues that seem immutable or paths that seem limited. Examples like those of artists like Rebecca Allen help the cause. An artist and a woman from computer technology's earliest days, she insists that it is "mandatory that artists of every discipline get involved and help mold what's happening with new media technology"…she goes on to say:

> What is really disturbing is that after all these decades new technology is still predominantly being invented by one type of person, a white male computer scientist or engineer, which is tragic. Diversity is still so desperately needed in the invention of technology that is completely changing humanity.

> *(Watson, 2020)*

**FIGURE 7.7** Rebecca Allen *Tangle of Mind and Matter* (2017). Image and permission courtesy of the artist. Additional thanks to Gazelli Art House.

Allen points out that so many aesthetic and technical decisions have already been made – and our technological culture is already deeply committed to computing as it exists now. What would it look like if input from a more diverse group were there at the beginning? (R. Allen, personal communication, April 14, 2023).

> At the beginning it was difficult to access the laboratories and work with digital technology, either because I was an artist or because I was a woman. But now they're starting to tell me it's because I'm too old and it's believed that 'digital natives', having been born into the digital age, understand it better. Instead, I believe I was lucky to observe and experience the entire evolution of immersive art from its inception. If you were born with a smartphone in your hand, your perspective is different. What can you invent?
>
> *–Rebecca Allen (Piga & Monti, 2022)*

## REFERENCES

*About the Lab Who we are + what we do + why we do it.* (n.d.). MIT Media Lab. Retrieved March 27, 2023, from https://www.media.mit.edu/about/overview/

Abrams, A.-R. (2019, November 16). Features | Craft/Work | Neon Lights: The Digital Art Of Rebecca Allen. *The Quietus.* Retrieved March 25, 2023, from https://thequietus.com/articles/27447-rebecca-allen-interview

Allen, R. (n.d.). Rebecca Allen. *Rebecca Allen.* Retrieved March 25, 2023, from https://www.rebeccaallen.com/projects/life-without-matter

Allen, R., Triantafyllidis, T., & Rickett, A. (n.d.). Rebecca Allen. *Rebecca Allen.* Retrieved March 27, 2023, from https://rebeccaallen.com/projects/the-tangle-of-mind-and-matter

Bailey, S. (2015, December 11). *Ian Cheng: Entropy Wrangler - 艺术界 LEAP. LEAP magazine.* Retrieved March 25, 2023, from https://www.leapleapleap.com/2015/12/ian-cheng-entropy-wrangler-2/

Featherly, K. (n.d.). Nicholas Negroponte | American architect and computer scientist. *Encyclopedia Britannica.* Retrieved March 27, 2023, from https://www.britannica.com/biography/Nicholas-Negroponte

Kerr, D., & Ashford, D. (2013, October 10). Ian Cheng. *BOMB Magazine.* Retrieved March 25, 2023, from https://bombmagazine.org/articles/ian-cheng/

Maeda, J. (2013, July 11). Artists and scientists: More alike than different - Scientific American Blog Network. *Scientific American Blogs.* Retrieved March 27, 2023, from https://blogs.scientificamerican.com/guest-blog/artists-and-scientists-more-alike-than-different/

Mandelbrot, B. B., & Blumen, A. (1989, May Royal Society). Fractal geometry: What is it, and what does it do? [and discussion]. *Proceedings of the Royal Society of London. Series A, Mathematical and Physical Sciences, 423*(1864), 3–16. https://www.jstor.org/stable/2398503

Piga, A. M., & Monti, S. (2022, June 28). Intervista a Rebecca Allen, in mostra a Düsseldorf. Artribune. Retrieved March 27, 2023, from https://www.artribune.com/professioni-e-professionisti/who-is-who/2022/06/intervista-rebecca-allen-arte-digitale-mostra-dusseldorf/

Rhizome. (2013, December 23). Prosthetic knowledge picks: The year of the Oculus Rift. *Rhizome.* Retrieved March 25, 2023, from https://rhizome.org/editorial/2013/dec/23/prosthetic-knowledge-picks-oculus-rift/

Szilak, I. (2016, July 27). Artist profile: Matteo Zamagni uses VR to hack the senses. *HuffPost.* Retrieved March 25, 2023, from https://www.huffpost.com/entry/artist-profile-matteo-zamagni-uses-vr-to-hack-the_b_5798d53be-4b0e339c23ffdca

Watson, K. (2020, September 17). Rebecca Allen on Kraftwerk, video games and artificial life. *Serpentine Galleries.* Retrieved March 27, 2023, from https://www.serpentinegalleries.org/art-and-ideas/rebecca-allen/

# CHAPTER 8

# Virtual Reality as a Medium

## INTRODUCTION

As seen in earlier chapters, virtual reality (VR) as a medium for the creation of artwork has been around for some time. While it is important with any artistic medium to understand the user's experience, the use of a computer as a medium is relatively recent. A source of friction in developing for the digital space is that while it is important to "master techniques to render digital media transparent to user," it is equally important to "render the media visible to and reflective of the user" (Bolter & Gromala, 2003, p. 6). As Jay David Boulter and Diane Gromala point out in their book *Windows and Mirrors: Interaction Design, Digital Art and the Myth of Transparency*, if users are only looking "through the interface, [they] cannot appreciate the ways in which the interface itself shapes our experience" (Bolter & Gromala, 2003, p. 9).

In no way does the current virtual experience replace or completely replicate the lived physical experience. Nor should it – in part, what is exciting about VR is the possibility of creation within a digital format, untethered to the specifics and limitations of physical reality. As a digital format, it is perfectly reasonable to create visible interfaces, to address the digital nature of the medium, to recontextualize how art is seen within the medium, and to play with the notions of "virtual" and "reality." Conversely, constantly breaking the fourth wall may also distract the user, pulling them away from enjoyment of the immersive experience. A balance must be struck – acknowledgment that the user is entering a computer-generated medium, and yet a willingness on the user's part to suspend disbelief in order to submerge themselves fully into the experience.

As a medium generated by the computer, VR fits nicely within the historical context of what is commonly called "new media art." In many ways, new media art can be understood as artworks created in concert with digital technologies and includes not just what we think of as computer art, but also film, video, and sound. In their book *The New Media Reader*, editors Noah Wardrip-Fruin and Nick Monfort open with a poignant question:

> how long will it take before we see the gift for what it is - a single new medium of representation, the digital medium, formed by the braided interplay of technical invention and cultural expression at the end of the 20th century?
>
> *(Wardrip-Fruin & Montfort, 2003, p. 3).*

In his essay for the book, Lev Manovich asks "what exactly is new media? And what is new media art?" (Manovich, 2003). In response, he breaks down new media art into eight subcategories: *cyberculture*; *distribution*; *data controlled by software*; *a mix between existing culture and software*; *aesthetics of all new media formats*; *faster algorithms*; *as metamedia*; and as *a reiteration of conversations around the early days of computing*. That Manovich approaches the terms so fully from so many different perspectives indicates how hard it is to pin down a more specific analysis of what new media art is. In fact, it is more helpful to think of Lev Manovich's original premise that new media "may be defined via reference to a foundational language or set of formal and poetic qualities identified across all sorts of new media objects and indeed across historical and social context" (Allen et al., 1994). In this definition, Manovich discusses a variety of aesthetic aspects of digital media – an emphasis on navigation through space, play, and games as essential to the interactive dynamics, as well as "the waning of temporal montage (and the rise of spatial montage)" (Antunes, 2020). For clarification, spatial montage can be understood as the "juxtaposition of more than one image within a frame. What constitutes a frame, however, can be subject to a great range of interpretation" (Sprengler, 2014).

A perfect example of this is found in some of Jacolby Satterwhite's work – multiple flat-planed images placed within a 360-degree 3D environment. In digital space, users can participate in new worlds, but they are also "connected to the history of the moving image, which has affected our assumptions about the mediated representation of the world" (Paul, 2008, p. 96). Artists exploring the virtual have a chance to build on the history of the moving image, but more specifically, those artists who understand and utilize the medium to its full potential have a chance to subvert audience expectations. As will be discussed later, therein lies the true power of the technical knowledge needed to develop VR – the ability to reinterpret how their participants see and interact with virtual space.

This idea of categorizing new media art within the terms "formal and poetic qualities" can be applied to an understanding of VR artworks as opposed to what can be called a "non-art experience." Manovich's description allows for a broad scope within new media art, as the emphasis on a "set of formal and poetic qualities" across multiple objects brings the work's concept and context to the fore rather than prioritizing technical aspects of a work. In fact, in *Preserving and Exhibiting Media Art*, Sarah Cook's chapter on curating new media art discusses her prioritization of the conceptual over the technical in curating new media artworks. Cook states that for a retrospective show on the history of new media art, she had to deliberately move away "from the media and technology part of its definition. After all, all technologies were once new. What seemed more important was selecting works where the artists continued to interrogate these larger, more resonant themes within their work" (Cook, 2013).

To untangle some of these threads around definition, one need only look to another important scholar in the world of new media art: Christiane Paul, author of *Digital Art* (2003). Paul uses the term "digital art" as a category that sits under the umbrella of "new media art," but points out that using the term "new" in defining "new media art" is problematic. Paul states, "what is supposed to be considered 'new' about the digital medium? Some of the concepts explored in digital art date back to almost a century…" (Paul, 2003, p. 7). What digital art most certainly does is to "collapse boundaries between disciplines – art, science, technology and design" (Paul, 2003, p. 22).

In *Digital Art*, Paul makes the distinction between art that uses "digital technologies" as a tool for the "creation of more traditional art objects" and "digital born, computable art that is created, stored and distributed via digital technologies and employs their features as its very own medium" (Paul, 2003, p. 8). It is worthwhile to explore how authorship of virtual artworks fits within this idea of digital technologies as tools versus mediums. For instance, using 3D drawing software such as Tilt Brush to create a VR artwork could be said to fit most of Paul's categories for the use of digital technology as a medium – although Tilt Brush could also be considered a digital tool to create something of a more traditional art object, such as a digital painting based on the aesthetics of paintings in the physical realm.

Using digital technologies as an artistic medium, according to Paul, "implies that the work exclusively uses the digital platform from production to presentation, and that it exhibits and explores that platform's inherent possibilities" (Paul, 2003, p. 67). Digital art as a medium also implies an invitation to participate in the work in one form or another. This could be done through gesture or clicking, but the invitation requires the audience to participate. In turn, the interactive work will respond in a dynamic fashion. In discussing *The Chalkroom*, Laurie Anderson points out that there are many paths to take and that the same person entering the piece at different times will have completely different experiences. The dynamism of the work fits what Paul describes as having "multiple manifestations and is extremely hybrid" (Paul, 2003, p. 67).

A technological life cycle where artists adopt new technologies, then those technologies become widely adopted, can lead to the degradation of the impact of some new media works. For example, interactive digital projection was an exciting novelty in 2000 but has now been adopted to the point that brick-and-mortar banks use it for advertising. If an artwork relied on the technology of digital interactive projection for its conceptual content, it is likely to have less impact today. The artists chosen for review in these chapters are interesting in that the themes of their work resonate with some of the themes found in contemporary art in general, such as identity, place, the body, time, memory, language, and spirituality. For example, Jacolby Satterwhite's family/self-portraits present themselves within the context of VR, but his work isn't about VR per se; his focus is more on "designing spaces where he can go wild, because they don't have to be built. They become Surrealist, outlandish, and queer" (Bullock, 2018).

Hsin-Chien Huang's VR work *Bodyless* (2019) is "based on the director's childhood memory during Taiwan's martial law period in the 1970s [and is] is a surreal VR experience in which the player becomes a deceased political prisoner's ghost in his journey to find his way home" (Antunes,

2020). Huang's technical proficiency in virtual space is expansive – he uses parametric modeling tools so that "shapes can be changed once parameters such as dimensions or curvatures are modified — removing the need to reshape the model from scratch" (Delgado, 2022). An exploration of his parametric modeling tools could easily be Huang's focus – in fact, generative art is a branch of new media artwork – but Huang is using his technical experience to give his audience an intimate self-portrait that "interweaves childhood memories and ultramodern technology to create a surreal fairytale environment through which we literally fly using virtual reality technology" (*Bodyless*, n.d.).

This doesn't mean that the medium of VR isn't an important consideration in each of these examples. The materiality of the medium is essential to interacting with these works. The idea is to strike a balance between technology, experience, and concept within the work. The combination of VR and the concepts behind new media artworks "not only reduces the distance between the experience and the art but also allows the experiencers to better understand what the artist wants to convey in the artwork" (Wu & Li, 2022).

Learning how software can be used to create work in virtual space gives rise to in-depth experimentation. Understanding not just the foundations of how software and hardware work, but also the "cognitive mechanisms" found in the experience of the user can all "be made to serve artistic intentions" (Cavazza et al., 2005, p. 9).

In his book *Information Arts* (2003), Steve Wilson laid the groundwork for talking about artists working in technology, asking that they not only interpret scientific knowledge but that they become an "active partner in determining the direction of research" (Wilson, 2003, jacket). Artist technologists work in ways that require self-education in order to "function non-superficially in the world of art, science and technology" (Wilson, 2003, p. 29). Understanding how VR works are made means that artists are "connected to both the art and the technical worlds…it asks artists to be willing, if necessary, to abandon traditional concerns, media and contexts" (Wilson, 2003, p. 29). Artists who have direct control over their output can engage with their audience in profound ways. Understanding the formal aspects of a work is important; each work is concerned with its "own materiality, which informs the ways in which it creates meaning" (Paul, 2003, p. 70).

Materiality, in a pragmatic sense, refers to the materials used to create an artwork. In the case of VR, the materials would be the software and hardware used to develop the artwork, as well as the hardware used to immerse oneself in the artwork. But materials can also be active parts of a work's concept and how the work is to be interpreted (Lehmann et al., 2012, p. 8). The materials "visual and haptic qualities" can open up an artwork for a specific interpretation, guiding "the choice of subject matter, personal and period style as well as aesthetic perception" (Lehmann et al., 2012, p. 8). Artist technologist Rebecca Allen stated that when she started making artwork in the 1970s, she "thought that computers had the potential to be the most important and powerful development in our society" and "was appalled that artists were running away from it" (Allen et al., 1994).

What is essential to the artworks in these pages is that the materiality is not what defines the work, but that the artist "couples his own movement and gestures – indeed, his very life – with the becoming of his materials, joining with and following the forces and flows that bring his work to fruition" (Lehmann et al., 2012, p. 9).

## IMMERSION AND INTERACTIVITY

Interactive VR technologies inherently demand that the user participates in the creation of the content while simultaneously being incorporated into the experience. This realization has dramatic implications for media and artistic works, as the traditional role of the content creator has been to dictate and frame the way in which the user interacts with and views artistic content. With VR, the back and forth between the work of the creator and their audience is central to the medium. This breaking of the traditional roles, accompanied by the transition away from "the rectangle," or the flat rectangular plane, which acts as a "canvas" for media and artistic works, requires new approaches.

Essential to the immersive nature of a VR system is that it "removes the distinction between the computer system and the user's environment. The system is the user's environment" (Haywood, p. 9). This means that any interfaces available to the user are through the virtual environment only. This immersive system is typically obtained through wearing some sort of head- or helmet-mounted display (HMD), where the user's visual and auditory cues and stimuli are entirely virtual. Non-immersive systems, also known as "out-the-window" systems, provide the user with a "bird's-eye" view of the virtual environment as if the user were looking out the window of a moving vehicle. Non-immersive systems allow the user to look away from the virtual environment and back to their real surroundings as needed. A non-immersive system typically requires the user to view a special screen or display device to operate in the virtual environment. Overlay or augmented reality systems are those that project a virtual image onto the user's view of the real environment through the use of heads-up displays (HUDs). Three-dimensionally capable systems like those of VR permit the user to maintain bodily contact with the real environment while simultaneously immersed in the virtual environment. It is the tension between the physical and mental dichotomies that allows for compelling experiences. Who better to explore and play with this than artists?

The possibilities that VR offers in terms of artistic creations mean that the audience interacts with the artworks as part of a world translated into a different time and space. In choosing to work with VR, "reality" is often used to refer to the non-digital world – shorthanded to IRL or "in real life." The issue with this is that our digital realms are incorporated into our reality – their insistent reminders and sirens' calls are intrinsically intertwined with the fundamentals of our physical selves. Separating the two is akin to creating artificial divisions between mind and body. How can we separate what we experience with our minds from what our bodies are doing?

VR is a way to experience a world, rather than a specific world in itself. VR reconciles the concepts of virtuality, by allowing the user to live the virtual as if it were real, but within a greater physical reality. Instead, it may be better to describe the experience inside VR and the headset as "virtual," "digital," or "immersive virtual" and refer to the experience outside the headset as the physical realm. Although realistically, everything takes place in the physical realm, having the language to talk about what happens in the headset is important.

What makes VR a "radical" form of insertion into the artwork is the fact that it "puts a screen right in front of a viewer's eyes…immersing the user in an artificial world and eliminating or augmenting the physical one" (Paul, 2003, p. 125). This deep dive into the mind of the artist goes beyond that of the flat screen. Things happen behind the viewer's head; they must move in order to experience all that is around them. The addition of interactivity "reflects the consequences of our actions and decisions back…but also refracts what it is given" (Penny, 1995, p. 133). The potential with the use of VR as a medium is that artists can "enjoy 'unrestricted' space for creative work while exploiting features that are not possible in the physical world" (Mu et al., 2022, p. 1).

A better understanding of the systems that underpin various immersive VR experiences can provide examples for artists to build on. Exploring virtual structures and systems can spark new ideas about how to approach the virtual space. While VR as an art form has been around for some time, there is still a profound need for investigation into how humans, with their corporeal bodies, interface with unrestricted, immersive digital space. For those interested in creating in the virtual space, it is valuable to discuss the structures that exist in terms of both understanding and developing for the work. In *Explorations in Art and Technology*, Linda Candy and Ernest Edmonds look at characteristics of "the relationship between the artwork, artist, viewer and environment" (Candy & Edmonds, 2002). They then break interactivity into four categories that help define levels of interactivity in a broad way (*static, dynamic-passive, dynamic-interactive,* and *dynamic-interactive (varying)*), rather than trying to narrowly define expectations for responsive works. What is appealing about these categories is that they are an answer to the question that many pose: *aren't all artworks interactive?* Candy and Edwards would answer yes, but also offer clarification in terms of the level of interactive engagement each type of artwork offers. Following are the terms that Candy and Edwards define:

## STATIC

This category of work can be best described as one in which the artwork might invoke an emotional response in the viewer, but the work itself has no interaction with its external surroundings. Artworks in this category would consist of paintings, non-responsive video, printed material, and maybe even tape recordings.

## DYNAMIC-PASSIVE

In this category, the art object has an integrated component that is responsive to very specific parameters, such as temperature, sound, or light. The observer can view these changes but is not the cause of them.

## DYNAMIC-INTERACTIVE

This category encompasses any sort of responsive input from the dynamic-passive category, with the added requirement that the viewer has an active role in affecting change in the art object. The response to viewer changes can be captured through sensors or cameras and would necessarily incorporate a noticeable reaction in the artwork.

## DYNAMIC-INTERACTIVE (VARYING)

This last category integrates both the dynamic-passive and dynamic-interactive requirements but adds another catalyst in the form of an artist update or artificial intelligence. Both artist update and artificial intelligence offer a system of "learning" that would provide new information to the art object and therefore the possibility of profound changes to the artwork's original specifications (Candy & Edmonds, 2002). This also creates a back and forth between the user and the artist, or an artificial intelligence proxy.

Candy and Edmonds propose that instead of talking about artworks, it is more helpful to view works that fall into the latter three categories as "art systems," as a system can integrate all aspects of the work, including the input from the human viewer (Candy & Edmonds, 2002). In creating an interactive VR experience, artists can design event systems that can integrate (or opt not to integrate) physics from the physical world. In that "human subjects show a strong propension to perceive causality between co-occurring events," VR offers artists a wonderful stage to experiment with what's expected versus what the artist decides to have happen (Cavazza et al., 2005, p. 4). In this example, causal perception refers to circumstances where if a viewer sees one event and another event happens, the viewer will try to understand the second event within the context of the first event's occurrence. Working within the medium of VR, artist technologists have the opportunity to create "artificial causality" which in turn "has the ability to create illusions or to distort…perception of events" (Cavazza, p. 5).

In developing work for VR, it has been "observed that as soon as people put on the HMD, many people start to look around and explore the virtual environment" (Song & DiPaola, 2015, p. 236). Studies have also shown that participants enjoy an embodied experience where they can physically look around rather than using a controller to rotate the imagery (Song & DiPaola, 2015, p. 238). In fact, the way in which users interact with the virtual environment can affect how the work is perceived. For instance, if a user puts on a headset and is confronted with content directly within their field of view, this differs considerably from experiences where exploration is required. Both are valid ways of interacting within the virtual environment, but both evoke different responses in their audiences.

Studies have shown that VR offers participants the ability to become very actively engaged with the artwork. In one study, participants' head elevation changed dramatically as the person in the headset "purposely lowered their heads…[seemingly] to take a look at a much lower object (often near ground level)" (Mu et al., 2022, p. 12). The study also found that users would bend over to avoid "obstacles" within the virtual environment and that participants "reached their hands out and tried to stroke the artwork" (Mu et al., 2022, p. 12). Observations from the experiments above "indicate that the multi-sensory experience may have a pivotal role in VR artwork" (Mu et al., 2022, p. 12). This sense of realism from within the digital environment creates an opportunity for a call and response from participants to the work – again, the level of immersion offered by VR opens up novel ways that artists can communicate with audiences.

## Building a Virtual Reality Experience

Understanding how VR artworks are developed can be helpful in terms of critiquing and creating this art form. There are some consistencies in how users tend to interact with VR works, in both how they move within the headset as well as what they expect in terms of interaction. This chapter's section's primary focus is on laying down the foundation for understanding how viewers approach a VR artwork in terms of navigation. In the past, much of the VR development was a combination of 3D graphics and the interfaces of the time, usually in an effort to simulate an experience from the physical world. More recently, VR experiences are finding influence and inspiration from the world of video games (Zyda, 2005).

Many analogies from the game design world work well in thinking about how to create in virtual space. For starters, most VR art is developed using some sort of game engine software. Game engine software can be set up as 3D environments and use various forms of scripting to prompt events or, in its most basic mode, to provide a 360-degree space for viewers to engage with. When used to their fullest, the following characteristics can set the tone for how participants interact with the work's core mechanics and offer a sense of collaboration in terms of users triggering events within the VR experience.

## Character

When a user puts on a headset to experience a VR artwork, it seems intuitive to let them be themselves. Unlike a video game, artwork in general tries to connect with its audience in an authentic way. Still, there are examples of works that utilize their audience's first-person perspective to shape the VR experience. In *Man Mask* (2016), Rachel Rossin places virtual eyes, nose, and ears atop the viewer's field of vision as they enter the headset. In doing so, she is breaking the fourth wall, requiring her audience to consider their particular perspective in a new way. In many ways, just acknowledging the role of the participant is important – are they voyeurs? Are they in on the joke? Are they participants in the experience? Do their interactions negatively or positively affect the immersive digital environment? So much of our world is viewed through unwittingly mediated perspectives – access through software portals like Facebook and TikTok happens because their free software mines user data, which they then sell to others. When posting on Facebook, is the user aware that their role is to provide financial opportunities and data on their personal preferences? The software is most definitely aware of the user's role and, in fact, develops algorithms that best suit the needs of the software company over those of the end users. This lack of self-awareness in engaging with the digital is interesting in itself, but it also offers artists working in VR an opportunity to play with this notion when creating work.

## CAMERA

A camera in the VR environment refers to the user's view, also called a first-person camera. Most often, when a person puts a headset on, their view replicates their vantage point in the physical domain. In Sandrine Deumier's *Lotus Eaters* (2021), scale replicates human-size interactions – figures appear to be about the same height as the user, massive sculptures tower overhead, and the viewer finds themselves surrounded by massive walls. It is important to remember that the view is what the viewer sees and to treat the movement accordingly.

A poor example of a flawed view comes from the video world. Early cellphone videos were often recorded from the perspective of a hand rather than a head. The end result is video that moves too quickly, perspectives that change in quick and unnatural ways, and angles that cause motion sickness in the viewer. Motion sickness can be caused by issues with lagging frame rates or latency, poor options for in-application locomotion, and disorientation due to an inability to make a correlation between their visual information and their physical location (Chang et al., 2020).

While it is important to address the user's physical comfort and develop VR works for the binocular vision of humans, it isn't a requirement that they enter or move through the VR work from one central vantage point. Lawrence Lek's *Nøtel* (2016–ongoing) starts off from a top down view of a building's architecture and then moves into the interior space. This broad perspective of the interior virtual space gives the user information they might not otherwise receive.

## CONTROL

The category of control relates to how the user interacts with the virtual space. The foundation for this stems from actions taken in the physical world, such as head movement, body movement, use of a controller, hand gestures, voice input, and the like. These multimodal inputs can then trigger events within the VR space. A sense of user control can also work with output feedback. One example of this is the use of haptics in a controller – a buzzing sensation felt but not necessarily always heard. Sound can be important here; it completes the feeling of an immersive environment but can also be used to guide participants.

## COMMUNICATION

Lastly is the unofficial "c" in game development "how to" – communication. Communication, as the fourth development category, can be understood as a dialog with the user – presentation of the work in the way it is meant to be approached. In Brendal Laurel and Rachel Strickland's work *Placeholder* (1993), communication is meant as an open-ended experience for users. Using local mythologies from locations in the Canadian Rockies, the work uses spatialized sounds and voices and simple animations to invite users into the open-ended virtual environment. Their approach varied from the standard interface of menus and dropdowns and used a goalless structure that allowed users to experience the work in whatever way best suited them. Contemporary VR tends to use this open-ended approach as well, but today's users are more familiar with interacting with digital environments and know that interactive works are an invitation to explore (Rogers, 2010).

In using VR as a medium, artists have moved into the realms of computer programming, electronics, interface development, and information architecture. In his book *Information Arts*, Steve Wilson encourages artists to expand how they think of themselves. Instead, he encourages them to reconsider the way they think about their research.

> There is a major categorical flaw in the way we think about scientific and technological research as being outside the major cultural

flow, as something for specialists. We must learn to appreciate and produce science and technology just as we do literature, music and the arts…Many artists have begun to engage the world of technological and scientific research - not just use its gizmos - but rather to comment on its agendas and extend its possibilities.

*–Steve Wilson (Wilson, 2003, p. xxiii)*

## REFERENCES

Allen, R., Brown, B., Galloway, K., Rabinowitz, S., Singer, A., & Iskin, R. (1994). Design and entertainment in the electronic age. *Leonardo, 27*(4), 347–351. https://doi.org/10.2307/1576012

Antunes, J. (2020, October 8). Bodyless: A surreal "must see" virtual reality experience. *ProVideo Coalition.* https://www.providecoalition.com/bodyless-a-surreal-must-see-virtual-reality-experience/

Bolter, J. D., & Gromala, D. (2003). *Windows and mirrors: Interaction design, digital art, and the myth of transparency.* MIT Press.

Bullock, M. (2018). Interview: Jacolby Satterwhite on how video games, art history, and sleep deprivation inspire his 3d interiors. Pin-Up, *25.* https://archive.pinupmagazine.org/articles/interview-3d-queer-artist-jacolby-satterwhite-on-video-game-environments

Candy, L., & Edmonds, E. (2002). Explorations in Art and Technology. *Crossings: EJournal of Art and Technology, 2*(1). https://crossings.tcd.ie/issues/2.1/Candy/

Cavazza, M., Lugrin, J.-L., Crooks, S., Nandi, A., Palmer, M., & Le Renard, M. (2005). Causality and virtual reality art. *Proceedings of the 5th Conference on Creativity & Cognition,* 4–12. https://doi.org/10.1145/1056224.1056228

Chang, E., Kim, H. T., & Yoo, B. (2020). Virtual reality sickness: A review of causes and measurements. *International Journal of Human-Computer Interaction, 36*(17), 1658–1682. https://doi.org/10.1080/10447318.2020.1778351

Cook, S. (2013). On curating new media art. In J. Noordegraaf, C. G. Saba, B. Le Maître, & V. Hediger (Eds.), *Preserving and exhibiting media art* (pp. 389–405). Amsterdam University Press. https://www.jstor.org/stable/j.ctt6wp6f3.18

Delgado, G. (2022, November 29). 3D artist and educator Hsin-Chien Huang takes VR to the world stage this week 'in the NVIDIA studio.' *NVIDIA Blog.* https://blogs.nvidia.com/blog/2022/11/29/in-the-nvidia-studio-november-29/

Lehmann, A.-S., Scholten, F., & Chapman, H. P. (Eds.). (2012). How materials make meaning. *Netherlands Yearbook for History of Art, 62,* 8–26.

Manovich, L. (2003). New media from Borges to HTML. In N. Wardrip-Fruin & N. Montfort (Ed.), *The new media reader* (pp. 13–26). MIT Press.

Mu, M., Dohan, M., Goodyear, A., Hill, G., Johns, C., & Mauthe, A. (2022). User attention and behaviour in virtual reality art encounter. *Multimedia Tools and Applications.* https://doi.org/10.1007/s11042-022-13365-2

Paul, C. (2003). *Digital art.* Thames & Hudson.

Paul, C. (2008). *Digital Art* 2e. WW Norton.

Penny, S. (1995). *Critical issues in electronic media.* SUNY Press.

Rogers, S. (2010). Everything I learned about level design, I learned from level 9. In *Level up!: The guide to great video game design* (pp. 14–16). Wiley. ISBN: 978-1-118-87716-6.

Song, M., & DiPaola, S. (2015). Exploring different ways of navigating emotionally-responsive artwork in immersive virtual environments. *Electronic Visualisation and the Arts,* 232–239. https://doi.org/10.14236/ewic/eva2015.24

Sprengler, C. (2014). Spatial montage, temporal collage, and the art(ifice) of rear projection. In C. Sprengler (Ed.), *Hitchcock and contemporary art* (pp. 91–117). Palgrave Macmillan US. https://doi.org/10.1057/9780230392168_5

Wardrip-Fruin, N., & Montfort, N. (2003). *The new media reader.* MIT Press.

Wilson, S. (2003). *Information arts: Intersections of art, science, and technology.* MIT Press.

Wu, X. & Li, Y. (2021). Experience mode of digital media art under virtual reality technology. *Advances in Computing and Engineering for Bionics and Medical Applications,* 2022, Article ID 5117150. https://doi.org/10.1155/2022/5117150.

Zyda, M. (2005). From visual simulation to virtual reality to games. *Computer, 38*(9), 25–32. https://doi.org/10.1109/MC.2005.297

# CHAPTER 9

# Artist Gallery – Jacolby Satterwaite and Rachel Rossin

## JACOLBY SATTERWHITE

Artist Jacolby Satterwhite was born in 1986 in Columbia, South Carolina. He received his BFA from the Maryland Institute College of Arts, Baltimore, and his MFA from the University of Pennsylvania, Philadelphia. Starting as a painter with formalist concerns and "quasi-pretentious, Bauhaus-y obsessions with texture, plans and lines," Satterwhite moved into 3D animation and found that it brought movement to the formal elements he explored as a painter. This move into the digital realm echoed his feelings of being a child and getting lost in the "infinite 3D arenas" of *Laura Croft: Tomb Raider, The Legend of Zelda: Ocarina of Time, Metal Gear Solid*, and *Resident Evil* (Bias & Satterwhite, n.d.). As a child, Satterwhite had cancer and played these video games in the hospital while undergoing chemotherapy. The years spent in the hospital as a 12- and 13-year-old gave Satterwhite a "skepticism around [his] mortality," which he has countered by creating art objects ever since. He states that the work he leaves behind "is a mortality defiance stand." His productiveness includes sculpture, video, performance, virtual reality (VR), and music, to name a few of the practices he has investigated (Small, 2014). Satterwhite neatly blends the physical world of objects and performance into and back out of the digital

DOI: 10.1201/9781003363729-9

world – in a way, his work is medium-agnostic; what is central to it is the theme of his personal narrative and experience. Satterwhite discussed how "personal mythology is embedded in the objects around us" and went on to say that "the objects and architecture [in his work] contextualize the bodies in the pictures" (Cornell, 2013).

Central to the theme of personal mythology, Satterwhite integrates volumetric digital line-form and physical performances, all of which inform his later works in VR. Most of Satterwhite's line forms subvert any feelings of cold digital aesthetics by originating from drawings created by Satterwhite's mother. As a young child, Satterwhites' mother Patricia was inspired by late-night television commercials to create and draw inventions of her own making. Beautifully rendered, her images riff on a theme. In one case, she investigates multiple creative ideas centered around the symbol Pi: a table that uses the symbol's form with table legs as curving bases to support the table's top; shoes that use the symbol to create a lacey high heel; a pitcher whose base shears away from a delicate spout. Self-taught, Patricia Satterwhite also composed and sang, managing "a mental health diagnosis that eventually rendered her homebound" (*Patricia Satterwhite*, n.d.). Ultimately diagnosed with schizophrenia, Patricia drew thousands of drawings that explored her ideas and inventions. In some cases, defying logic, the drawings spoke of her desire to connect and share. Hopeful, she ultimately wanted to submit her ideas to the television shopping network QVC for instantiation. Satterwhite translates his mother's drawings into his own video and VR works – often directly, by re-drawing the work into virtual space, but also by creating an object in the physical realm, like a 3D print, and then digitizing that physical print. Satterwhite offers that there is an "animistic attitude" in his work – he states that "the soul and spirit of my videos, photographs and drawings are objects" (Cornell, 2013). Satterwhite's work obsessively reinterprets objects, objects rendered and re-rendered in multiple ways – parts of works finding their way into later works, usually output differently, whether through a change in material or a change in materiality – objects that start on paper end up 3D printed, then again 3D animated.

A foundation of these re-interpreted objects are Satterwhite's mother's immense self-produced works. Patricia Satterwhite not only created thousands of drawings but also made hundreds of a cappella recordings. Poignant and heartfelt, the songs melded top 40 riffs with folk and gospel. Jacolby was commissioned by the San Francisco Museum of Modern

Art to make an album based on his mother's songs. Jacolby teamed up with Nick Weiss from Teengirl Fantasy and worked for two years to produce the record (Small, 2014). Jacolby Satterwhite states that he ultimately wanted the record to be a VR album in an effort to defy the way music is heard when it is streamed. Instead, he wanted to bring the music "back to the experience in a certain way [to make it feel] sculptural" (Small, 2014).

## DOMESTIKA

In 2017, Satterwhite created *Domestika*, a VR piece that uses music from the album he created with Weiss. In *Domestika*, Jacolby integrates music from the album into the virtual space. The melodies echo hauntingly as the immersed viewer explores a complex and layered world where mechanical tentacles are whipped around by figures encircled at the top of a dystopian carouse, and larger-scale figures that resemble Jacolby walk as if on a treadmill. These larger figures are lashed to the tentacles, and the treadmill sits atop clear figure-scale globes encased in what appears to be rusted steel tubing. Gold-framed screens play pastel-colored scenes in the background, and in the middle ground, another figure sits atop a chrome winged pegasus with what appears to be a woman's braided head in place of a horse's head.

Satterwhite describes his method of creating these virtual worlds as an "attempt to re-route personal trauma" and "beautiful compositions that use data language" for his subject material. Satterwhite's digital worlds explore themes of public space, the body, ritual, and story. Satterwhite uses his own body as a central reference, and one sees this in his replication of his body for all 3D-modeled figures, as exemplified in sculptures and digital drawings where he inserts his own figure in replications of famous historical paintings. Satterwhite's repeated use of his figure allows for "dealing with the body as a personal mythology and the body as a modernist measurement too, like measuring your own body as a medium" (Small, 2014). Satterwhite states that having digital animation and modeling programs at his disposal allowed him to "lend itself to more dynamic drawing principles. When I trace my movements digitally I make very interesting things happen with line, composition, light and shadow" (Bias & Satterwhite, n.d.). Satterwhite's body becomes a "repetitive presence, dancing alongside multitudes of digital avatars, mythological creatures-turned-machines…leather-clad performers and muses- all of which move ritualistically to Satterwhite's choreography" (Miller & Ravich, 2014).

**FIGURE 9.1** Jacolby Satterwhite *Domestika* (2017). Image permission courtesy of the artist, via Mitchell-Innes and Nash.

Satterwhite's work pulls Black queerness to front and center stage, enveloping the viewer in a riotous world of sensual movement that evokes a joyful present of carnal pleasure and subverts a past of historical oppression by rewriting it in a technological future where "chains donning the S&M workers' bodies on the spaceships…are emblematic of a different Diaspora – one where both the white and black body is punished in captivity *with pleasure*" (Ames, 2017).

## WE ARE IN HELL WHEN WE HURT EACH OTHER

More recent VR work includes *We Are In Hell When We Hurt Each Other* (2020), which was included as part of Satterwhite's solo exhibition at the Mitchell-Innes & Nash gallery in New York City. As an artist who works in technical mediums, Satterwhite is able to fully realize his artistic voice in immersive work. Satterwhite's ability to create objects for the digital 3D space means that he can pull in multiple themes from his lexicon for his creative practice. In *We Are In Hell When We Hurt Each Other,* Satterwhite discusses repetition in his work as circling back to things. This circling back allows him to translate various forms of media into other forms of media – recombinations that, as he states, give the work "emotional spirit because I understand how to use the tools enough to convey a lot more than I was able to before. It has more Jazz. I've learned to be more lyrical and free...I feel like I'm less of a tech artist now- I've revived some of my artistry" (Small, 2014). In the virtual world of Satterwhite's imagination, it is impossible to make a blanket statement of what each object represents in connection to contemporary society, as society "pollutes objects with meanings with history, politics, and social anxiety." Instead, Satterwhite envelopes the objects into his personal mythology and shows how they are "resonant with meaning beyond their function" (Cornell, 2013).

*We Are in Hell When We Hurt Each Other* breaks many 3D world conventions as the piece works to pull flat, 2D memories from the past in order to give them new life in the expansive, exotic world of virtual space. Flat-planed photos, videos, and Patricia's handwritten notes are integrated alongside dancing permutations of Jacolby's figure. These lower resolution relics from the past are artfully integrated and replicated across virtual

**FIGURE 9.2** Jacolby Satterwhite *Domestika* (2017). Image permission courtesy of the artist, via Mitchell-Innes and Nash.

**FIGURE 9.3** Jacolby Satterwhite *We Are In Hell When We Hurt Each Other* (2020). Image permission courtesy of the artist, via Mitchell-Innes and Nash.

**FIGURE 9.4** Jacolby Satterwhite *We Are In Hell When We Hurt Each Other* (2020). Image permission courtesy of the artist, via Mitchell-Innes and Nash.

space. As there are many other unusual and opaquely fashioned objects in each scene, these flat renderings become yet another component of a personal story writ large. Patricia's songs intertwine with the contemporary digital dance music created by Jacolby and Weiss, with various figures responsively dancing across scenes in the virtual universe. Based on Jacolby's choreography, which is in itself built on an archive of the movement of 270 people, the figures represented vary from creatures composed of digital representations of 3D-printed objects to realistic representations of Satterwhite in 90s-style aerobics wear.

Some figures wear their gold-lame skin loosely, like a cloak; other figures present themselves as feminized versions of Jacolby, wearing their skin like armor. In his performative work, Satterwhite states, "I disrupt logic. I force the viewer to assimilate to my standards. Psychologically that's a way of pushing back reductive recognition" (Bias & Satterwhite, n.d.). In Satterwhite's surreal virtual worlds, the multiple forms that his body takes subvert the various contemporary narratives about race, sexuality, and space. Instead, the focus is on Satterwhite's 3D-generated bodily movements – these figures move in response to echoes from without – they find their origin in his performances in the physical world. Ultimately though, Satterwhite feels that "the context for my body isn't planet Earth, its virtual reality" (Bias & Satterwhite, n.d.).

Satterwhite describes wearing masks for his first three years of performing because he wanted audiences to "think about a strange post-race and post-gender body operating in the world" (Bias & Satterwhite, n.d.). Satterwhite's hybrid objects in the virtual world inspire him "to perform in a way that queers the meaning of the object, dissolving the political potential of the object in relationship" to his body (Cornell, 2013). Algerian philosopher Franz Fanon discusses the colonization that a body of color experiences through the external projection of others. Fanon states that the fact of blackness forced Fanon to discover that he could be reduced to an "object in the midst of other objects" (Fanon, 2008). Fanon writes that the colonization of his mind means that "not only must the black man be black, he must be black in relation to the white man" (Fanon, 2008, p. 111). In turn, Satterwhite's media translation purposely "queers the meaning of the object, dissolving the political potential of the object in relation to [his] body" (Cornell, 2013). In an interview for *Dismagazine*, Satterwhite discusses reading author Sara Ahmed, who talks about how the "phenomenology of race and sex shows us how bodies become racialized and sexualized in how they 'extend' into space…It requires a reorientation of one's body such that other objects, those that are not reachable on the vertical and horizontal lines of straight culture, can be reached" (Ahmed, 2006, pp. 99–100).

The space that VR offers is a new frontier, allowing diverse artists to explore and reinvent what semantic meanings are associated with objects and bodies once those objects and bodies are rendered in virtual 3D space. Free from "'fleshy meat-space' artists can fashion new aberrant identities and sexual lives beyond the biological constraints of their bodies" (Ames, 2017). Satterwhite notes that while his virtual worlds are surrealist, they are tethered to the tactile, in part because of the work's foundation in the analog world. Satterwhite states, "realism is inevitable there because I'm using Maya and After Effects to trace a drawing or a real performance in front of a green screen. There aren't that many misleading graphic embellishments" (Bias & Satterwhite, n.d.). His ability to translate media from one realm (the physical) to another (the digital) echoes the conceptual content of his work: a recombination of memories, familial influence, past trauma, and contemporary personal expression. VR is, in many ways, a territory free from entrenched expectations. Collapsing the time-based tradition of video and film, VR offers a fully immersive space that allows for an intimate insertion into the creative mind of another. Indeed, Satterwhite's move into the virtual may be part of his conceptual relationship to his work. He states, "I think queer and abstraction are synonymous. I just say queer because it's more a spatial term. My digital work, performance, and sculpture is a resistance to traditional fine art practices such as painting. In my opinion, queer means finding utopian free autonomous space for being a brave individual" (Bias & Satterwhite, n.d.).

## RACHEL ROSSIN

Rachel Rossin is an artist technologist who started experimenting with code at age eight. Born in West Palm Beach, Florida, in 1987, Rossin began painting around the same time she began coding and went on to receive a BFA from Florida State University, Tallahassee. The ability to code is important to Rossin, as "the reality is that all programmers are self-taught because the sands are always shifting" (*Interview with Virtual Reality Artist, Rachel Rossin*, 2019). Rossin works in a wide variety of digital and physical mediums, and an article in 2016 dubbed Rossin as one of the "Five Rising Artists You Must Know," stating that "Rossin bridged the gap between the white cube and the floating, limitless digital world" (Comita et al., 2016). Like Satterwhite, Rossin's practice moves fluidly between the physical and the virtual. In many of her exhibitions, she blends VR experiences for the Oculus Rift with oil paintings and sculptural elements – the content of one informing and influencing the other in recursive waves. Like Satterwhite, Rossin uses her VR experiences to give the participant an experience outside the boundaries of their own skin. Rossin is very intentional in her choices around VR as a medium. She states,

> I do regard its best-use as a phenomenological tool, and that is what I am aiming for in the way I program my works. Of course, that is not the exclusive purpose in and of itself but it is important to note that every VR work I've made employs the user's perspective as the game mechanic or "arbiter."

> *(R. Rossin, personal communication, March 17, 2023)*

This idea that the viewer's gaze, important to the history of how art and its subject matter are perceived, affects the *content* of Rossin's work is a powerful one. The responsibility of a viewer's gaze has been given negligible consideration in the past – although an artist's choice of subject matter (think: reclining female nude) influences what an audience expects to see. Rather than offering a buffer between viewer and work, Rossin allows/invites/requires the user in the headset to see the consequences of their presence.

When she was young, Rossin would play video games and save a variety of assets. When she became more completely immersed in her artistic practice after school, Rossin was able to recover these early assets – including the first avatar she used, a generic male. In a version of masking her presence in online games, Rossin took on this male avatar "for safety... looking for some kind of neutrality" (*Rachel Rossin's Digital Homes*, 2021). Later on, when Rossin first moved to New York City, she used a male pseudonym to apply for freelance computer programming jobs (Pechman, 2018) (V112 vmagazine.com/article/rachel-rossin-turned-a-fake-identity-into-virtual-reality/). Rossin found that she was offered more jobs under her male pseudonym than if she represented herself as a female.

## MAN MASK

Her VR piece *Man Mask* references her early experiments into virtual space identity politics. In 2017s *Man Mask*, Rossin creates a VR world where the viewer looks through the face of a *Call of Duty* character. The viewer sees the back of the eyes, nose, and mouth and looks through the face at the virtual scene. In the scene, Rossin has placed hacked assets from the COD game in order to place characters in active military maneuvers throughout a grassy, deconstructed landscape. Dulcet birdcalls and running water are heard in the background. A different scene in the VR piece is evocative of a large swimming pool where bodies and objects intermittently splash down. *Man Mask* has been described as "a guided meditation through landscapes taken from the game *Call of Duty: Black Ops*, drained of violence and transformed into an ethereal dreamworld" (First Look, 2017).

Although the audience looks through the face of a man, Rossin's feminine voice is heard periodically, a very intentional move on Rossin's part. As many females know, interaction with others through cyberspace – whether through gaming, social media, even e-commerce – can mean opening oneself up to various forms of abuse. This harassment "frequently occurs when users identify themselves as female. A host of other violent acts are discussed or threatened. Thus, the idea of cyberspace as a safe haven for women equal to that of the book has not been realized" (Flanagan, 2009). Through the immersion afforded by VR, Rossin performs "a body-awareness meditation from inside a 'Call of Duty' character...inside this exploded video game world" (Birnbaum, 2019). In *Man Mask*, the physical body of the viewer wears a layer of inside-out "face" that allows them to interact with *Call of Duty* active soldiers, who are in turn representatives of others who engage the game's portal in a multiplayer role. In an interview with Rossin, the interviewer, Daniel Birnbaum, states that there is "sometimes a critical impulse attached to VR, that it's somehow solipsistic. I always say that reading a novel is also something you do alone" (Birnbaum, 2019). In a discussion about *Man Mask* with Rossin, she points out that "I lead a body-awareness meditation and speak directly to the user (thereby using the byproduct of their reflection on the dissociative experience from inside VR)" (R. Rossin, personal communication, March 17, 2023). In that most VR experiences are offline and/or single player, *Man Mask* offers a siloed space that allows for reflection and a conscious redirection of the visual experience to one of embodiment.

## I CAME AND WENT AS A GHOST HAND

Rossin says that "we think about (technology) as this 'other' but it has so much to do with ourselves, with our desk drive" (Pechman, 2018). In *I Came and Went as a Ghost Hand* (2017), Rossin uses photogrammetry

**FIGURE 9.5**   Rachel Rossin *Man Mask* (2016). Image and permission courtesy of the artist.

software to scan her surrounding domestic spaces. Photogrammetry is a technique that compiles thousands of photos taken at multiple angles, which are then reconstructed in order to render them as 3-D models. Rossin pulls these 3D models generated by the photogrammetry methods into software "such as Unity that enables her to alter them by applying the forces of physics to certain portions of the scene" (Stinson, 2015).

Moving through *I Came and Went as a Ghost Hand*, the viewer is struck by the juxtaposition of the matte, yellow virtual environment and the shrapnel of domestic spaces familiar to most of us. A disembodied hand floats above all, the fingers tiptoeing their way across the fragmented landscape. The realistic interiors are drawn from Rossin's own apartment – easels with paintings sit in living rooms lit by natural sunlight; leafy green plants float in space; the interior of a refrigerator reveals a door of condiments. Some of the edges of these scenes are pixelated and ragged – it is as if these scenes of domesticity are torn from physical reality and tossed into a weightless world of no consequence. These torn edges are remnants of "the user's gaze" as it "carves into the game world creating a record of their time with a raycast entropy script" (R. Rossin, personal communication, March 17, 2023). When someone puts a headset on and enters the piece, their presence actually affects the digital world – where they have looked is torn away, leaving these ragged edges.

Uninhabitable and fantastical, Rossin finds a reference to this space in her youth spent close to the ocean. Rossin's time underwater felt similar to her time playing video games; "the surface tension of the water felt very similar to the surface tension of the virtual screen…there's this thing that was just out of reach beyond this surface" (Westfall, 2021).

Familiar with C#, the programming language of the gaming development platform Unity, Rossin points out that while the photogrammetry feels like a scan, they were really renderings from the "space of [her] imagination" (London, 2020). Her process of development on the Unity platform makes *I Came and Went as a Ghost Hand* seem like it references physical reality, but it is a combination of her current studio, her childhood backyard, and the contents of her refrigerator. The ragged edges that appear on the small domestic scenes are actually generated by the viewer's gaze. As viewers walk through the 3D world, their gaze decimates whatever part of the scene they are looking at. Using a raycast, Rossin states that the viewer's gaze eats away "parts of these memories, these models, the spaces where the paintings were made from, which I would reset every 24 hours. So every viewer had a different perspective; each had a different role in viewing the piece and was taking a part of it with them" (London, 2020). Raycasts are interaction techniques that trace a trajectory from a starting position along a straight path with an end point either at

**FIGURE 9.6** Rachel Rossin *I Came and Went as a Ghost Hand* (2015). Image and permission courtesy of the artist.

a predetermined range or at the intersection with a virtual object. It follows what is basically a line to see if it collides with anything. In this case, the raycast is an operation that starts from the viewer's gaze out to the 3D photogrammetry models of Rossin's domestic world. Rossin states that raycasting is the "way bullet logic is scripted in 'shooter' games," again an echo of her video game play from childhood.

Rossin exhibits *I Came and Went as a Ghost Hand* and other VR work alongside her oil paintings in her solo show "Lossy" at NEW INC in New York City. Lossy is a term in the digital world that refers to compression/decompression "codecs" that, when used, remove digital information from the file getting compressed. File formats such as .gif and .jpg are small and light, but in order to make such a nimble file format, the computer must delete digital information. An algorithm is used to estimate what is noticeable to the human eye, and the codec works to rid the file of what it deems as imperceptible. Rossin states that she is "making paintings inspired by lossy algorithms (i.e. mesh decimation, polygon-reduction, and .jpg compression) and using these algorithms as a narrative thread and metaphor for entropy," a process "of degradation or running down or a trend to disorder" (Definition of Entropy, 2023; *Rachel Rossin's Lossy Exhibition Blends Virtual Reality with Oil Painting*, 2015). Pulling from the VR work and re-interpreting what *should* be in the VR space, Rossin's paintings upend "traditional notions of portraiture, landscape, and still life" as they "inform and reflect the technological installation, an inversion of the most sacred of standards—age-old techniques with the flare of advance guard contemporaneity" (Rossen, n.d.). Lush with vibrant color, her paintings bend and distort planes of physical reality. World views are upended, and scenarios are fragmented.

This "disorder" reveals much in its study of disintegration. Rossin's work defies and utilizes Clement Greenberg's theory of the primacy of materials. Greenberg felt that there were inherent qualities specific to each artistic medium and that painting's flatness contrasted markedly with artists' attempts to recreate a scene through the use of a painted illusion. Rossin addresses her use of mediums, saying that "the most interesting thing for the medium usually is the thing it's most suited for" (Westfall, 2021). Rossin uses the tension between the flatness of the canvas and the vibrancy of her original, RGB, digital references to "re-create spaces that didn't exist" (London, 2020). Rossin's painting *After GTAV 2015* references the video game *Grand Theft Auto V* and offers a rich palette of vibrant

**FIGURE 9.7**  Rachel Rossin *Lossy* (2015). Image and permission courtesy of the artist.

**FIGURE 9.8**  Rachel Rossin *Lossy* (2015). Image and permission courtesy of the artist.

golds and oranges. This palette is pulled directly from that of the game; in fact, the subject matter – sunset over the ocean – is directly referenced from a scene in *GTA V*. In the game, this ocean is explorable: "the player has access to scuba suits and two submarines: the Submersible and the Kraken. While exploring the bottom of the ocean, the player may come across a number of places of interest, such as wrecks" (Pacific Ocean, n.d.). Rossin's illusion built on illusion uses contemporary references that will provoke a wide variety of responses from viewers. Those familiar with the game may have feelings of nostalgia; others of a different generation might see what they think is a more direct reference to the ocean and its imagery. In the folding of the landscape, the viewer is invited to puzzle out what is digital about the original content...Rossin states that "the exhibition posits that our relationship with reality isn't comprised of a separate virtual and real but looks more like a gradient between the two—with most of our modern lives being lived in the action of hopping from screen to screen" (Rachel Rossin-Lossy, 2015) Rossin describes her work as "looking for something that's essential to our lived experience—what it's like to have a body, what it's like to lose people that you love, what it's like to be a part of the messiness and contradictions of that. It goes beyond the medium" (Westfall, 2021).

**FIGURE 9.9** Rachel Rossin *After GTAV* (2015). Image and permission courtesy of the artist.

In interviews, along with referencing writings from Susan Sontag and Hannah Arendt, Rossin discusses Robert Smithson's writings as influential in terms of thinking about her own work. In *A Sedimentation of the Mind: Earth Projects*, Smithson writes, "The earth's surface and the figments of the mind have a way of disintegrating into discrete regions of art. Various agents, both fictional and real, somehow trade places with each other" (Smithson, 1996). Rossin's "Lossy" exhibition of oil paintings and VR experiences allows her oil paintings to reference the digital through painted subject matter that folds in on itself. In her paintings, a realistic scene with crisp edges abuts single color fields painted on the canvas. In that calculus is a study of the rate of change, it can be argued that Rossin's paintings are snapshots of the ever-moving virtual world – when viewers don a VR headset, they can access the digital work from a multitude of vantage points – how and why Rossin chooses to capture any single perspective is a specific part of her painting's compelling nature. Rossin does not discuss her work in reference to the language of technology. Instead, she states that "when you think about it, technology is the promise of being able to live forever, ideas of utopia. Whereas being human is very much rooted in loss…which, in shorthand for Smithson, is entropy" (Westfall, 2021).

## THE SKY IS A GAP 2017

In 2019, Rossin had a solo show at the Zabludowicz Collection in London and revisited an earlier VR work, *The Sky Is a Gap* (2017). Rossin discusses the difficulty in integrating the installation space with the VR content, in that she felt immersion was an essential part of the show. In an article with Litro Magazine, Rossin says that she desired a space where she "could overtake the viewer and pull back when she needed to" (*Interview with Virtual Reality Artist, Rachel Rossin*, 2019). *The Sky Is a Gap* is part of a bigger installation entitled *Stalking the Trace*, which had multi-channel video projections surrounding the VR work. In the installation, "the primary game mechanic uses the user's position in space to scrub through 3-Dimensional disasters" and references the fluidity of movement through time-based videos (R. Rossin, personal communication, March 17, 2023).

Parts of the exhibition reference Michaelangelo Antonioni's *Zabriskie Point* (1970). At the end of *Zabriskie Point*, the protagonist daydreams that a new resort-like real estate development in the desert is blown apart. The film is loosely about American society and radical movements, but the ending is directly evocative of the Yucca Flats, a Nevda-based atom bomb test, where a "Survival City" was built by the U.S. Army. In order to observe how buildings, people, and their stuff would survive at various distances from a nuclear blast, mannequins from J.C. Penney were clothed and arranged throughout the silent city (Atomic Bomb Test, 1953). While this concept of disrupted domestic scenes echoes in Rossin's later works, Rossin states that overall the installation and final VR work are "talking about the body—the inherent frailty and how easy it is to fool ourselves into believing that all we need is an accelerometer in this virtual world" (Westfall, 2021). Rossin uses "moments of explosions and reworks them into an experience through which we understand the link between space and time through the form of our own movements" (Westfall, 2021). This is done on a larger scale in the physical world, where the gallery space is taken over by projections that evoke zoetropes. As the visitor enters the gallery and walks down the hallway toward the VR installation, there is an "illusion of a before or after image or walking through...an animation device" (Westfall, 2021). The animation projected onto the walls moves forward as the visitor moves forward. If the visitor stops, the animation stops. The exhibition addresses "control and consent in relationship to the phenomenological experience of loss," including how a participant in the VR headset "is the arbiter of destruction by their participation" (R. Rossin, personal communication, March 17, 2023).

## CONCLUSION

What is remarkable about both Satterwhite's and Rossin's works is how each of the VR creations explores and pushes the boundaries of digital interaction and virtual space. Through Satterwhite's performance and representation of the body, participants find themselves in a landscape that is at once surreal and familiar. The figures in his works have a lively vibrancy that creates a sense of an intimate relationship upon viewing. As the figures dance, exploring their own virtual limbs and torsos, the underlying sense of joy in digital expression is palpable. The way that Rossin pulls from her own environment and past to create spaces that viewers interact with using their gaze means that no one who puts on a headset to view her work is aloof or outside the experience. These two digital natives are artist technologists creating works that aren't about VR per se; rather, they are making full use of the medium to express themselves. Anyone hoping to enter the VR world should take note of Satterwhite and Rossin.

## REFERENCES

Ahmed, S. (2006). *Queer phenomenology: Orientations, objects, others.* Duke University Press.

Ames, A. (2017, March 31). Review: Jacolby Satterwhite's virtual reality performance at SFMOMA imagines a black, queer, S&M future. *Artspace.* https://www.artspace.com/magazine/interviews_features/close_look/review-jacolby-satterwhites-virtual-reality-performance-at-sfmoma-imagines-a-black-queer-sm-54680.

*Atomic Bomb Test in Nevada w/ JC Penney Mannequins 34512.* (1953). PeriscopeFilm. https://www.youtube.com/watch?v=NWJ7XI2_zQ8.

Bias, Z., & Satterwhite, J. (2023). Adjust opacity. *DIS Magazine.* https://dismagazine.com/discussion/61413/adjust-opacity/.

Birnbaum, D. (2019, April 26). Possibilities of creation. *Frieze Week Magazine.* https://www.frieze.com/article/possibilities-creation.

Comita, J., Zhong, F., Russeth, A., & McGarry, K. (2016, November 2). Meet five rising artists for the future. *W Magazine.* https://www.wmagazine.com/story/meet-five-rising-artists-for-the-future.

Cornell, L. (2013, February 1). *Techno-animism.* https://www.moussemagazine.it/magazine/lauren-cornell-techno-animism-2013.

Definition of Entropy. (2023). *Merriam-Webster dictionary online.* https://www.merriam-webster.com/dictionary/entropy.

Fanon, F. (2008). *Black skin, white masks.* Grove Press.

*First Look: Artists' VR.* (2017, February 1). Rhizome. https://rhizome.org/editorial/2017/feb/01/first-look-artists-vr/.

Flanagan, M. (2009). Navigating the narrative in space: Gender and spatiality in virtual worlds. *Art Journal, 59*(3), 74–85. https://doi.org/10.1080/00043249.2000.10792016.

*Interview with Virtual Reality Artist, Rachel Rossin.* (2019, December 23). Litro. https://www.litromagazine.com/usa/2019/12/interview-with-virtual-reality-artist-rachel-rossin/.

London, B. (2020, June 26). *Rachel Rossin* (1.06). https://www.barbaralondon.net/rachel-rossin/.

Miller, W., & Ravich, N. (2014, April 25). *Jacolby Satterwhite is going public.* Art21. https://www.youtube.com/watch?v=p6jQ3ImmWLU.

Pacific Ocean. (2023). *GTA Wiki.* Retrieved March 30, 2023, from https://gta.fandom.com/wiki/Pacific_Ocean.

*Patricia Satterwhite.* (2023). Mitchell-Innes & Nash. https://www.miandn.com/artists/patricia-satterwhite.

Pechman, A. (2018, April 10). Rachel Rossin turned a fake identity into virtual reality. *V Magazine.* https://vmagazine.com/article/rachel-rossin-turned-a-fake-identity-into-virtual-reality/.

*Rachel Rossin-Lossy.* (2015, October 2). Art Week. https://www.artweek.com/events/united-states/art-opening/new-york/rachel-rossin-lossy.

*Rachel Rossin's Digital Homes.* (2021, May 5). Art21. https://art21.org/watch/new-york-close-up/rachel-rossins-digital-homes/.

*Rachel Rossin's Lossy Exhibition Blends Virtual Reality with Oil Painting.* (2015, October 28). New Inc. https://www.newinc.org/archive/rachel-rossin-blends-virtual-reality-with-oil-painting-2jgej.

Rossen, R. (2023). *Rachel Rossen.* https://rossin.co/.

Small, R. (2014, December 19). The digital creator. *Interview.* https://www.interviewmagazine.com/art/15-faces-of-2015-jacolby-satterwhite.

Smithson, R. (1996). A sedimentation of the mind: Earth projects. In P. Smithson & R. Smithson (Eds.), *Robert Smithson: The collected writings* (pp. 100–113). University of California Press.

Stinson, L. (2015, November 13). Rachel Rossin's trippy paintings of reality as seen through VR. *Wired.* https://www.wired.com/2015/11/rachel-rossins-trippy-paintings-of-reality-as-seen-through-vr/.

Westfall. (2021, February 19). Rachel Rossin. *Killscreen.* https://killscreen.com/rachel-rossin/.

# CHAPTER 10

# The Embodied Conceptual Space

## INTRODUCTION

In many ways, interactive virtual reality (VR) artworks "break" the boundaries traditionally found in artistic settings and interactions. The level of immersion within the work is unique and offers an experience for the participant that is not common to other digital forms. This immersion allows users to interact with every aspect of the artist's virtual work and enforces them to leave the physical environment behind. The focus of this chapter is the tension between a user's physical body as it exists within the suppressed physical environment and the virtual environment that fills their eyes, ears, and, in some cases, nose. As Christiane Paul points out in her important book *Digital Art*, the "concept of disembodiment radically denies the physicality of our bodies and the reality of our interaction with computers, which still very much is a physical process" (Paul, 2003, p. 125). At the core of this discussion are the concepts of embodiment and interactive agency and the profound effect that they have on the audience/viewer dynamic and emergent meaning in artistic works (Jerald, 2016).

## THE SENSES

Integral to our experiences and our interactions as we move through our world are the senses, both individually and in combination. Vision, hearing, taste, smell, and touch give us information about the objects that

DOI: 10.1201/9781003363729-10

surround us, how those objects react to us, and what we might expect from them. Each works to convey information to our brain, with vision accounting for nearly 80% of environmental information (perhaps the reason so many discuss contemporary art within the framework of *visual arts*) (MacKenzie, 2013). Indeed, in a VR experience, vision and hearing are the two senses most catered to, with some applications incorporating tactile (touch) responses in the form of controller vibration. In some cases of interactive, responsive VR, our senses also play a dual role: that of a sensor and a responder (MacKenzie, 2013). Our senses work to not only collect information from environmental stimulation but also to respond to that stimulation.

This process may occur remotely, such as through the reception of stimulus through space, as seen with lightwaves, or it might occur mechanically, such as through direct contact, as experienced through touching a textured surface. This process can also occur chemically, such as through the binding of chemicals with receptors, as in the case of smell (Marshall et al., 2019). It is through these senses that the cognitive function of perception occurs. In many ways, "senses are the portals to the mind" (Biocca, 2006). By using their senses, people are able to perceive the structure of the environment around them and base their responses on their lived experience. A user's perception is a "basic element in examining the characteristics of a virtual space and [plays] a key role when it comes to the degree at which the physical and symbolic differ or blend" (Paul, 2003, p. 95).

This perception leads to an important cognitive function called kinaesthetics. Kinaesthetics describe a situation where a combination of senses are used to create a mental map of where one's body sits in space, how that body is moving, and where the body is at any given time (Marshall et al., 2019). Kinaesthetics become especially important in VR, as the VR suppresses input from the user's physical environment. Instead, all vision, most sound, and sometimes touch or smell are provided by the immersive experience of the user. Headsets have incorporated headphones that play sounds and music from the virtual experience, and in at least one case, artists, such as Winslow Porter, included the use of specifically developed scents to enhance the user's immersive virtual experience.

Even hand movements can be mediated in the virtual environment; whereas some headsets offer hand-tracking, those that require controllers occupy the participant's hand movements and disallow touching the physical environment. In this way, VR modifies the participants' experience of their physical environment through the dampening, elimination, or minimization of sensorial stimuli (Biocca, 2006). These repressed stimuli are then replaced with the predominantly visual and auditory stimuli created by the VR system. The greater the number of senses stimulated by the VR system, the greater the potential impact an experience may hold, but this is also where the potential danger of VR as a medium exists (Jerald, 2016). The act of severing someone's physical environment from what they are experiencing through their senses can cause a sense of distortion or distress. Often, when a user's senses are misaligned, the mixed signals perceived lead to *simulation sickness* (Marshall et al., 2019). In many cases, when an inexperienced individual is in an extensively immersive virtual experience, there are attendants in the physical realm who act as "spotters," making sure the participant is safe and stable.

## EMBODIMENT

The sensory process builds an experience of embodiment. At its most basic, embodiment is the concept of interaction with the *other*, with the *other* defined as anything not of one's self – including other people, external objects, and the physical environment outside of corporeal form (Porrovecchio, 2020. Embodiment, then, is defined as the subjective experience of having a body, where each sense processes stimuli to cumulate in a sense of space (Skarbez et al., 2018). Embodiment is not solely a sensory process, however. Instead, the body can be viewed as "a representational medium for the mind," a sort of primordial display (Biocca, 2006). Through body language, actions, and movement, our bodies become *responders* in addition to *sensors*. In this way, embodiment becomes a tool for communication (Smith & Neff, 2018). At the core of this communication is the interaction one's form has with another, be that another human, environmental, natural, or synthetic. It is precisely this matter that makes attending to the user's experience within an artwork paramount – ignorance of what the user experiences, how they respond, and what they might feel hinders an artwork's impact.

In an artistic sense, embodiment is found "in the contemplation of works of art and of natural objects, and it occurs insofar as the preliminary activities of creation by the artist, or of recreation or 'learning' by the spectator, have been completed" (Berndtson, 1960). This back and forth between an audience and an artwork is often described as an emotional provocation for the viewer; as a connection occurs, the user intuits the meaning/context/experience of the work and thus has an emotional response that unites. To understand this better, it's important to understand when a sense of embodiment is "broken by an act of analysis." The disconnect between viewer and artwork is categorized by a loss of feeling for the open, intuitive responsiveness experienced within embodiment; instead, "embodiment and aesthetic perception cease, giving way to the bifurcation typical of ordinary experience" (Berndtson, 1960).

Embedded within the concept of embodiment is the idea of *presence.* According to Jason Jerald, author of *The VR Book: Human-Centered Design for Virtual Reality,* presence in embodiment is the cognitive effect a viewer experiences of having the medium (such as the pages of a book) fall away and instead attending to the content (such as the story, message, event, or character) contained within (Jerald, 2016). While not required for presence to occur, immersion is often the mechanism for presence in VR works. As Jerald points out, immersion occurs when a VR system is **extensive** in terms of the range of senses stimulated; **matching** in that there is a congruence between senses; **surrounding** as one might experience with 360-degree content; **vivid** in the quality of presentation; **interactive** by allowing a user to affect the virtual world; and **plot informing**, which means that there is a consistent portrayal of experience, events, and behavior within the world (Jerald, 2016).

Thoughts, feelings, and behaviors are rooted in our bodily interaction with virtual space (Meier et al., 2012). What's interesting is that ultimately the experience is dynamic – within any experienced time frame, the embodied experience fluctuates and changes (Porrovecchio, 2020). Through lived experiences, we learn. Take, for instance, a small child who tries to insert a square peg into a round hole. They may try to repeat the experience until dissatisfied and defeated, only then to take an alternate route: that of inserting the square peg into the square hole. Similarly, as a user enters an interactive work, they must reach out and explore in order to experience the entirety of the work. Early interactions may not yield desired results, so the person in the virtual space must reach out and try again.

Physical movement, repeated effort, and immersion all combine forces to bring someone into the virtual space, giving them the illusion that they are actually there – that what they see, hear, and (maybe) feel constitutes their reality; that their presence is within that world. These actions, taken to create a sense of embodiment, are essential in that the "digital does not represent the parameters of space as we know it in other media forms" (Paul, p. 94). In more commercial realms, the response to creating a sense of embodiment is to try and create a hyper-realistic illusion. Creating a simulation can be interesting, but it should in no way be the main goal for the creation of all VR experiences. The virtual world offers a chance to explore and inhabit in ways that are impossible in the physical world – additionally, there are some pitfalls that can interfere with the creator's intended experience. One misstep of hyper-realism in the virtual is the creation of characters who imitate the real "as we get closer to reality... only up to a point. If reality is approached, but not attained, some of our reactions shift from empathy to revulsion" (Jerald, 2016, p. 49). Called the uncanny valley, this effect can mar a user's experience, causing the user to experience a tremendous feeling of unease. Unsure if the feeling of imminent danger is realistic or overblown, the perception of someone or something as "creepy" can break the artistic embodied link that a person can experience with an artwork. Instead of seeking an accurate simulation of the physical, creating worlds that provide a "sense of spatial stability" has been proven to be a more effective way of integrating someone into virtual worlds (Jerald, 2016, p. 50).

Edmond Couchot argues that immersion in the virtual means an "exclusively symbolic space, purely made up of information. What we experience as space is actually the product of complex mental processes and cyberspace is an extension of consciousness" (Paul, 2003, p. 95). One aspect of this notion that completely misses the mark regarding immersive virtual environments is the interplay of one's body with the immersive space. In the headset, a participant can use their physical body to make gestures or movements in order to cause a reaction from the digital environment, but it would be "an oversimplification to claim the body is in virtual reality...the body, we might say, is partially present" (Penny, 2019, p. 61). Immersion is, in many ways, a form of illusion. What saves users in the virtual space – what tethers them to the experience in spite of it being an "exclusively symbolic space" is the idea of *self-embodiment*. When a user looks down in VR and finds themselves disembodied, they latch on to a sense of presence in whatever way they can.

Most often, this comes through an echo of one's physical movements represented in the virtual space. A hand gesture in the physical realm is replicated by a floating 3D version of a hand – grabbing the controller causes the application to grab an object in virtual space (Jerald, p. 48).

Human self-perception is actually quite complicated: "we don't necessarily perceive ourselves objectively and how we perceive ourselves, even in real life, through the lens of subjectivity can be quite distorted" (Jerald, 2016, p. 48). Studies have shown that one "automatically associates the visual characteristic of what is seen at the location of the body with one's own body" (ibid.). The adaptability of human perception allows for fluidity in response to circumstances – this makes sense evolutionarily (adaptability and responsiveness in terms of a quick change of circumstance are excellent traits), but it also means that users can adapt to, conform to, and, if appropriate, enjoy the virtual world presented to them.

It makes sense, then, that individual differences can affect the process of embodiment. How connected or disconnected a person feels from their body may contribute to a sense of unease, nausea, or blissful immersion. Examples that can contribute to why people experience the embodied experience in VR differently can be one's prior experiences, personal beliefs, or even one's sensory acuity – or how responsive to stimuli each user is. Contemporary research is taking a deep dive into studying external stimuli's effect on participants. Exertion games, such as those from the Exertion Games Lab housed at Monash University, make full use of the senses. Exertion games are defined as "a digital game that utilizes physical exertion interactions where the physical effort is a key, if not the dominant, determinant in reaching the game's goal" (Mueller et al., 2016, p. 5). Essentially, exertion games are experiences that take stimuli to an extreme in order to create a greater emotional, psychological, and physiological response in the user. This can be seen in *Inter-Dream* (Semertzidis et al., 2019), a multi-sensory VR artwork where users lay on a bed in the installation space with a VR HMD on. Calming music plays while displayed on the HMD are procedurally generated visuals affected by the user's current cognitive state. Brain activity is monitored by EEG, which is then fed back into the visuals the user experiences. Quite literally, the visual experience is a sensory loop where a user is driven by their own perceptions. The visuals, sound, and tactile experience fold into their physical states, driving the entire experience forward.

*You Better Eat to Survive* is another exertion game that makes use of a seldom used sense in human-computer interaction: taste (Arnold et al., 2018). In a collaborative VR experience, one user is equipped with an HMD and another is not. The goal is for the VR user to escape from a deserted island by solving puzzles – however, from time to time they will "blackout" and be unable to see until their partner feeds them in the real world. A sensor is attached to the VR user's cheek and detects when the player chews. Echoing the common survival tactic in the gaming world of eating to gain health, *You Better Eat to Survive* ties a user's physical body into their digital experience. Eating in the physical realm returns the user's "strength" and allows them to see again and press forward. By attending to this under-used sense, that of taste, that sense becomes central to the experience and creates an impactful work.

## FROM AUDIENCE TO USER

One would be remiss to discuss interaction without mentioning the notion of affordances. Affordances are what the virtual environment "offers the animal, what it provides or furnishes, either for good or ill" (Gibson, 2011, p. 127). While affordances were originally contextualized in the realm of psychology, their impact has spread throughout a variety of fields, most notably (for the purposes of this discussion) human-computer interaction (HCI). For HCI, affordances are the actions, things, and possibilities offered to a user by the system, whether it be a command prompt, graphic user interface, or VR environment. These systems not only expect user participation but explicitly rely on said participation (Vincente, 2020). They demand the user to actively engage via control of the form and content contained in the experience (Lee & Kim, 2009). This runs counter to the museums or galleries in which static or dynamic-passive works are typically displayed. Save for some installations, like performances or similar works, static artworks are placed on a wall or in a room with boundaries that prevent direct interaction, manipulation, or contact with the work. Instead, viewers must not touch and are relegated to "seeing with their eyes." Here, the patrons are undeniably fulfilling the role of an audience member; that of a spectator. This transition from user to audience member occurs when interactive mediums, such as VR, offer a space with which to reach out and connect.

Affordances in VR emerge from two distinct sources. The first is from the technology itself, which is the functional, mechanical, and technological properties of the VR system used. Technological affordances include 360-degree displays, tracked hand controllers, speakers/headphones, and devices like sensor vests. Often, the artist has limited control over these affordances, apart from whether or not they choose to utilize them. When artists are specific about the technology used, then they access the second source of affordances: the overall design and integration of the work. These secondary affordances are mechanics of the experience; they may be digital or physical in nature, depending on the specific artistic implementation. The mechanics decide how interaction takes place and with what – artistic experimentation can find a home here, as designing mechanics most often sits within the software and code. Of course, while affordances are dictated by the artist and their intent, engagement with any individual affordance by a user cannot be guaranteed.

VR is unique in the degree to which the virtual is affected by the physical. Many mediums boast the benefit of interactions, such as gaming or websites; however, in these mediums, the interactions are abstracted. Interaction is input through human interface devices (HIDs) such as keyboards, mice, or gamepads. In these situations, a complex interaction is simulated through keystrokes and button presses, abstracted through the devices designed for these computer systems. VR, instead, capitalizes on the user's full form. In a VR experience, if a user were to pick an object off the floor, they would have to bend over, reach out with their physical hand, and initiate a grab. While the "grab" movement will vary depending on the system, it most often uses a pressure-sensitive button on a hand controller. After grabbing the object, the user must return their arm to their side and stand back up.

## MECHANICAL MESSAGE

In discussing virtuality artworks, so much of the work's message can be contained within the *mechanics*. For it is the mechanics that give rise to the overall experience (Hunicke et al., 2015). Described in the *MDA Framework* proposed by Hunicke et al., *mechanics* are the specific components or rules that, when combined, give rise to *dynamics*, that is, the interactions between the mechanics with each other and the user. These dynamics then lead to the overall *aesthetics*, or feeling, conveyed by the experience (Hunicke et al., 2015). In a sense, the mechanics are the building blocks of the overall message conveyed by an experience. Their impact on what stories, meanings, and messages emerge from an artwork cannot be denied.

An excellent example of mechanics at work in an artwork can be seen in the ongoing series of physical board games/artworks found in *The Mechanic Is the Message* by Brenda Romero. Her 2008 addition to the series, *The New World*, uses the game mechanics to create a deeply impactful experience centered around the slave trade. In the art game, the players are tasked with packing small figurines into a box with the explicit goal of maximizing the number of figures that can be arranged in the confined space. While playing, every time a player places a figure, they are forced to confront the horrific conditions that many Africans were subjected to when stolen from their homes. Romero's board game *Train* (2009) explores similar territory, asking "will people blindly follow the rules?" and "will people stand by and watch?" The game starts with players organizing yellow figures into box cars, but as the game progresses, the players are made aware that the train's destination is Auschwitz. It is then that the players must decide whether they will continue to follow the game rules, or reject them in favor of their own. In each game, the mechanics play an integral role in expressing the overall narrative, meaning, and message contained within the game. Lessons that can be translated to the design and implementation of VR artistic works.

## EMERGENT MEANING

Works such as Brenda Romero's hint at a trend unique to interactive experiences: the emergence of meaning through interaction. That is, meaning

**FIGURE 10.1** Brenda Romero *Train* (2009). Image and permission courtesy of the artist.

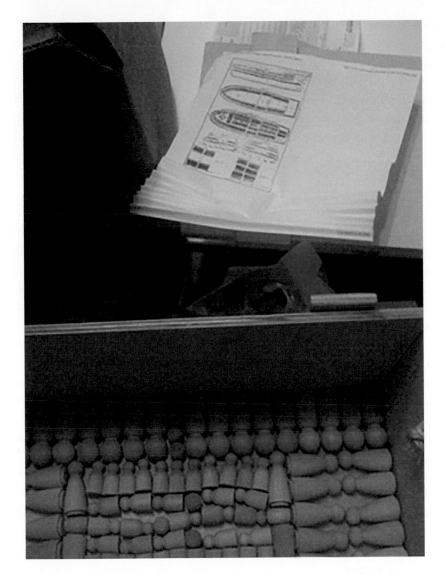

**FIGURE 10.2** Brenda Romero *The New World* (2008). Image and permission courtesy of the artist.

appears or is revealed through the process of interacting with the work (McCormack & Dorin, 2001). Users are caught in an interactive feedback loop with the work, where the user and the system each "listen," "think," and then "speak" (Chew & Mitchell, 2020). This cycle is the process by which the user affects the world, the world responds, and the user impacts future events (Jerald, 2016). A simplistic example of emergent meaning would be in a situation where a user may topple a virtual tree, thus affecting the digital world. The toppled tree then falls on top of another object, causing it to be destroyed – the destruction of the object is a situation where the virtual world responds. Lastly, a situation occurs where the user needs that object but is unable to obtain it – the emergent meaning of a situation where the user impacts a future event. But what if the user had chosen not to topple that virtual tree? Later, when the player needed the object, they would be able to obtain it. This is a key aspect of emergent meaning: the player's choices, actions, and interactions shape the experience. They impact, if not dictate, the meaning.

An example of emergent meaning can be seen explicitly in a study conducted by Hjaltason et al. (2015). The researchers designed a game that randomly chooses from a set of mechanics when play begins. This means that in every playthrough, the goals, affordances, environment, and interactions differ. After players played the game, they were asked to describe their experiences in narrative form; each described it through a different story. Some players described being supervillains or criminals, while others discussed their role as an explorer, one user described their experience escaping evil penguins. Vital to each individual's experience was the narrative of their generated experience – a narrative created through their unique mechanical experiences (Hjaltason et al., 2015). This research study created vastly different experiences for its players, but instead of chaotic random components, the carefully chosen mechanics combined to create unique and meaningful experiences for its users. Consider the somewhat opposite game of *Train* again; while *Train* has set, explicit rules and mechanics, players were still able to make choices not explicitly permitted by the game once they learned the truth about the experience. The meaning found within both the research study and Romero's board game comes through the rules of engagement and interaction.

Examples of emergent meaning can also be found in VR artworks, such as Laurie Anderson and Hsin-Chien Huang's *Chalkroom* (Anderson & Huang, 2017). *Chalkroom* presents a visually stunning artwork reminiscent of grade school chalkboards. Every aspect of the environment has a dusty, dirty quality comprised of dark grays and chalky whites; this is in direct contrast to the clean digital visuals common to most digitally generated VR works. In *Chalkroom*, words are scrawled on every surface and float ethereally off the walls toward the user. A user's progression through the space is accompanied by cryptic narration with phrases such as "things are made of words." Contained within the experience are a number of hidden rooms for users to discover, each with their own unique elements. In one, a tree is erected in the center of the room with its foliage composed of various letter and numeric forms; in another, ominous light cubes illuminate unsettling images and phrases on the surface of the environment. This leads to varied and unique experiences with each playthrough and between users. For each user and each use, a different experience emerges – experiences that tell different stories and convey different messages. It is a freeing experience that the viewer is expected to create for themselves. As Laurie Anderson describes, "Chalkroom is a library of stories, and no one will find them all."

## HISTORICAL ANTECEDENTS

There are striking similarities between VR artistic works and the 1950s and 1960s *Happenings*. These artistic events, popularized by Allen Kaprow, would invite people into a space (or environment) to interact with others. This included actions such as licking jam off of a car or destroying objects in space. When describing *Happenings*, Kaprow called for the elimination of audiences, a "collage" of events, an emphasis on space, a relation to sport or play, an emphasis on chance, and questioned the ability for any event to be repeated (Kaprow, 1956; Sontag, 1962). This mirrors much of the discussion surrounding VR art, with VR art: shifting audiences to users, emphasizing digital embodiment in a space, being akin to a collection of tools or games rather than an object or collection, and containing variability across users and subsequent uses.

In many ways, it may be apt to consider VR works in a similar vein as improvisational mediums. This is due to the necessity of interactivity and user engagement for construction and continuation of narratives (Aylett & Louchart, 2003). In a sense, a VR user is more akin to an improv actor than a traditional viewer. They are an interactor in an interactive narrative (Swartjes & Theune, 2009. Essentially, they are fed a premise, situation, or other narrative and environmental variables to respond to and affect in real time, much like an improv actor on stage.

## RENEGOTIATING AUTHORSHIP

All of these factors – the embodied nature of VR, the shift from audience to user, and the emergent meaning from mechanics – lead to a renegotiating of artistic authorship. A 15th-century painting of a still life can have hidden meaning in its visual metaphor. The audience views the artistic work, and hopefully the embedded meaning is conveyed. But this is not the case with immersive and interactive art works. Instead, with a VR work, the artist creates a world with affordances, and the user is then invited into that space in order to interact with the system. How they sense, perceive, and respond to the stimuli and affordances presented by the virtual environment is dependent on the particular user.

## CONCLUSION

It is important that artists who choose to work in the VR medium consider the embodied interactive experiences that give rise to emergent meaning, as it is not sufficient to simply place a user in a 3D environment. Instead, the artist must challenge established assumptions regarding control, interaction, and visualization (gracanin). This begins by considering the user's point of view and the affordances they are able to utilize. Through attention to the interactive feedback loop, the embodied experience, and the provided affordances, along with considerate adjustments to each, meaning can be manifested in meaningful ways (Chew & Mitchell, 2020). In VR, the user "is the storyteller here" (Pillai & Verma, 2019, p. 5). When a user is lost in the experience, when they can move past a sense of disembodiment, when they can connect with the digital work, there is an amazing sense of control within the environment. One can fly through layers of code or text as they do in Char Davies' *Osmose*, or one can thread narratives from words floating in space as they do in Anderson and Huang's *Chalkroom*. The liberation afforded users of virtual works can be intoxicating, and it would seem that the ability to offer that experience would be appealing to an artist. Stepping out of physical reality into digital reality means that:

> One does not take one's body into VR. One leaves it at the door while the mind goes wandering, unhindered by a physical body, inhabiting an ethereal virtual body in pristine virtual space, itself a 'pure' Platonic space, free of farts, dirt, and untidy bodily fluids.

> *Simon Penny "Consumer Culture and the Technological Imperative"*

# REFERENCES

Anderson, L., & Huang, H.-C. (2017). *Chalkroom*. Laurie Anderson. https://laurieanderson.com/?portfolio=chalkroom.

Arnold, P., Khot, R. A., & Mueller, F. "Floyd." (2018). "You better eat to survive": Exploring cooperative eating in virtual reality games. *Proceedings of the Twelfth International Conference on Tangible, Embedded, and Embodied Interaction*, 398–408. https://doi.org/10.1145/3173225.3173238

Aylett, R., & Louchart, S. (2003). Towards a narrative theory of virtual reality. *Virtual Reality*, *7*(1), 2–9. https://doi.org/10.1007/s10055-003-0114-9.

Berndtson, A. (1960). Beauty, embodiment, and art. *Philosophy and Phenomenological Research*, *21*(1), 50–61. https://doi.org/10.2307/2104788.

Biocca, F. (2006). The cyborg's dilemma: Progressive embodiment in virtual environments. *Journal of Computer-Mediated Communication*, *3*(2). https://doi.org/10.1111/j.1083-6101.1997.tb00070.x.

Chew, E. C., & Mitchell, A. (2020). Bringing art to life: Examining poetic gameplay devices in interactive life stories. *Games and Culture*, *15*(8), 874–901. https://doi.org/10.1177/1555412019853372.

Gibson, J. J. (2011). *The ecological approach to visual perception* (17th pr). Psychology Press.

Hjaltason, K., Christophersen, S., Togelius, J., & Nelson, M. (2015). *Game mechanics telling stories? An Experiment*. International Conference on Foundations of Digital Games.

Hunicke, Robin & Leblanc, Marc & Zubek, Robert. (2004). MDA: *A Formal Approach to Game Design and Game Research*. AAAI Workshop - Technical Report. 1.

Jerald, J. (2016). *The VR book: Human-centered design for virtual reality* (1st ed.). ACM, Association for Computing Machinery.

Kaprow, A. (1956.). *Assemblages, environments, and happenings*, 13.

Lee, M., & Kim, G. J. (2009). Effects of heightened sensory feedback to presence and arousal in virtual driving simulators. *Proceedings of the 8th International Conference on Virtual Reality Continuum and Its Applications in Industry - VRCAI '09*, 151. https://doi.org/10.1145/1670252.1670285.

MacKenzie, I. S. (2013). *Human-computer interaction: An empirical research perspective* (1st ed.). Morgan Kaufmann is an imprint of Elsevier.

Marshall, J., Benford, S., Byrne, R., & Tennent, P. (2019). Sensory alignment in immersive entertainment. *Proceedings of the 2019 CHI Conference on Human Factors in Computing Systems*, 1–13. https://doi.org/10.1145/3290605.3300930.

Mccormack, J., & Dorin, A. (2001). Art, emergence, and the computational sublime. *Proceedings of the Second International Conference on Generative Systems in the Electronic Arts*, Victoria, Australia, 5-7 December 2001. Centre for Electronic Media Art, VIC, Australia, ISBN: 0-7326-2195-X, pp 67–81.

Meier, B. P., Schnall, S., Schwarz, N., & Bargh, J. A. (2012). Embodiment in social psychology. *Topics in Cognitive Science*, *4*(4), 705–716. https://doi.org/10.1111/j.1756-8765.2012.01212.x.

Mueller, F., Khot, R. A., Gerling, K., & Mandryk, R. (2016). Exertion games. *Foundations and Trends® in Human–Computer Interaction*, *10*(1), 1–86. https://doi.org/10.1561/1100000041

Paul, C. (2003). *Digital art*. Thames & Hudson.

Penny, S. (2019). *Cognition, computing, art, and embodiment*. The MIT Press, p. 540. ISBN 9780262538237.

Pillai, J. S., & Verma, M. (2019). Grammar of VR storytelling: Narrative immersion and experiential fidelity in VR cinema. *The 17th International Conference on Virtual-Reality Continuum and Its Applications in Industry*, 1–6. https://doi.org/10.1145/3359997.3365680.

Porrovecchio, A. (Ed.) (2020). *The SAGE International Encyclopedia of mass media and society*. (Vols. 1-5). SAGE Publications, Inc., https://doi.org/10.4135/9781483375519

Semertzidis, N. A., Sargeant, B., Dwyer, J., Mueller, F. F., & Zambetta, F. (2019). Towards understanding the design of positive pre-sleep through a neurofeedback artistic experience. *Proceedings of the 2019 CHI Conference on Human Factors in Computing Systems*, 1–14. https://doi.org/10.1145/3290605.3300804

Skarbez, R., Brooks, Jr., F. P., & Whitton, M. C. (2018). A survey of presence and related concepts. *ACM Computing Surveys*, *50*(6), 1–39. https://doi.org/10.1145/3134301.

Smith, H. J., & Neff, M. (2018). Communication behavior in embodied virtual reality. *Proceedings of the 2018 CHI Conference on Human Factors in Computing Systems*, 1–12. https://doi.org/10.1145/3173574.3173863.

Sontag, S. (1966). Happenings: an art of radical juxtaposition. In Sontag, S. (ed.) *Against interpretation*, Penguin Classics, 263–274.

Swartjes, I. M. T., & Theune, M. (2009). *Dramatic presence in improvised stories*. University of Twente.

Vicente, P. (Ed.) (2020). *The SAGE International Encyclopedia of mass media and society*. (Vols. 1-5). SAGE Publications, Inc., https://doi.org/10.4135/9781483375519

# CHAPTER 11

# Artist Gallery – Laurie Anderson and Hsin-Chien Huang

## LAURIE ANDERSON

Perhaps best known for her song *O Superman*, Laurie Anderson has been a pioneer in terms of incorporating new media and multimedia into her art works. Spanning a variety of mediums, including performance art, experimental music, film, and sculpture, Anderson started her career in the 1970s as a performance artist, and her career continues to this day (Anderson, 2023b). She began performing at a young age as a violinist with the Chicago Youth Symphony, and in 1969 she received her BA from Barnard College, continuing her education in 1972 to receive an MFA from Columbia University (Britannica, 2023). Early works included collaborations with William S. Burroughs, John Cage, Philip Glass, and Lou Reed (Anderson, 2023b). These collaborations and artistic movements from the 1970s experimental scene, such as Happenings, influenced much of her early work.

One such example of her work is *Handphone Table* (1978) – a five-foot table conceals a sound system that emits low-range vocal tones (Anderson, 2023c). Gallery attendees can only hear the sound by placing their elbows on the table and covering their ears with their hands. Where before no sound was heard, when covering one's ears with elbows on the table, the

DOI: 10.1201/9781003363729-11

sound was very clearly heard. When originally completed, the work aimed to explore both sound and material, taking significant influence from Anderson's musical training. Her work *Automotive* (1969) is arguably her first performance piece and was an orchestral performance using car horns (Anderson, 2023). *Duets on Ice* (1975–1977) was performed throughout the 1970s and found Anderson playing a duet with an altered violin, with the bow hair and strings replaced with a prerecorded audiotape and tape head. When performed, Anderson wore ice skates embedded in blocks of ice – the performance ended once the ice melted (Britannica, 2023).

An early adopter of many technologies, Anderson would incorporate these into her performances. Anecdotes abound – how in the late 1980s she stepped on stage to perform. Her outfit, considered somewhat androgynous at the time, consisted of a collared shirt, pants and a tie with a piano on it. Imagine the audience's surprise when she began to play the tie – it was actually a synthesizer. Anderson's career is long and varied, not only does it consist of museum exhibitions, performances on stage, and virtual reality (VR) works, but she was selected as NASA's artist in residence in 2002, which in turn inspired her one-woman show *The End of the Moon*, which was released in 2004 (Anderson, 2023a). The performance was a 90-minute show exploring a number of topics related to contemporary life and culture. While many of her performances and works utilized technology, The *End of the Moon* featured only her voice and violin, which points to her dedication to *art*. Anderson very clearly uses her artistic expression as her guide, and rather than letting the technology drive what she makes, she clearly considers it as a means to an end – a medium that will support her concepts and vision.

## HSIN-CHIEN HUANG

This openness to technology and innovative nature led to her crafting a complex, interactive CD-ROM with Hsin-Chien Huang called *Puppet Motel* (1995). At the time they came out, CD-ROMs were a breakthrough technology that allowed for images, videos, sound, and interactivity. The web at that time was not robust enough to host video and sounds – or, alternatively, videos would have to be downloaded and played locally. CD-ROMs avoid these sorts of delays and allow for immediate responses. *Puppet Motel* puts users "adrift on an ocean of repeated images, ubiquitous voices, and mesmerizing rhythms. Navigating PUPPET MOTEL is a challenge in itself; the map is your memory of what you've already seen, with objects functioning as signposts" (Anderson, 2019). The collaboration with Huang turned out to be a long and fruitful one. Of particular interest to this discussion are her endeavors with VR artistic development in conjunction with Hsi-Chien Huang. Anderson and Huang worked collaboratively on both *Chalkroom* (2017) and *To the Moon* (2019), both of which explore many pertinent aspects of VR technology a common theme in Huang's work (Huang, 2021).

Hsin-Chien Huang is an artist "obsessed with stories" (Huang, n.d.). When he was four, he lost vision in his right eye; then at fourteen, he received a cornea transplant in Sri Lanka. With it came not only a new sight but also a new enlightenment: "life and flesh are interchangeable and given" (Huang, n.d.). This also led to his obsession with stories, as he now reads stories through the eyes and the gift of an unknown deceased. He graduated from the National Taiwan University and then received a Master's in Design from the Art Center College of Design and Illinois Institute of Technology (Huang, 2018). Along with his artistic endeavors, Huang is also a professor of design at the National Taiwan Normal University (Delgado, 2022) and has worked as a researcher with the Interval Research Corporation (Huang,2018). He also served as the Art Director at both Sega and Sony Computer Entertainment, overseeing development on games such as *Geist Force* and *Kinetica* (Huang, 2018). In addition to the numerous collaborations with Laurie Anderson, including *Chalkroom*, *A Trip to the Moon*, and *Aloft VR* (2017), Huang has created numerous VR artistic works on his own, including the following: *Bodyless* (2019), *Kuo Hseuh-Hu: Three States of Home Gazing VR* (2019), and *Samsara* (2021).

## CHALKROOM

In *Chalkroom* (2018) (Huang & Anderson, 2018), the user is presented with a dark and textured virtual environment reminiscent of grade school chalkboards. The black walls are comprised of blocks covered in chalk drawings, messages, and stray lines. This gritty environment is in direct contrast to the sleek, often science fiction or technology-focused virtual environments presented by many VR experiences. Sometimes text exists – floating freeform in *Chalkroom's* environment; these texts are sometimes sentences or fragments of a phrase and are ghostly white and gray. Sometimes individual letters float through the void, loosened from their original sentence, and are now adrift in the hallways of the virtual space. In some places, ominous cubes emit stark white light, illuminating a haphazard conglomeration of walls fused at angles – creating a broken space filled with crevices and hidden corners. Various frames form portals around doorways and entrances, their luminous properties casting light on the virtual backdrop. As the experience is mostly in the dark, the beams of light found periodically through the work give any surrounding chalk imagery a luminosity akin to a star or the bioluminescence of a deep sea dweller. Eerie digital music complements the ominous visuals, further highlighted by snippets of Anderson's voice narrating some of the cryptic phrases surrounding the user. Anderson describes the work as a "collection of stories" (*Laurie Anderson Interview*, 2017), wherein the user floats through without clear guidance or a path to explore and discover on their own. In this sense, they are the directors of their story. Hidden in the experience are so many puzzles, rooms, and stories that no one user would likely find them all.

As the user flies or moves through the space, secret passages and areas reveal themselves, inviting exploration. Anderson states that for her, stories are about time and about memory – in *Chalkroom*, there are "lots of stories hidden away that people can fly through and find" (Huang, 2018). A light projected from the vantage point of the viewer's gaze helps to guide and illuminate the path in front of them as they wend their way through the work. Various other objects also decorate the world, such as chairs that replicate themselves, creating snake-like arcs through the air. At times, views of the greater skybox come into focus, revealing the monolithic structure that the user is navigating. Chalky, almost snow-like, particles fall from the sky.

The experience is poetic, and its foundation on open-ended narratives allows a participant the chance to bring their experiences and personal stories to bear when interpreting the work. Each user's experience will differ substantially due to the non-linear, self-driven progression. Balancing abstract and figurative, sometimes "words become a nebula that users can interact with using their hands" (Huang, 2018). Instruments appear in primary colors, and the user's hands turn into mallets that play notes when they come into contact with the abstract forms. In discussing the work, Huang references the belief in Chinese culture that "on the 49th day after a person passes away, their memories go into the world" (Huang, 2018). In creating *Chalkroom*, Huang expresses the hope that those who travel through the space feel something akin to moving through their own minds and memories.

**FIGURE 11.1** Anderson and Huang *Chalkroom* (2017). Image license all creative commons via www.livrolab.com.br.

The means of locomotion further emphasize the ethereal, disembodied aesthetic of *Chalkroom*. The work implements a hand-steered flying mechanic for moving through the work (*Laurie Anderson Interview*, 2017). This mechanical interaction choice reflects the overall aesthetic and meshes quite well with the visual and auditory components. When users first put the headset on, they begin in a familiar place – one central room that the application reverts to when started. The ability to fly through the series of rooms allows the user to experience multiple spaces and interact with many objects and rooms, but soon the path becomes more like a labyrinth – no clear way to go. Instead, the experience becomes about one's process of moving through the space and the memories and feelings that arise. Anderson states that she wanted participants to feel free; in fact, she says that she is "an artist because she wants to be free" (Huang, 2018). Freedom comes in the virtual space because even though users' feet say, "I'm in a room, I feel the floor," and their eyes say, "I'm in great danger, I'm about to fall," users believe their eyes, not their feet. This is why Anderson likes VR. As she says, "VR lets you look around for yourself, you are in control" (Huang, 2018).

*Chalkroom* is a direct and intentional contrast to the sleek, futuristic experiences offered by most VR experiences. The artist's intention was to create a gritty, dark, and dirty experience (*Laurie Anderson Interview*, 2017), an aim that they executed masterfully. This intentional focus creates a very particular aesthetic where all aspects of the art – the sound, visuals, interactions, atmosphere – work together to entice and compel the viewer. This focus on the aesthetic experience over the graphic fidelity (often referred to as simply graphics) should be important to any aspiring VR artist and something to strive for. Simply put: every aspect of the work feels like it fits and coincides perfectly with the other components. This not only includes the visual and auditory aspects, which are often the focus of digital works, but also the interactions.

Several artistic institutions have housed *Chalkroom* installations, including Mass MoCA in North Adams, MA, the Louisiana Museum Literature Festival in Humblebæk, Denmark; the 74th Venice International Film Festival in Venice, Italy, where the work received the best VR experience award; and the Taipei Museum of Fine Arts in Taipei, Taiwan (Anderson & Huang, 2017). At each event, the work has garnered rave reviews:

> The best thing in Ms. Anderson's show is *The Chalkroom*, a gallery covered in raw, white-on-black graffiti that expands into a haunting multi-chambered journey if you use its virtual reality component: her indelible voice on audio serves as the guide. It establishes Ms. Anderson as one of the artists VR was invented for.
>
> *(Sheets, 2017)*

Indeed, this collaborative work between Anderson and Huang capitalizes on and exemplifies the aspects that make VR such a compelling medium.

## A TRIP TO THE MOON

*A Trip to the Moon* (2019) offers a similar visual aesthetic to *Chalkroom* in that both are predominately grayscale. *A Trip to the Moon's* (2019) inspiration differs from *Chalkroom*, as *A Trip to the Moon* isn't about the handwritten grittiness found in memories of school but is instead inspired by the silvery light of the moon as it appears in the sky at night. In creating the work, artist Huang said he started with an investigation of "how this big giant rock relates to [his] life" (Louisiana Channel et al., 2018). Both artists did extensive research, and Anderson used inspiration from her two NASA artist-in-residence stays (the first and the last) to think about how to approach this project.

Huang and Anderson started with scientific research about how the moon was formed, but as they worked on the project, many, many directions were investigated: Chinese painters, Russian astronauts, personal experience, political beliefs...Anderson says that ultimately "let's just call it an unknown territory rather than the moon" (Louisiana Channel et al., 2018). *A Trip to the Moon* consists of a collection of different stories inspired by our lunar satellite and begins by catapulting the user into space toward the familiar white orb in the night sky (Anderson & Huang, 2019; To the Moon, 2019). As the participant gets closer, ominous, surreal landscapes emerge, like a lone mountain with its inverse mirrored along its base or a flower composed of moon rock. From the ethereal void particles fall which at first resemble snow, but closer inspection reveals them to be chemical symbols. Turning to the sky, the viewer is presented with an endless expanse of black and stars. Some of the starscapes reveal ghostly sketches inspired by the "constellations." Hanging among these is a half-illuminated view of planet earth. On the surface of the moon, ghostly constructions of animals are present. These animals are fabricated from the same chemical symbols that fall from the sky: birds, a giraffe, whales, and other creatures float in the air, reconstituted from their chemical origins but now stuck in time. At another location, objects move across the sky: spawning crystals, a ship, a polar bear, bees, democracy, the symbol for infinity – many are objects and things that are disappearing from our own world.

As with *Chalkroom*, the experience is explored through the use of several well-thought-out mechanical design decisions. Again, a hand-driven steering technique is utilized for locomotion (*Laurie Anderson & Hsin-Chien Huang Interview*, 2018). The steering emulates how one might physically move in space: by floating and using forces to propel oneself through a weightless, or near-weightless, environment. A tension between the user's actual, physical body and how they are represented in physical space is further explored through the morphing of their avatar's form (Anderson & Huang, 2019; Hsin-Chien Huang Youtube). They begin the experience as astronauts but then lose their bodies, a mechanical and narrative design choice that emphasizes the importance of embodiment against an ethereal background. Their form then returns but morphs from chemical symbols to that of an entirely different creature. While embodying an alien creature, the user is presented with different interaction choices as they now interact using long tendrils instead of human hands. Each of these choices helps to explore the thematic material as a dichotomy of physical achievement and spiritual achievement.

Huang states that when someone enters the work, they can experience it from multiple angles. Users can experience the work from a "mystical point of view, a research point of view, a political point of view," and participants "become the astronaut" (Louisiana Channel et al., 2018). At first, the user's avatar is a representation of an astronaut, but as they progress through the experience, their form changes. Eventually, the user loses their body, only to have it replaced with a shell composed of large prime numbers. They then further mutate into an alien-like creature with tentacles for arms. These alien arms can be used to interact with and decimate the rock scenery in the environment. Throughout the experience, Anderson's experimental violin music highlights surreal elements. Cryptic messages are read, such as "Do you know the reason I love the stars? Because we can't hurt them" (Anderson & Huang, 2019). Anderson says that as a child she "knew she was from the sky," and this has never been more clear than in the virtual experience of *A Trip to the Moon* (Louisiana Channel et al., 2018). Much like Anderson and Huangs' previous collaborative works, *Moon* provides a sense of awe and wonder to those who experience it. While immersion in the virtual experience encourages a suspension of disbelief and asks the user to come along for a ride, in Anderson and Huang's works, it is the artists' amazing vision that allows participants the ability to "live" in the surreal.

*A Trip to the Moon* touches on several meaningful themes of embodiment (or lack thereof): technology, mythology, human curiosity, and human ingenuity. Humanity's fascination with space, the stars, and the moon has always been "underpinned by the almost timeless notion of adventure, the dreams of space that have inspired humans for centuries" (Still, 2019). *A Trip to the Moon*'s surreal mythologies, scientifically inspired visual language, and exploration of different forms of life emphasize much of our romantic fascination with the mysterious heavenly bodies beyond the near atmosphere.

## ALOFT VR

In Anderson and Huang's *Aloft VR* (2017) (Huang, 2022), the user begins their journey on an airplane. They are the solo passengers in the slate gray fuselage. As the experience progresses, the plane begins to fracture and dissolve – starting from the cockpit with decay working its way toward the user. As the plane falls apart, the pieces begin to circle around the user in a tornado. The user's hands are tracked using a Leap Motion – which is a device that tracks hands and other objects in space and removes the need for hand controllers. This hand freedom allows users in the virtual space to grasp objects as they float by – objects such as a fire extinguisher or a charger block. When these objects are held close to the user's ear, they whisper stories of their past; as the stories unfold, it becomes clear that generation after generation of humans has faded from the world. The scenery progresses and changes as the user continues to float through their journey; the surrounding hurricane changes to a deserted wasteland and back again. Eventually, a typewriter is presented to the user. As they interact with the relic, words float through the air in front of them, spawned from the typewriter. Each of these words can be grasped, moved, and discarded, making *Aloft* as much about leaving stories as experiencing them.

There are two endings to the experience that are dependent on the user's actions throughout. If the user spends too much time holding onto objects and refusing to let go, they are presented with a book at the experience's conclusion: Dostoyevsky's *Crime and Punishment*. After flipping through the pages of this tome, the letters explode outward and float away into the vortex. Shortly after this, the user's hands change from ghostly outlines

**FIGURE 11.2** Anderson and Huang *Aloft VR* (2017). Image and permission courtesy of Hsin-Chien Huang.

**FIGURE 11.3** Anderson and Huang *Aloft VR* (2017). Image and permission courtesy of Hsin-Chien Huang.

**FIGURE 11.4** Anderson and Huang *Aloft VR* (2017). Image and permission courtesy of Hsin-Chien Huang.

to more photorealistic arms, slowly being drenched and caked in blood. Regardless of how hard the user tries to shake or wipe the blood away, the red continues to overtake their flesh. However, if the user is able to "let go," they will find themselves transported to a tranquil lake scene. Several cherry blossom trees release petals that float ever so gently to the water.

The user's view starts to move toward a carved stone cavern until they are completely enveloped. Finding themselves at the bottom of the lake, they are greeted by a monk statue stoically contemplating the peaceful scenery.

Branching endings dependent on user choice are commonplace in many interactive experiences, especially games. This relinquishing of control in terms of creating an artwork capitalizes on one of the most compelling aspects of VR as an artistic medium: the shift of the participants' role from *viewers* to *users*. What is particularly compelling in the case of *Aloft VR* is that the exact mechanics behind how the endings arise are not explicitly communicated to the user. Instead, their unprimed choices to interact with the environment inevitably change the experience.

## BODYLESS

> Fifty years ago, they destroyed my body. I thought this is the cruelest thing that they could have done to me. But fifty years later, with new technologies they stole my face, reduced and distorted my kinsmen's and countrymen's memory about me. I am no longer a full man. I have become a symbol to deceive people, a commodity in the digital world to be traded…At last, I find myself being erased completely from the world.
>
> *(Huang, 2020a)*

*Bodyless* (2020, 2021) was created by Hsin-Chien Huang and is a historical narrative work inspired by a period of martial law in Taiwan in the 1970s (Huang, 2020a). The experience draws from stories told to Huang during his childhood by his mother. The user begins the experience in an overgrown cell with a deceased man lying on the floor, covered with a newspaper blanket. In his outstretched arm, he holds a photo. His flesh pulsates and shifts between high-fidelity rendering and a low-polygon abstraction. In *Bodyless*, the user "experiences the journey through the eyes of an old man who was a political criminal under a government's secret experiment. After his death, he becomes a ghost and descends to the underworld" (Antunes, 2020).

Looking up from the dead man's body, the user can see a group of insects fluttering around and vegetation protruding from the walls. The ceiling fades into a seemingly endless void. Moving further into the experience, the user floats around a cell block overgrown with vines and trunks. Light

**FIGURE 11.5**  Hsin-Chien Huang *Bodyless* (2019). Image and permission courtesy of Hsin-Chien Huang.

**FIGURE 11.6**  Hsin-Chien Huang *Bodyless* (2019). Image and permission courtesy of Hsin-Chien Huang.

floods into the space from barred windows and corridors, but the yellow tinting prevents observation of the outside world. Cages are placed on the concrete walls, reinforcing the oppressive motifs provided by the source narratives. As the user explores, they move beyond the cell to encounter

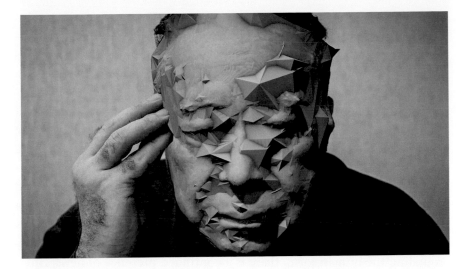

**FIGURE 11.7** Hsin-Chien Huang *Bodyless* (2019). Image and permission courtesy of Hsin-Chien Huang.

various other environments inspired by the stories told to Huang. One of the first things found outside of the prison is a shanty town that simultaneously appears to be both floating atop and submerged beneath water. The buildings levitate in the space, with a ripple-like effect shining down on them. In the center is a large tree-like structure with two massive pink leaves wavering in the ripple. While the sun is present, there is a hazy, almost smog-like effect permeating the scene. A different environment offers an overgrown room with a similar smog hanging in the air. As the user enters, they must weave through the vegetation to reach the far side of the room. This end is covered in images, newspapers, and other printed materials that are meticulously arranged on the walls. Below one of the displays is a desk with further materials.

Many of the environments take inspiration from traditional Taiwanese culture. One such environment presents a wooden shrine bathed in golden light and embroidered with gold trimmings. In the center of this space is a female performer. Her robe matches the golden highlights of the carved wooden space. As she dances, a group of butterflies obscures her face, preventing a clear view until the user is almost on top of her. Outside of the shrine is a murky swamp-like environment where other shrines, trees, and structures lay decayed and decrepit among the black water. Juxtaposing this scene that honors tradition are views into contemporary Taiwanese culture and life, such as the environment where the user navigates a miniature city placed atop a kitchen table. The buildings are modern; skyscrapers built from concrete and steel are hung with neon signs – electrical wires strung from rooftop to rooftop. At the table, a bodiless figure sits reading a newspaper, surrounded by modern furnishings such as a television, refrigerator, stove, etc. This motif is further explored in another environment where the user floats through a large megastructure where the walls are all black displays with animated grids of ASCII characters texturing the walls. Throughout the experience, the human forms shift between high-fidelity representations and low-polygon abstractions, such as those used in the initial cell environment. Other abstractions and obscurings of the human form are also presented, such as a wireframe of dancing figures or using insects to cover the dancing figure. Along with these motifs surrounding the human form, there is a continued presence of newsprint – from the initial blanket to burning lotus blossoms and boats made from newspaper.

*Bodyless* won the NewImages Festival Golden Mask Award, the Los Angeles Film Awards Best Virtual Reality Award, and an Honorary Mention from Prix Ars. One central theme is how modern technologically enabled oppression compares to the 1970s state of martial law in Taiwan. Huang explores Taiwan's political history, viewing it through the narratives of Taiwanese folklore surrounding "Ghost Month" (Huang, 2020a). It is believed that during "Ghost Month," the gate to the afterlife opens to allow ghosts to visit their families (Huang, 2020a). In *Bodyless*, this opening of the gates leads to corruption from mechanical forces that degrade the human form and memory into geometric shapes. These reduced forms are output into geometric shapes as the low polygons are easier for governmental policies to ingest, reduce, process, and control. At the center of the work lies conflict – the conflict between tradition and technology and the conflict between people and oppressors. In particular, the tension between tradition and technology makes the use of VR for this work a particularly powerful choice, as VR is often discussed in contemporary times as one of the next and best advancements in entertainment media forms. In this work, "martial law governing and ultramodern digital technologies are fused into a dark oppression against folk's living and beliefs" (Antunes, 2020). The theme of a body's dystopian morphing by invading technological elements is not only in line with Huang's interest in the corporeal form but also plays upon the element of embodiment intertwined with

VR technology. This interplay between the theme and one of the driving factors that makes VR so enticing for artworks helps to drive the themes of *Bodyless* home.

## KUO HSEUH-HU: THREE STATES OF HOME GAZING VR

*Kuo Hseuh-Hu: Three States of Home Gazing VR* (2020) is a VR homage to the painter Kuo Hsueh-Hu. Born in 1908, Hsueh-Hu is one of Taiwan's most renowned painters (Cheung, 2021). At the age of 19, he was featured in the "Three Youths of the Taiwan Fine Arts Exhibition" alongside Chen Chin and Li Yu-shan (Cheung, 2021). He left Taiwan for China in 1941 due to difficulties stemming from World War II. He would later return after the completion of the conflict, but left again in 1964 for Japan and then to the United States, which became his place of residency until his passing in 2012 (Cheung, 2021). Huang's VR work *Kuo Hseuh-Hu: Three States of Home Gazing VR* pays homage to Hsueh-Hu and his life by not only allowing the user to view his workspace but also by making the paintings come alive and allowing them to break the frame and step inside of the works.

This type of VR experience is a step closer to "art as entertainment" than Huang's other work. Indeed, the use of a deceased painter's work as the foundation of a VR work could seem a bit like "interactive virtual art fabrication" rather than a collaboration, but in *Kuo Hseuh-Hu: Three States of Home Gazing VR* Huang creates and contributes to environmental scenes and complex interactivity that are in-depth and integral to the work. An opposite example that fits the bill of "art as entertainment" is Immersive Van Gogh, which takes Van Gogh's paintings and turns them into 3D spaces. The Van Gogh immersive adds little new to the visuals and interactivity and definitely does not belong in a book that prizes artists that create and innovate with technology. With a slight twinge, we believe *Kuo Hseuh-Hu: Three States of Home Gazing VR* belongs in a book founded on the vision of artist technologists. We feel a great deal of respect for Hsin-Chien Huang and his technical craftsmanship and artistic skill. We also want to acknowledge that the ideas of "ownership," "authoring," and "appropriating" do vary from culture to culture, and put all of these thoughts forward with the understanding that we as authors are limited by our own cultural values.

*Kuo Hseuh-Hu: Three States of Home Gazing VR* opens with a fade into Hseuh-Hu's studio. In the center is a large wooden table covered in pots, vials, containers, and painting tools, each filled with brightly pigmented materials presumably used for the glue color painting Hsueh-Hu was known for. Among these tools of the trade is a radio set that springs to life shortly after the fade, emanating a "tuning" sound. Once interacted with, a particle effect consisting of several golden glowing orbs floats from the radio to one of the four paintings hanging on the walls. As the particles touch the painting, it begins to glow. Once observed by the viewer, it begins to animate; the visuals change to Hseuh-Hu's painted Taiwanese cityscape, which bustles with lively figures moving and frames shifting. Once the animation is complete, the particles move to the second painting – a scene of boats on the open sea. Like the previous painting, this one soon animates with accompanying music and sound effects, all of which highlight the subject. The particles then move to a third painting of a festival scene; however, unlike the previous two paintings, this one does not animate. Instead, the user steps into the painting and is transported into a separate environment clearly inspired by the work. At first, the figures in the street are eerily still until the user bangs a gong that has spawned in their hand. Soon after, the figures begin to animate, and the festival scene is in full effect. The user is then invited to explore the scene via a street cart. Throughout the experience, the particle effects highlight objects that can be interacted with, such as a flower that draws a butterfly near or a child handing the user a traditional piece of jewelry. Once the tour of the festival is complete, the particles highlight a doorway that serves as a return to the workshop. However, the new workspace has changed. A table with various painting tools still exists, but other furniture, materials, and objects now decorate the space. A radio once again springs to life, inviting interaction from the user, which returns them to the original workspace.

*Three States of Home Gazing* allows the user to literally step into the paintings of Kuo Hsueh-Hu. It provides "an alternative approach to a two-dimensional viewing of museum artworks, through interaction with illustrations in immersive and expansive environments, enhancing the overall museum experience" (Huang, 2021). The work is a historical reenactment, an homage to Kuo Hsueh-Hu, and a good example of "breaking the rectangle." Each of the workshop scenes presented in *Three States of Home Gazing* is a semi-historical reconstruction of the locations in which Hsueh-Hu practiced painting. Furthermore, the paintings depicted in the experience are stylized historic and traditional scenes of Taiwanese life, which allows the user to explore and experience not only the historical settings but also the culture embedded in these settings.

As an artist constantly uprooted, Hsueh-Hu often expressed feeling homesick, yearning for his youthful days in the Dadaocheng area of Taipei (Huang, 2020b). In creating Three States of Home Gazing, Huang is acutely aware of the life surrounding the artistic work. Both homesickness and a sense of longing were intertwined into the digital VR representations of Hsueh-Hu's work (Huang, 2020b). This melancholy but respectful tone reverberates throughout the experience, with the sound, visuals, and interactions all contributing to the feeling of loving and longing. As the user moves through the street scene, they are presented with traditional gifts and participate in traditional experiences. These experiences are presented in a way that emphasizes the love in longing.

## SAMSARA

*Samsara* (2021a) grants the user the opportunity to experience multiple different lives throughout the experience. Through this exploration, it explores how humanity advances, both technologically and spiritually (Huang, 2021b). Many of the embodied experiences are exceptionally cruel or dark. At first, the user begins as a human, but experiences the scenes as a variety of different characters. In one environment they float through a gallery of violent atrocities, the next environment sees them as a famished refugee on the brink of death facing off against militant individuals. Later they assume the role of a person mere seconds away from perishing in a nuclear holocaust. Another role sees the user play the antagonist as a suicide bomber.

Eventually, the user breaks from the bonds of Earth and assumes the role of an astronaut. They begin in a space vessel, but it soon shatters around them leaving them floating above the planet. Soon after the user also breaks free from the bonds of the human form beginning with an environment where other bodies, including their own, are held captive in futuristic pods with arms deconstructing them. Eventually, this leads to the user assuming forms other than human including a whale, and what can only be described as an ethereal being. While in these forms they use sound to explore their environment and move through a mindscape representative of the themes presented in *Samsara*.

*Samsara* received an honorary mention from the 2022 Prix Ars Electronica Computer Animation exhibition. In 2021, it received the South by Southwest Film Festival Jury Award, and in 2021, it received the Cannes XR Best VR Story Award. It begins as a cautionary tale in which resource wars have led to the devastation of earth forcing mankind to leave behind their home, but emphasizes that it is only through spiritual progression that true advancement can occur (Huang, 2021b). Again embodiment plays a key role in the experience drawing from the concept of embodied cognition; the notion that our experience is mediated through our corporeal form (Huang, 2021b). This concept is at the core of VR experiences as the digital environment is experienced, interacted with, and processed through the physical form of the user. By capitalizing on the use of VR to explore concepts related to embodied cognition Huang emphasizes the message that in order to truly empathize with others we must experience through their corporeal forms.

## CONCLUSION

The works of Laurie Anderson and Hsin-Chien Huang capitalize on many of the enticing aspects of using VR technology for artistic works. Their lack of linear design of the works such as *Chalkroom* creates a unique and novel experience between different playthroughs of the experience. This grants the user greater control over the experience. The user is also empowered through the emphasis on player interaction and choice, such as in *A Trip to the Moon* and *Aloft VR*. With VR artistic works, it is of the utmost importance to consider the participant's experience and how they will shape the interaction. By intentionally relinquishing control of the experience to the user, Anderson and Huang create artistic works that captivate, engage, and collaborate with users.

The heavy focus on the user's form among Anderson and Huangs' works (such as *A Trip to the Moon* and *Bodyless*) emphasizes the embodied nature of VR. As the user interacts with the virtual worlds presented in these works through their physical form, the user's reflection in the virtual world may warp, affect, or otherwise change how the user's body is viewed. This exploration is in line with Huang's interest in the body as a narrative element and his philosophy that "life and flesh are interchangeable and given" (Huang, n.d.). In many ways, the works of Anderson and Huang can be seen as augmentations of the corporeal form. Not only do they provide simulated stimuli to create visions and experiences impossible in the physical realm, but the user's avatar can be manipulated and changed to present a novel, potentially enlightening, embodied experience.

Anderson and Huang also work to break 'the rectangle' that permeates historical representation of artworks – these metaphors of mirrors, windows, and frames are found throughout western artistic practice. In *Three States of Home Gazing VR*, Huang literally moves the user from an external viewer *into* the paintings of Kuo Hseuh-Hu. When discussing *Chalkroom*, Anderson describes the problem with art being overly represented inside a frame by pointing out that in VR "people forget to look up and back and around because [they] are so oriented to stereo and things in front of us" (Anderson, 2017). Due to the widespread establishment of windows, mirrors, and frames within artistic practice, the artistic viewer has been conditioned to think, respond, and interact in specific ways that are challenged by VR works. Anderson and Huang have created works that truly capitalize on and emphasize the benefits and intrigue possible when using VR for artistic expression.

## REFERENCES

Anderson, L. (2023a). *About*. Retrieved March 26, 2023, from https://laurieanderson.com/about/.

Anderson, L. (2023b). *Artnet*. Retrieved March 26, 2023, from https://www.artnet.com/artists/laurie-anderson/biography.

Anderson, L. (2023c). *The art story*. Retrieved March 26, 2023, from https://www.theartstory.org/artist/anderson-laurie/.

Anderson, L. (2019, August 3). Laurie Anderson - Puppet Motel (1995 Mac version). *The Internet Archive*. Retrieved March 30, 2023, from https://archive.org/.

Anderson, L. (2023). *Britannica*. https://www.britannica.com/biography/Laurie Anderson.

Anderson, L., & Huang, H.-C. (2017). *Chalkroom*. Laurie Anderson. https://laurieanderson.com/?portfolio=chalkroom.

Anderson, L., & Huang, H.-C. (2019, June 10). *To the Moon VR installation*. https://www.youtube.com/watch?v=GJcjcWcSItk.

Anderson, L., & Huang, H.-C. (Directors). (2022, March 7). *Aloft VR installation*. https://www.youtube.com/watch?v=ejH70EQkFQc.

Antunes, J. (2020, October 8). Bodyless: A surreal "must see" Virtual Reality experience by Jose Antunes. *ProVideo Coalition*. Retrieved March 30, 2023, from https://www.providecoalition.com/bodyless-a-surreal-must-see-virtual-reality-experience.

Biennale Cinema 2019 | Bodyless. (2019, July 19). La Biennale Di Venezia. https://www.labiennale.org/en/cinema/2019/venice-virtual-reality/bodyless.

*Chalkroom*. (2018, January 15). Laurie Anderson. https://laurieanderson.com/?portfolio=chalkroom.

Cheung, H. (2021, April 4). Taiwan in time: Yearning for home. *Taipei Times*. https://www.taipeitimes.com/News/feat/archives/2021/04/04/2003755048.

Delgado, G. (2022, November 29). 3D artist and educator Hsin-Chien Huang takes VR to the world stage this week 'in the NVIDIA studio'. *NVIDIA Blog*. https://blogs.nvidia.com/blog/2022/11/29/in-the-nvidia-studio-november-29/.

Hsin-Chien's New Media Art Project Bodyless. (2020). https://hsinchienhuang.com/pix/_3artworks/i_bodyless/p0.php?lang=en.

Hsin-Chien's New Media Art Project Kuo Hsueh-Hu: Three States of Home Gazing VR. (2020). https://www.hsinchienhuang.com/pix/_3artworks/i_threeStatesOfHomeGazing/p0.php?lang=en.

Huang, H.-C. (2021). *Les Ailleurs*. Retrieved March 26, 2023, from https://lesailleurs.art/en/auteur/hsin-chien-huang-2/.

Huang, H.-C. (n.d.). *Artist statement*. Retrieved March 26, 2023, from https://hsinchienhuang.com/2_bio_cv.php?lang=en&detail=3.

Huang, H.-C. (2018). *ZKM*. Retrieved March 26, 2023, from https://zkm.de/en/person/huang-hsin-chien.

Huang, H.-C. (Director). (2019, June 10). To the Moon VR installation - Laurie Anderson x Hsin-Chien Huang. https://www.youtube.com/watch?v=GJcjcWcSItk.

Huang, H.-C. (2020a, March 1). *Bodyless*. https://hsinchienhuang.com/pix/_3artworks/i_bodyless/p0.php?lang=en.

Huang, H.-C. (2020b, May 1). *Kuo Hsueh-Hu: Three states of home gazing VR*. https://www.hsinchienhuang.com/pix/_3artworks/i_threeStatesOfHomeGazing/p0.php?lang=en.

Huang, H.-C. (Director). (2020c, August 31). *Kuo Hsueh-Hu: Three states of home gazing VR*. https://www.youtube.com/watch?v=9yJ6u2Y-Zqc.

Huang, H.-C. (2021a, August 25). *Samsara VR teaser*. https://www.youtube.com/watch?v=9IygU6BpINQ.

Huang, H.-C. (Director). (2021b, September 30). *Samsara behind the scene*. https://www.youtube.com/watch?v=wDIudBwhOvA.

Huang, H.-C. (Director). (2022, March 6). *Aloft VR installation*. https://www.youtube.com/watch?v=ejH70EQkFQc.

Huang, H.-C., & Anderson, L. (2018, January 16). 沙中房間創作介紹 Chalk Room VR trailer. *YouTube*. Retrieved March 30, 2023, from https://www.youtube.com/.

Laurie Anderson | Biography, Art, Performance, O Superman, Home of the Brave, Lou Reed, & Facts | Britannica. (2023, March 2). https://www.britannica.com/biography/Laurie-Anderson.

*Laurie Anderson & Hsin-Chien Huang Interview: A Trip to the Moon*. (2018, December 25). Louisiana Channel. https://www.youtube.com/watch?v=bncsR45hxGU.

*Laurie Anderson Interview: A Virtual Reality of Stories*. (2017, September 14). Louisiana Channel. https://vimeo.com/233785242.

Louisiana Channel (Director). (2017, September 14). *Laurie Anderson interview: A virtual reality of stories*. https://www.youtube.com/watch?v=zHT016FbR30.

Louisiana Channel, Anderson, L., & Huang, H.-C. (2018, December 25). Laurie Anderson & Hsin-Chien Huang interview: A trip to the moon. *YouTube*. Retrieved February 30, 2023, from https://www.youtube.com/watch?v=bncsR45hxGU&ab_channel=LouisianaChannel.

Sheets, H. M. (2017, May 26). A museum where giant art has room to breathe. *The New York Times*. https://www.nytimes.com/2017/05/26/arts/design/mass-moca-new-building.html.

Still, J. (2019, June 13). Laurie Anderson: "It's a great time to be creating new realities". *The Guardian*. https://www.theguardian.com/culture/2019/jun/13/laurie-anderson-new-realities-to-the-moon-manchester-international-festival.

*Three States of Home Gazing Ar by Hsin-Chien Huang*. (2021, February 25). A'Design Award & Competition. https://competition.adesignaward.com/design.php?ID=120342.

*To the Moon*. (2019). MIF t/a Factory International. Retrieved March 26, 2023, from https://factoryinternational.org/to-the-moon/.

# CHAPTER 12

# Output and Access of Artistic Virtual Reality Content

## INTRODUCTION

> And we have a small, extremely literate power elite—the people
> who go into the Metaverse, basically—who understand that infor-
> mation is power, and who control society because they have this
> semi mystical ability to speak magic computer languages.
>
> *(Stephenson, 1992, p. 57)*

Popular culture has provided many depictions of virtual worlds throughout the decades. *Neuromancer* by William Gibson describes a virtual reality (VR) world called the "matrix." *Star Trek: The Next Generation* and
onward feature the holodeck, which uses force field projections to create
virtual environments. *Snow Crash* by Neil Stephenson introduces the concept of the "metaverse," which is a term that has become increasingly popular over the past several years due to its coopting by the company known
as Meta (formerly Facebook). Many concepts from *Snow Crash* have found
their way into the digital space, such as avatars, immersive 3D user interfaces, and constant network connectivity. However, what has been decid-
edly ignored in Stephenson's vision of a technologically advanced future

DOI: 10.1201/9781003363729-12

as well as Gibson's ideas in *Neuromancer* is the capitalist hellscape empowered by technocracy. Rather than cherry picking from Stephenson's book, it makes more sense to address all of what *Snow Crash* describes – turning a blind eye to a potential issue is rarely just or correct.

Science fiction often serves as a projection of the future, providing hopes, promises, and warnings of things to come. This is exactly why it is imperative that artists interested in working with VR as a medium must understand the complex interplay between VR hardware, the companies using that hardware, the software used for development of artistic VR works, and their own artistic visions. The use of commercially available headsets offered in conjunction with software storefronts such as Facebook or Steam has dramatically increased the accessibility of the technology for artistic purposes; however, it has also led to a complicated and difficult-to-navigate space for the uninitiated. As such, this chapter aims to provide general guidelines and commentary about the current state of VR and how to approach the technological pitfalls, concerns, and challenges.

## A META PROBLEM

Steam is an application and platform that allows people to purchase and download games, interact with other players, stream live content, and generally connect with a greater gaming community. Known for their intensive and up-to-date data collection, Steam surveys serve as a strong indicator of which direction the gaming, software, and hardware markets are moving. The Steam Survey allows users to opt to share their current hardware configuration and peripherals. This includes VR headsets. In the August 2022 survey, 42.04% of users used an Oculus Quest headset and 9.59% used an Oculus Rift (Statista, 2022). Combined, this accounts for 51.63% of all the headsets used for Steam VR applications. The second largest share from a single hardware producer is the Valve Index at 13.16%, and purchases are on the rise for ByteDance's (parent owners of TikTok) Pico headset (Statista, 2022). Because of the Pico headset's relationship with Chinese-owned ByteDance, some companies, government entities, and schools are unwilling to bring the headsets onto their campuses due to national security concerns. Some of these same groups have (albeit different) issues with the Oculus Quest, Rift, and other Meta hardware due to their producing parent company. There are a plethora of reasons as to why Meta headsets account for such a large share of the VR space, starting with the fact that the cost for entry into the VR space is at a lower price point. The Quest line also supports both tethered (connected to a PC) and untethered standalone use. What is particularly interesting about Meta's lead in headset market shares boils down to the structure, goals, and organization of the company producing these head-mounted displays. The company has invested billions into research and development surrounding VR; as such, it is beneficial to consider their motivations for such a heavy investment.

Meta is predominantly a company focused on buying and selling data, specifically user data (Fuchs, 2017). Started in 2004 with the internet platform Facebook, Meta generously offered free use of its social network platform to anyone connected to the internet over 13 years old. The company funds itself by gathering data on its users and reselling that data to interested parties; namely marketing and advertising entities. It also generates funding by gathering user data in order to sell ads and target content to each user's specific interests. Meta clients can use this targeted content to also sell ads and to implement political strategies built on psychological schema. Another strategy central to the company is the acquisition of other technology platforms (such as the original Oculus VR) that may either threaten competition or allow the company to expand into other technological realms (Fuchs, 2017). This desire to expand into other technology spaces is more than likely the motivation behind the 2014 acquisition of Oculus VR for around $2 billion ("Facebook to Acquire Oculus," 2014). In doing so, Meta gained significant leverage over the VR landscape.

As Meta is, at its core, interested in user data, it should come as no surprise that they eventually shifted their Quest line of headsets to be a data collection avenue. In 2020, the then-named Facebook announced that they would require any new users on Oculus headsets to login using a Facebook account ("Facebook Accounts on Oculus," 2020). There was a significant backlash from the VR user community, with some concerns arising from parents concerned about giving children access to social media accounts and other concerns arising from those worried about data privacy. Additional worries were expressed by users who had purchased the head-mounted displays prior to this change. Some of these users felt that had they known a Facebook account would be required to operate the Oculus, they would not have purchased the headset in the first place. In part due to the reaction from the VR community, the decision to require a Facebook account was rescinded.

Instead of a Facebook account, users could use a Meta account in lieu of a Facebook account ("Introducing Meta Accounts," 2022).

In the new branding of Facebook's parent company, it is worth unpacking the choice of the name Meta – taken from the root of Neal Stephenson's 1982 coined term *metaverse*. Stephenson's *Snow Crash* takes place in a cyberpunk dystopian world that follows a former pizza delivery driver named Hiro Protagonist, a courier on skateboard named Y.T., and a virtus named Snow Crash that, when downloaded, causes the viewer's computer to crash and brain damage to "hackers" who view the file. The societal context surrounding the protagonists and the denizens of the metaverse is one where the federal government has ceded most of its power and territories to private companies and corporate entities. The *metaverse* described in the novel is essentially a VR-based world accessed by an internet-like network populated by millions; it is also one of the delivery methods for the Snow Crash virus (Stephenson).

Chohan (2022) describes a metaverse as a connected network of virtual environments that emphasize social connection mediated through virtual and augmented reality technologies. Through these technologies, individuals interact with not only each other but also with simulated virtual environments. Mystakidis (2022) highlights the "post-reality" nature of the concept. Rather than try to separate the physical realm from that experienced in the virtual, post-reality offers a combination of them both – an enhanced version of each. Both VR and augmented reality technologies play with the relationship between the physical world and the digital; in VR, this is done through the interaction triggered by a participant's physical movements; in augmented reality, this is done through an overlay of the digital onto the physical. In both cases, the technologies use multisensory interactions to shape, alter, and create realities.

Hanza (2008) explored the concept of the metaverse through a variety of case studies and the online virtual world platform Second Life. Created by the San Francisco-based Linden Lab in 2003, *Second Life* is a "vast 3D-generated virtual world and platform filled with user-generated content where people can interact with each other in real-time. It also hosts a thriving in-world economy" (Villar, 2022). Participants enter the *Second Life* virtual world through their computers and use *avatars* (another word coined by Stephenson) to interact with one another. Not exactly a game, but more akin to an open world explorer, participants in the *Second Life* virtual world can do almost anything that they do in real life, "such as watching movies, listening to music, playing games, going to parties, buy-ing or selling stuff, and creating new content for the world, be it items or even buildings" (ibid.). The open community allows its users to represent themselves in any way they want, with a multitude of purchasable or self-programmable options for their avatars, domiciles, and/or environments. *Second Life* has its own currency and has minted an in-world millionaire. Linden Lab creator Philip Rosedale read Neal Stephenson's *Snow Crash* when it came out and was inspired by the book's "two worlds: the real world and the global, highly realistic online space called the Metaverse" (Maney, 2007). At the time he read the book, Rosedale knew it was too early in the internet's infancy to create a second world like the metaverse, but the wait ended when "Nvidia released a significant advance in com-puter graphics with its GeForce2 card" (Maney, 2007).

During the acquisition of Oculus in 2014, Meta founder Mark Zuckerberg stated: "mobile is the platform of today, and now we're also getting ready for the platforms of tomorrow" ("Facebook to Acquire Oculus," 2014), suggesting that the company anticipates widespread adop-tion of reality technologies. In fact, the rebranding of Facebook to become Meta seems to be acutely in line with their interest in establishing *their* metaverse (Kraus et al., 2022). Adoption of a metaverse by a greater popu-lation will take time, just as adoption of computers and mobile phones took time (Fernandez, 2022). When the metaverse does become widely adopted, Meta has a leg up on the competition not just in terms of their dedication to virtual research but also by controlling 51.63% of VR hard-ware, which is tied to Meta software (Statista, 2022). Whatever the future of VR holds, Meta will have a profound influence in terms of shaping the reality of the metaverse.

## A CANDLE THAT BURNS TWICE AS HOT…

Hardware and software obsolescence further compound issues around the learning curve for VR development. As with any new or emerging technology, the newest innovation can quickly become outdated. This has been the case with a variety of early VR platforms, such as Google Cardboard, WebXR, the Oculus GO, and early versions of the Oculus Rift. Some companies are leaving VR development, while others are belatedly entering it. Back in 2014, when VR was (again) on the upswing, Google produced "headsets" out of cardboard containing special lenses. These devices allowed users to see 360 video content using a smartphone rather than dedicated VR hardware. The user could load an online video file or executable application on their phone and then insert the phone into the cardboard cutout to use as a viewer. Despite being inexpensive, popular, and easily accessible, Google eventually killed the platform (Nardi, 2021).

The Oculus GO suffered a similar fate as Meta shifted their focus to the more powerful and versatile Quest line of headsets (Bithray, 2021). Both of these discontinuations make sense, given the features and capabilities of these two platforms in comparison to other head-mounted display options. Unfortunately, their ends also meant the loss of a development platform as well as the ability to see the works created for this medium. In more traditional artistic works, like painting, sculpture, and drawing, there is a sense of longevity that exists with the pieces. These traditional formats do not require specific hardware to be viewed. An individual does not need to be using a specific VR headset with a specific computer configuration to experience an artistic work created in graphite. The temporal nature of hardware and software development for VR can make working in the medium more difficult. While artists who worked in neon also suffered as technology developed, it seems that working in VR requires artistic adaptability. If a work was created to be viewed on the Cardboard, GO, or another platform that has since been discontinued, the artist may need to port their work over to a newer platform or potentially recreate the work.

In fact, both the Cardboard and Oculus GO platforms have shifted to open-source and unlocked platforms (Peters, 2019; Whitwam, 2021). This does increase the overall lifespan of these development tools, as it allows enthusiasts to continue supporting and accessing the hardware and software required. Unfortunately, there is no guarantee due to the reliance on community support for longevity. There is also a question of hardware availability, regardless of platform status. Due to the discontinuation of the Oculus GO, it is no longer possible to purchase GO hardware, and as such, there is a dwindling number of headsets available. Eventually, even if tools and support still exist to develop for the platform, there will no longer be headsets to display those works. This creates further challenges for artists interested in using VR for their work and creates a need for planning around upgrades and content preservation.

## PRESENTATION OF WORK

In addition to hardware and support, there are also important considerations regarding the distribution and presentation of VR artwork. While this phenomenon isn't really anything new, as even woodcut print blocks are subject to issues around distribution, with digital mediums in general and VR specifically, there are some unique considerations. It is entirely possible to set up a VR headset in a traditional museum or gallery setting and restrict the experience to solely that location (which may allow for the inclusion of other physical objects to enhance the experience); it is also possible to distribute the artistic work to anyone with a compatible VR system. Although displaying the work solely in the museum comes with the downside of restricting the audience, it allows the artist control over the physical environment in which the work is experienced.

## MONETIZATION

The use of commercial platforms such as Steam for distribution of VR artistic works produces questions regarding monetization, or how the artist gets paid. Unfortunately, the use of emergent technologies like VR is associated with increased costs of creation. Even with advancements such as standalone headsets (like the Meta Quest 2 or Vive Focus), the cost of "materials" to create VR experiences can be higher than the cost of creating other visual works. In addition to a headset, a semi-powerful personal computer is required to develop. Additional software costs may also exist for producing models, graphics, animations, and other files associated with development.

Some of these costs can potentially be recouped through monetization, and while for many exhibiting in a museum or gallery is the end goal, publishing through game distribution platforms (such as Steam or Epic Games) allows for the artwork to be sold to each and every user. In terms of multiple copies sold for distribution, there are some complications around the questions of uniqueness and authenticity. As digital files are infinitely reproducible, does the quantity of experiences out in the world degrade the overall value or quality of the work? This question is not new, as printmakers have been struggling with this idea well before computing technology emerged; their answer was to limit the print run of different works.

Some emerging trends, such as non-fungible tokens that rely on blockchain technology, have tried to address issues of authenticity and access to digital works. Blockchains are essentially databases that store information electronically in digital format. Because blockchains have an irreversible "timeline of data," they allow digital files to be theoretically locked in stone and part of the one-way timeline. Chains are formed by blocks of information/data being linked to one another; each "block is given an exact timestamp when it is added" (Hayes, 2022). Artworks held in the blockchain format allow for an alternative method not just for storing but also for owning and authenticating digital work. Because the blockchain format makes it easy to track transactions, a digital artwork's ownership and value can be closely monitored. Digital art is often more difficult to "own than 'traditional' art…the issue of shareability again affects the work's value. Blockchain allows art collectors to own digital art in a completely new way" (Pires, 2021). These digital artworks can take the form of limited-run, non-fungible tokens that can be bought and sold online. The notion of limited runs "stands in stark contrast to most digital creations, which are almost always infinite in supply. Hypothetically, cutting off the supply should raise the value of a given asset, assuming it's in demand" (Conti, 2023). However, this technology is not without its faults and criticisms, as there have been issues with authentication and authenticity of works.

As discussed in previous chapters, one of the important and defining elements of VR artistic works is not the files or the distribution of the content, but rather the unique embodied experience each individual user experiences when they don a headset. Due to this, many notions associated with the traditional distribution and dissemination of artistic materials are reexamined. For example – in viewing a virtual environment, is there a difference between experiencing it in one's living room versus a fine art museum? This digitality also begets another dilemma – the malleability of the experience over time. Unlike most physical works of art, digital files can be fairly easily modified and manipulated. If an artist decides that they wish to modify the existing work and then update the experience on the platform they have distributed, the work on that platform will force an update on the end user. This forever alters and changes their instance of the artistic program. Similar to downloadable content or expansion packs used in gaming, the ability to update adds new, changed, or varied content to an already existing work. While possible with other mediums, this form of updating is often not considered commonplace. Updates also create a different economic ecosystem surrounding digital artistic works. Not only is there the opportunity to produce an initial sale, but there is also the possibility to charge for artistic "add ons." Because these abilities differ so widely from how more traditional artworks are sold, a conversation is needed regarding the distribution and dissemination of virtual art works. Probably one of the most important aspects to consider with each of these points is that the discussion of VR artistic work is now essentially a discussion of artistic *software*.

## THE REALITY OF REALITY

VR technology, as it stands today, did not manifest out of nothing. Rather, it is the culmination of decades of work not only on VR systems but also on computing as a whole and related fields such as psychology, sociology, and communications. The worlds and experiences created within a VR headset will not be the sole creation of Meta or any other single corporate entity, but a culmination of effort by an unfathomable number of individuals throughout contemporary society and culture. An important component of VR's development is the hardware, and it is very often that only a company like Meta or ByteDance has the resources to develop and produce affordable and competent hardware.

Currently, this necessitates reliance on hardware developed by international corporate companies, which may ultimately cause tension between what creators produce inside the head-mounted displays and the desires of the corporate companies that make them. In most cases, this tension emerges from corporate changes in developer licenses, updated end-user license agreements, and international political differences in approaching free speech for artists. Artworks that confront a corporation's policies or a country's human rights record may be vulnerable to content and/or distribution restrictions. While it is difficult to avoid this when using a corporate headset, it should be noted that there are options for open-source Arduino-based "build it yourself" headsets – as VR communities continue to create, it may be worth investigating non-commercial routes.

## THE ONLY LIMIT IS YOUR SKILL

The reality of developing artwork for immersive 360-degree experiences is that it is highly technical. Even with free or low-cost game engine software, integrated packages, and dedicated developer support, artists using the medium of VR will often need to know programming languages, computing principles, how to create and work with 3D models, and keep abreast of trends in hardware development. It's also important to know the theoretical concepts surrounding VR and its design, but it is up to artists to explore the medium and how it is understood in ways that go beyond conventional structures. While it is possible for a VR novice to produce compelling work using open-source software and public output, mastery of each skill required for VR artistic creation takes years.

As with any mastery of an artistic medium – it takes a high level of craftsmanship and experience to create artwork that can explore compelling concepts. Comparably, video games usually take several years to develop and are typically collaborative efforts between different teams focused on a wide variety of the game's aspects. Sometimes these teams number in the hundreds, with specific groups focusing on sub-categories within the overall project. Within this sort of development space, there are typically multiple specialists in design, computer science, and art working together. While the exact number of individuals and total time varies depending on a variety of factors, there is a significant commitment required to develop these types of projects, even with the use of game engines, integrated packages, and prebuilt assets. To develop *from scratch*, as is sometimes favored in the greater artistic community, would require significantly higher levels of skill, especially to attain the same level of polish that is afforded by consumer software. This level of skill doesn't even account for the complex hardware of the head-mounted display, which to create on one's own requires a completely separate additional skill set.

## RESTRICTION OF CONTENT

As mentioned, this tradeoff of using commercially available hardware and software comes with a variety of potential pitfalls and sacrifices. First are the potential limitations on artistic vision and creation. Often, novice VR artists seek low- to no-code development options; however, these can limit the functions and scope of content, as low-code platform creators have already made hundreds, if not millions, of choices regarding what aesthetics and interactivity are available to their users. Rather than being "low" or "no code," it may be more appropriate to consider these options as *precoded* in that another individual or entity has developed a significant portion of the functionality, which will inherently shape any subsequent works that use these tools.

A similar complication exists with platforms such as Acute Art and VIVE Arts. While both platforms provide valuable collaborative (and/or maybe what might be called VR fabrication) services to artists to produce important artistic works, there is still a potential sacrifice of control at play. Similarly to low- to no-code platforms, there can be a lack of depth in how artists unfamiliar with code understand the complexities of interactivity and the ways that it can be explored. To explain a bit more about what might be lost in the transition, a story that many artists have experienced may help. Often, in graduate school, an artist scholar will take a class outside of their field of expertise. Take, for example, a new media graduate student who enrolls in a ceramics course during their grad school tenure. While the graduate's new media work is at an advanced level of skill and mastery, that expertise doesn't necessarily translate to the medium of ceramics. It is unlikely that one course in ceramics would provide enough skill and theory in *that* medium to parallel the knowledge and expertise the new media artist has gained in their *own* field. This isn't to say that these platforms aren't enabling valuable artistic endeavors to take place, but rather that there are tradeoffs between full artistic control and ease and assistance with the technical development of these works. Sometimes an issue is that it may not make sense for a particular artwork to be developed for VR. As Rachel Rossin aptly points out, "It is important to me as an artist and a viewer to not be wholly tempted by the novelty of VR (or any technology/'new media' for that matter) and often find that artists will shoehorn ideas into the medium that don't need to be there" (R. Rossin, personal communication, March 16, 2023).

Many of the works created in collaboration with artists and platforms like Acute Art and VIVE Arts are beautiful, compelling, and work completely within the VR format. Some of the artists who have collaborated with these platforms already work across a variety of mediums and are easily able to translate their concepts and ideas into the immersive realm. These artists have chosen to express themselves in this medium and have integrated their mode of expression with their original concept. What is perhaps a bit jarring is seeing the works of artists who are either long deceased, not necessarily known for their work in interactive mediums, or whose priority may be more about marketability than actual interest in immersive interactive virtual worlds. While it is encouraging to see artists interested in VR, when a high-profile artwork isn't successful in itself (rather than being successful due to the high profile of the artist who created it), that can damage the repertoire of other VR artworks. If a work by a big name isn't successful, sometimes galleries and museums are less likely to bring in other VR works to display.

Additional issues arise around VR artworks that are reinterpretations of pre-existing works. If an artist originally worked in the medium of paint or graphite, what does it mean to re-interpret the work digitally? Is the reinterpreted work still a product of the artist's, or is it a technological experience decorated with the original artist's work? Often called "entertainment" rather than art, these reinterpretations usually involve a production company that will take images from a famous artist, like Vincent Van Gogh, and convert the objects in the original painting to 3D objects in virtual space. The VR experience comes from walking around in a Van Gogh painting – bereft of its original textures, original color palette, and intense detail. Taking a photograph of a painting can alter the appearance of the original considerably – often the photo's output varies in color due to how the painting is lit, what time of day the photo is taken…it can mean that the viewer's experience of the art work's digital versions can be a far cry from that of the original. Smith (2003) points out that the "image in a digital museum is just a surrogate; we do the viewer a disservice if we pretend that the surrogate can satisfy" (Smith, 2003, p. 11). Reproductions like these may jeopardize what artists originally intended for their work, not to mention the artistic authenticity lost in appropriation of artwork originally meant for two dimensional display.

## CONCLUSION

There is a tremendous amount of potential and promise in using VR as an artistic technology; however, there are some important constrictions and embedded structures. For starters, there are the potential challenges posed by those that control the distribution and advancement of the technology – such as companies like Meta, ByteDance, and newer entrants on the scene like Apple. Because access to affordable headsets tends to be through corporations that also control distribution software, artists may find it necessary to rely on these commercial systems. Without tools like headsets and online storefronts, the process of developing and building work in VR can become a bit cumbersome and daunting. There are also very real technical challenges that an artist turned developer will face, especially at the novice level. With all of these considerations, it may seem daunting to begin working with VR, but realistically, there is an element of self-selection for artists interested in creating for the immersive space. Up for the challenge, the artists who find themselves creating digital works are rewarded by being on the cutting edge of a new medium – therefore, their experiences and experiments are an important part of the story.

# REFERENCES

Bithrey, R. (2021, 01 Dec). How Long Should You Use VR For? Remember to take a break! VR Games. https://www.gfinityesports.com/vr/how-long-should-you-use-vr-for/

Chohan, Usman W., Metaverse or Metacurse? (February 19, 2022). Available at SSRN: https://ssrn.com/abstract=4038770 or http://dx.doi.org/10.2139/ssrn.4038770.

Conti, R. (2023, March 17). What is an NFT? Non-fungible tokens explained. *Forbes*. Retrieved March 29, 2023, from https://www.forbes.com/advisor/investing/cryptocurrency/nft-non-fungible-token/.

Fuchs, C. (2017). *Social media: A critical introduction*. London: Sage. 2nd Edition ISBN 9781473966833.

Hayes, A. (2022, September 27). Blockchain facts: What is it, how it works, and how it can be used. *Investopedia*. Retrieved March 29, 23, from https://www.investopedia.com/terms/b/blockchain.asp.

Kraus, Sascha, Kanbach, Dominik K., Krysta, Peter M., Steinhoff, Maurice M., & Tomini, Nino (2022). Facebook and the creation of the metaverse: radical business model innovation or incremental transformation? *International Journal of Entrepreneurial Behavior & Research*. https://www.emerald.com/insight/content/doi/10.1108/ijebr-12-2021-0984/full/html

Maney, K. (2007, February 5). The king of alter egos is surprisingly humble guy Creator of Second Life's goal? Just to reach people. *USA Today*. https://usatoday30.usatoday.com/printedition/money/20070205/secondlife_cover.art.htm.

Mystakidis, S. (2022). Metaverse. *Journal Encyclopedia*, *2*(1), 486–497.

Nardi, T. (2021, March 30). Google Calls It Quits With VR, But Cardboard Lives On. Hackaday. https://hackaday.com/2021/03/30/google-calls-it-quits-with-vr-but-cardboard-lives-on/

Peters, J. (2019, Nov 6). Google is open sourcing Cardboard now that the Daydream is dead. The Verge. https://www.theverge.com/2019/11/6/20952495/google-cardboard-open-source-phone-based-vr-daydream

Pires, S. (2021, February 10). Crypto art: How artists are selling their work on blockchain. *My Modern Met*. Retrieved March 29, 2023, from https://mymodernmet.com/crypto-art-blockchain/.

Smith, D. (2003, Fall). The surrogate vs. the thing. *Art Documentation: Journal of the Art Libraries Society of North America*, *22*(2), 11–15. https://www.jstor.org/stable/27949259.

Stephenson, N. (1992, June). *Snow Crash*. Spectra.

Villar, T. (2022, April 11). What is second life? A brief history of the metaverse. *MakeUseOf*. Retrieved March 29, 2023, from https://www.makeuseof.com/what-is-second-life-history-metaverse/.

Whitwam, R. (2021, October 25). Oculus Gives Discontinued Oculus Go a New Lease on Life with Unlocked Software. ExtremeTech. https://www.extremetech.com/extreme/328486-oculus-gives-discontinued-oculus-go-a-new-lease-on-life-with-unlocked-software

# CHAPTER 13

# Conclusion

## INTRODUCTION

This book's origins are found in a paper we presented at 2019's 17th International Conference on Virtual Reality Continuum and Its Applications in Industry, published by the Association for Computing Machinery and entitled *The Artistic Approach to Virtual Reality* (Kelley & Tornatzky, 2019). After presenting the paper, we realized that there was quite a bit more to say about the history of artists working in immersive virtual reality (VR), contemporary artistic approaches, and the theories and methods used to develop works. Once we started writing the book, we received a variety of interesting questions that are worth addressing here in the conclusion. Some of the questions ran along the lines of, "Why write a book about VR? Doesn't it make more sense to document this digital medium digitally?" "Why write about virtual reality? Hasn't its popularity waned?" "Why learn to code and model in 3D when you can hire a company to do so?" Or, conversely, "Virtual reality is the future; soon everyone will be immersed in a headset and making virtual content!" and "Everyone should have a headset; it will be the future of education, training, the workplace, entertainment, etc."

## WHY WRITE A BOOK?

In doing research for the original paper on VR as a medium for making artwork, it became apparent that some more permanent and extensive documentation was necessary. As academics, we have access to many articles published in journals, but these are not widely available. Additionally,

DOI: 10.1201/9781003363729-13

the majority of articles addressing VR as a medium within the continuum of new media/digital art were published some time ago. As for books that look at VR as a form of immersive art, at the time of this writing, few to none exist other than Oliver Grau's *Virtual Art: From Illusion to Immersion* (Grau, 2003). In describing new media artists, Grau states that these artists "sound out the aesthetic potential of advanced methods of creating images" while exploring new ways of manipulating perception – all while researching "innovative forms of interaction and interface design…thus contributing to the development of the medium in key areas" (Grau, p. 3). Grau's definition is exactly what we had in mind when selecting artist technologists to discuss in these pages. Creating for VR isn't without historical context and precedent; these just needed to be delineated in a written form that was accessible to a wider audience, more permanent than an article written for an online magazine, and more thorough and in-depth than a chapter in a journal.

## VIRTUAL REALITY IS NO LONGER RELEVANT

With layoffs in the industry, perceived waning public interest, a multitude of commercial missteps, and a slowing of sales for multiple aspects of the VR industry, many people asked us why we would still write a book about something that seems to be suffering from waning interest. As it turns out, we are writing a book about VR because we are personally interested in it as a medium outside of its level of popularity. In fact, we are mostly interested in humanity's relationship with computer technology and the ways that artists offer explorations of that relationship. In the same way that artists have been consistently creating work for the virtual space since the late 1980s, we aren't necessarily interested in exploring the latest hardware releases or how corporations are going to use VR to their ends, but instead want to experience what artists have to offer using these immersive technologies.

## VIRTUAL REALITY IS THE FUTURE OF EVERYTHING

Art can offer a new perspective on what immersive digital work offers us as humans. That perspective is best gained when the sweetness of an artistic experience is sprinkled with a little salt. To be an artist who understands the technical aspects of creating a digital work is to hold a space for criticality of the medium. In our opinion, VR should not be the default medium for all contemporary works, nor should work be created for it just because of its popularity. The artworks covered in these pages utilize the medium of immersive space, but the best works uncover and investigate the tension, euphoria, and sense of unreality found in the dissociation felt by a body immersed in the virtual medium, the sensory illusion provided by the system, and the technologically enabled mysticism enabled by the virtual aspect of VR.

## HISTORICAL CONTEXT

While much of the discussion surrounding VR technology highlights the novelty of the technology, this perceived 'newness' is not as merited as the general public may believe. Instead, VR and its sister technologies, collected in the mixed reality continuum, are built upon nearly a decade of academic and commercial research and invention. Each collaborative step forward has informed and fueled the advancement of contemporary VR systems. This in turn has allowed for the emergence of tremendous opportunities for the artistic technologist, as discussed in Chapters 2 and 3. Beginning with early vision experiments related to stereoscopic viewing, such as the Wheatstone Stereoscope, there is a clear foundation for the head-mounted displays commonly associated with contemporary VR systems.

These foundations would spawn a variety of important experiments, inventions, and artistic works including *Sensorama* (1965), Ivan Sutherland's *Head Mounted Display* (1968), and *The Ultimate Display* (1965). In turn, these advancements would spark the philosophical imagination of artists and researchers alike, leading to conceptual as well as technological advancements. Works such as Krueger's *Artificial Reality* describe the psychological aspects of transportation and immersion in a virtual world. Other concepts such as *Avatars* and the *Metaverse* are also products of these thought experiments. Scientific and technological advancements also fed into VR. This includes haptics and input research such as the *Data Glove*, developments in gaming, and research into graphics and human-computer interaction. Research, exploration, experimentation, and conceptual thinking have helped to establish VR not just as a commercial technology but as an artistic medium of limitless potential. This potential emerged long before the first HTC Vive and Oculus Rift headsets. Early works capitalized on the opportunities provided by VR modeling language (VRML). Like HTML, VRML allowed for the creation and distribution of three-dimensional vector graphics. This in turn spawned a multitude of interactive and VR artistic works, including *Traveler* (1995), *Conversations with Angels* (1998), and *Osmose* (1995).

Some works also saw collaborations between artists and researchers. These collaborations allowed artists to gain access to early VR systems to explore and push the boundaries of what these technologies could do. Works such as *Placeholder* (1992) saw Brendan Laurel collaborate with Rachel Strickland to explore concepts related to virtual environments, collaborative interaction, and metaphysics. It was also not uncommon for artists to be brought on board projects with not only researchers but military and industrial entities to create works such as Furness's *Super Cockpit* (1960s). On a positive note, contemporary corporate approaches to commercial VR headsets and the proper support from current computing technology offer more artists the opportunity to develop for VR, unlike the VR wave of the 1990s, which in turn led to a VR winter.

## TECHNICAL COMPONENTS

As discussed in Chapter 4, while the best VR experiences live and die by their conceptual content, there are undeniable technical components to the technology that are important for VR artists developing in the medium. Much of these technical components are deeply rooted in the historical explorations of computer science research, particularly that of human-computer interaction. Each development produced another aspect of VR to consider – from stereoscopic rendering to input and output methods to rendering techniques. VR is any system that suppresses the physical environment in favor of a simulated virtual environment. In the case of this book, much of the discussion has been focused on head-mounted displays where the user dons a headset, often paired with motion controller input devices; however, much of the discussion can be applied to other VR systems and tangential technologies. Additional input and output devices may also become a bigger part of the discussion, including gestures, haptic feedback, or even olfactory systems.

## MEDIUMS AND TOOLS

To simply recreate our physical reality in any given VR experience is to make light of VR's affordances. This is why, as discussed in Chapter 8, it is imperative to consider what VR offers as a medium rather than solely as a tool. In this regard, VR should be viewed through the lens of new media art. As forms of new media (such as the internet, digital video and photos, and video games) have emerged, there has often been tension around adopting these mediums as art. Understanding theoretical and developmental approaches to VR means that artists can work within the medium's strengths, but it also gives them the opportunity to break the rules. In this case, the medium isn't just about the immersive headset, but there is also a focus on the software used to create what is seen in the headset. This can be something as commonplace as existing open-source modeling software, or it can be something as specialized as a custom-written program in a preferred programming language. Software development further plays on the notions discussed in Chapter 4, where the artwork becomes as much an exploration in human-computer interaction as it does an artistic endeavor, and most successful new media works being acutely aware of this fact.

What is unique in regards to VR and new media artwork is the reliance on a digital space. Digital artistic artifacts are inherently different from traditional artistic works in so much as they are composed of binary encodings, regardless of the 'medium' chosen. This comes with a host of considerations and affordances, such as interactivity, malleability, and reproducibility. However, there is an inherent difference between using these new technologies as a medium and as a tool. For instance, the program *Tilt Brush* aims to provide a VR painting experience. While there is novelty in having a 3D painting displayed in a virtual setting, artwork of this sort can be seen as a digital tool for painting in a binary environment rather than a VR work of art. Instead, a true VR work capitalizes on everything the medium affords: capturing cognitive elements, its interactive nature, its innate immersiveness, and how it addresses multiple senses. In some regards, this does demand that the artist look beyond the visual characteristics and traditional conceptual ideation to think through the lens of the technology, as further discussed in Chapters 6 and 10. A deeper understanding of the development process requires consideration of aspects such as character, camera, control, and communication (as VR is inherently about communication) within the context of the immersive virtual space.

## CONCEPTUAL SPACES OF VIRTUAL REALITY

In addition to the developmental aspects considered in Chapters 4 and 8, there are also two major conceptual spaces to consider in regards to VR art: the visual space, as discussed in Chapter 6, and the embodied space, as discussed in Chapter 10. Each of these provides a lens through which to consider the design, development, and implementation of VR artworks. The visual conceptual space draws from the long history of both western visual artistic practice and human-computer interaction. The embodied conceptual space draws from psychology and cognitive science. The visual aesthetics of artistic works are often a key focus, and within those aesthetics there are a number of historically established motifs tracing back to the Renaissance era that have shaped much of the conceptions and thought regarding visual artistic works, namely windows, mirrors, and frames. The window metaphor in artistic practice typically references the notion that the viewer is external to the work and that the flat rectangular picture plane offers a view into the artistic space. On the other hand, using the mirror metaphor refers to the notion that the flat rectangular picture plane reflects something back at the viewer, such as the state of affairs in a given culture, an aspect of the human body, or some innate desire. What is key to understanding these metaphors is that they place the viewer outside of the work. This separation of viewer from artwork is a notion further cemented by the inclusion of a frame – it bounds the artwork and further ties it to the flat rectangular plane. The metaphors of windows and mirrors have unduly influenced the technological development of user interfaces. One need not look further than the *windows* metaphor in windows icon menus and pointer-based interfaces. This is not to say that metaphors are negative, as they do provide a valuable service by providing a conceptual framework to aid users in completing tasks, but it is important to consider the roots of these underlying metaphors and how they may be adjusted, affected, and reshaped, especially when presented with technology such as VR that challenges the established conceptualizations of visual artistic works.

One key challenge to the historically established roles of artwork and viewer is the innate, embodied nature of VR technology. This embodied space draws from the notion that humans exist and interact with their environment through their corporeal forms, whether that environment is physical or digital. Users intake virtual stimuli through the five senses: sight, smell, taste, hearing, and touch. These perceived stimuli are then processed by the individual's mind – a process mediated by past experience. When in a virtual environment, a participant can be led to the psychological state of transportation or presence (which are closely linked but have slightly different sources for the similar cognitive state), wherein the user feels as if they are "there". However, certain aspects must be present and attended to by the artist in order for this effect to take place. The sense of presence emphasizes the role of the audience member as a user rather than a passive observer. As such, it is imperative that the VR artist consider the affordances presented to the user: what can they do in the work? How do they fit into the work? In essence, the user has now become an active participant in the creation of their artistic experience, something that is not often emphasized (although it may be present) in traditional artworks. This interactivity creates unique emergent meaning through interactions that are outside of the artist's control.

## EXPERIENCING (VIRTUAL) REALITY

In addition to the historical context, the virtual as a medium, and embodied/conceptual spaces of VR artistic works, there are external influences that profoundly affect any sort of development. These influences are related to the commercial distribution of both VR systems and supporting software. Often a double-edged sword, commercial entities provide accessible tools and avenues for artistic expression using VR, but often require dependence on companies with potentially conflicting interests and the power to nullify any artistic endeavors through changes in policies. While concerning, the reality is that it is difficult for any individual to completely develop every aspect of a VR system and the supporting software, as well as their artistic work, by themselves. Even the most adept VR artists must rely on hardware and software provided by external corporate entities to create their works. However, it is important for the artist interested in exploring VR as their chosen medium to not only understand how to create works but also the external elements that drive decisions related to hardware and software used in VR development, as these decisions can lead to the premature death of an artistic vision from obsolescence of hardware and discontinuation of software, changes in corporate direction, or redirection in terms of user bases. These changes and considerations also further call into question the traditional roles of artistic viewership and dissemination. Issues such as monetization of work, presentation of work, and distribution of materials become the "problem" of the artists. While it is still possible to exhibit work in a more traditional museum or gallery setting, there are a host of other distribution avenues provided by the software used for VR artistic creation. Displays of VR artworks within more traditional art world settings can offer a form of vetting that can bring commercial success to an artist. This doesn't mean that other forms of distribution are less valid, and in fact, they may offer artists a broader platform with which to share their visions.

## THE ARTWORKS

The best part of writing this book has come from reviewing the works of talented artists willing to learn the software and hardware necessary to create immersive VR artworks. Experiencing each artist's work has given us as authors a much broader understanding of what is possible in the medium. We purposely described each work in detail in order to emphasize how diverse each artist's approach was. The detailed descriptions also offer readers access to virtual works, whether or not they have a headset or the ability to enter the immersive space. These descriptions also document each work at this point in history – what are artists thinking about and how are they conveying these thoughts in this medium? We are eternally grateful to these artist technologists – their vision, hard work, and generosity have afforded us many intimate and moving experiences.

> In the future, I think VR will have a very big impact, which will come if we directly influence people's perceptions of themselves. If today I was to look at myself through the eyes of another creature or through the eyes of the other sex, or through a different cultural background, I think this is the greatest challenge and VR's next wave of influence.

> *(Huang & Anderson, 2018)*

## REFERENCES

Grau, O. (2003). *Virtual art: From illusion to immersion.* MIT Press.

Huang, H.-C., & Anderson, L. (2018, January 16). 沙中房間創作介紹 Chalk Room VR trailer. *YouTube.* Retrieved March 30, 2023, from https://www.youtube.com/.

Kelley, B., & Tornatzky, C. (2019). The artistic approach to virtual reality [conference paper]. *Proceedings of the 17th International Conference on Virtual-Reality Continuum and Its Applications in Industry,* Article 36 ed., 1–5. User Interface, Virtual Reality, Art, Interaction, Storytelling, VR, User Experience. https://doi.org/10.1145/3359997.3365701.

# Index

Note: *Italic* page numbers refer to figures.